PAWNS

THE PLIGHT OF
THE CITIZEN-SOLDIER

ALFRED A. KNOPF   NEW YORK   1972

THIS IS A BORZOI BOOK
PUBLISHED BY ALFRED A. KNOPF, INC.

Copyright © 1971 by Peter Barnes

All rights reserved under International and Pan-American Copyright
Conventions. Published in the United States by Alfred A. Knopf, Inc.,
New York, and simultaneously in Canada by Random House of Canada
Limited, Toronto. Distributed by Random House, Inc., New York.

ISBN: 0–394–43616–4
Library of Congress Catalog Card Number: 72–136344

Manufactured in the United States of America

FIRST EDITION

FOR VALERIE, REGINA, AND LEO

I'M JUST A FINGER, A FRAGMENT
OF A FRANKENSTEIN MONSTER.
—*Lieutenant William L. Calley Jr.*

ACKNOWLEDGMENTS

IN THE COURSE of gathering material for this book, I met many people who went out of their way to be helpful. Among these were three military information officers: Major Mike Styles, Marine Corps Recruit Depot, San Diego; Major Frank Lancaster, Correctional Training Facility, Fort Riley, Kansas; and Major Lester Smith, Book and Magazine Section, Office of the Secretary of Defense, in the Pentagon. They assisted me even though they knew I disagreed with them on many points. I would like to thank them and, at the same time, absolve them of any responsibility for the views expressed in this book.

Many junior officers, particularly in the Judge Advocate General's Corps, were also enormously helpful. They spoke to me in a decidedly unofficial capacity. I would especially like to thank Captains Richard Lasting, Bill Peacock, Don Segretti, and Brendan Sullivan.

I am also indebted to Francis Heisler, Richard Silver, Edward Sherman, Bette-B Bauer, Congressman Mario Biaggi, and my vigilant editor, Dan Okrent. A generous grant from the Louis M. Rabinowitz Foundation made the research for this book possible.

Most of all, I would like to thank the hundreds of enlisted men who passed on to me their experiences and thoughts. This book, in a very real sense, is both about them and by them. I cannot name all of them here, but they know who they are. My special thanks to Corporal George D. ("Skip") Roberts and Private Gavino Tinaza, Marines both.

P.B.

AUTHOR'S NOTE: Because of the delays involved in publishing, the rank, military status, and assignment of many of the individuals mentioned in this book have changed since I was last able to contact them or check on them. Some have retired or been discharged from the service. Since it was not possible to reach again every person mentioned, I have used the rank and assignment that was last known to me. My apologies to anyone who is thereby literarily "demoted."

CONTENTS

PREFACE

ABOUT TWO years ago I became convinced that a major civilian appraisal of the military was needed. I was working in San Francisco at the time, as a correspondent for *Newsweek* magazine. Like many college graduates who came of military age after Korea but before Vietnam, I had had very little contact with the Army. Without much difficulty, I had been deferred first as a student, and then for minor medical reasons, until I had passed the magic age of 26. Having thus escaped the burden of personal service, I preferred to think as little as possible about the armed forces, concentrating instead on a civilian career and civilian diversions and leaving things military to men who wore uniforms.

My interest in the inner workings of the military was first aroused in a serious way by an event which occurred in San Francisco in October 1968: the "mutiny" in the Army's Presidio stockade. Of course, like most Americans, I had become aware of the growing influence of the military in our national life; of the enormous defense budget, with its consequent distortions of our social priorities; of the vast powers exercised by the so-called military-industrial complex; of the increasing militarization of our foreign policy; of the impact of the Vietnam War upon young people. But I had never given much thought to the military from the point of view of the human beings inside it. As an outsider, I had always viewed the military in monolithic terms, as a kind of gigantic, self-contained organism that had been swallowed whole, like some unpalatable but necessary medicine, by an otherwise democratic society. It had not occurred to me that if I looked inside the military organism itself, I would find a continuous stream of human beings in various stages of digestion, absorption, and elimination. Nor had I recognized that I should be concerned on purely humanitarian grounds about what was happening to these fellow humans—young men in America born just a few years later than I—or that the problem of controlling the military was very much related to the manner in which these men were treated.

In brief, I had until this time scarcely given a thought to these matters. But here on a crisp Monday morning in San Francisco were twenty-seven confused and frightened kids sitting down in an Army prison yard and crying for attention and help. How, I wondered, had these desperate soldiers been thrown together in a stockade in the first place? To what end and for what compelling reasons did our government declare their act of sitting passively on the grass to be a crime of monstrous proportions, punishable, if a handful of Army officers so determined, by death?

Other questions plagued me. A succession of American Presidents, encouraged by military and civilian advisers, had committed large numbers of soldiers to combat in Southeast Asia without a congressional declaration of war, with scarcely any prior public debate, and with little visible relation to the defense of legitimate national interests. It seemed incongruous that, in a democracy, so few men could compel so many to fight in a war that was so questionable. This was surely not what the Founding Fathers had had in mind when they had incorporated in the Constitution a slew of safeguards against unwanted presidential wars. Among the most serious questions raised by the long and unhappy conflict in Southeast Asia, it seemed to me, were these: What can be done to restore the traditional limits on the power of the President to wage war? And, as an extension of this first question, what can be done to protect young Americans from being used as implements of the illegitimate exercise of that power?

Then came the reports of a massacre of Vietnamese civilians by American soldiers at Mylai, and with the reports, yet more haunting questions: How many GI's trained by the military and given the order—or at least the sanction—to kill, would have behaved like the members of Charlie Company? What would *I* have done at the age of 20, or even 29? I was not sure. I still am not.

Spurred by these questions, I set out to write this book. My goal was threefold: first, to examine the powers that the military exercises over the lives of millions of American citizens; second, to consider the legitimacy of those powers; and finally, to search for responsible ways to limit them.

In approaching a subject so large and complex, I felt it necessary to look at the past as well as the present. What has traditionally been the role of the military in the United States? How did it acquire the powers and functions it possesses today? Several excellent writers, notably Russell F. Weigley, Walter Millis, and Samuel P. Huntington, have explored these questions with admirable skill and thoroughness, and in my own discussion of America's military past I have relied heavily on them.

Informing myself about the present characteristics of the American military, on the other hand, was a much more arduous task; it was necessary to interview literally hundreds of enlisted men, officers and veterans. For the better part of a year, I lugged my typewriter and tape recorder around to more than a dozen Army, Navy, and Marine Corps bases. Most of these were on the West Coast, but I also drove east to Washington, D.C., and stopped at several military posts along the way. Recognizing that many enlisted men, as well as official military spokesmen, have a tendency to exaggerate, I made a concerted effort at each major base to check stories for accuracy and to obtain the viewpoints of both ordinary GI's and high-ranking officers. This was not always easy.

While most GI's are embarrassingly eager to unburden themselves, many dissident soldiers are, with reason, suspicious of unknown faces asking questions. Military intelligence agencies use many spies with many covers; they have not been able to stifle dissent within the ranks, but they have unquestionably succeeded in spreading fear. A number of times I had to argue long and hard that I was not an agent (not always an easy thing to prove these days) before I was able to communicate freely with GI's. On other occasions, soldiers who had no doubts about my credentials as a reporter were afraid to speak with me for fear of being assigned to combat duty or suffering some other form of retaliation.

My problems with military officialdom were of a different nature. Few high-ranking officers were willing to speak with me without clearance from their base's Public Information Office, and the primary function of a Public Information Office, despite the title, is not to facilitate the public's access to information but to restrict that access to those few facts and versions of reality which the generals and colonels want to give out.

Early in November 1969, for example, I asked to interview a number of officers at Fort Ord, California. Major General Philip B. Davidson, commander of the base, stalled my request for more than two months. (The reason, I learned, was that he had been displeased by an article I had written in *The New Republic* on the Presidio "mutiny.") Finally I was granted the interviews I sought. To make sure, however, that no one said anything the slightest bit out of line, General Davidson ordered his information aide, Major Barry Winzeler, to sit in on every interview, taking notes on a clipboard. Major Winzeler, I should add, was at least a more subtle guardian of whatever it was he was guarding than was the burly master sergeant at Fort Hood who, as he physically threw me out of "his" administration building, profanely informed me what he thought of civilians who tried to talk to "his" men.

Despite these and other problems, I believe I was able, through perseverance and a certain amount of deviousness, to obtain almost all of the factual information I needed. The armed forces may not welcome civilian inquiry, but they are still open enough and full of enough unfrightened individuals to be unable to conceal very much for very long.

It was not my intention, in writing this book, merely to heap criticism upon the military. The armed forces have been much condemned of late, and often, in my opinion, unfairly. Most of the difficulties in which America finds itself today can be blamed on civilians and on the nature of American society as a whole. If America's role in the world has become misguided and destructive, it is largely because civilians have both caused and allowed this to happen.

What concerns me, however, is not who is to blame, but what can be done. It is for this reason that I believe it necessary to focus on the military's powers over American citizens, on the way it transforms Myrtle Meadlo's son, and millions like him, from "good boys" into murderers, gas pump men into stockade prisoners, high school grads into obedient policemen of the world. Congress can and should reassert its powers in the field of foreign policy. The draft laws can be modified or even abolished, though I would not favor the latter course. But unless the powers of the military itself are curbed, I don't think much progress will be made.

After a great deal of thought and consideration, I have come to believe—and it is the underlying thesis of this book—that what America needs is a humane, competent fighting force that can capably defend the nation but not so readily engage in undeclared and non defensive wars. It also needs an army that does not strip its members of the basic rights and dignities that the Constitution guarantees to citizens. I am satisfied that such an army can be created through reforms of the present military organization, though I recognize it will not be easy.

How do you go about reforming the American army? The first and most essential need, without which all else is futile, is for public awareness and concern. And here one encounters a curious phenomenon: although millions of Americans are veterans, and millions more come of draft age each year, the public knows remarkably little, and tends to care even less, about what happens to human beings inside the army. There is a pervasive feeling that internal military matters should be left to the military, a feeling often buttressed by the notion that any serious criticism of the military is somehow unpatriotic. Another widespread impression (promoted, naturally, by the army) is that nothing can be done to change things anyway: soldiers will come and go, many will have their gripes, but this is the way the army is—always has been, always will be.

In fact, however, the military is not nearly so immutable as it makes out. In fact, too, the army and its officers are quite responsive to public opinion. So change *is* possible—if people demand it and work for it.

In the final chapter, and occasionally elsewhere in the book, I offer a series of what I believe to be constructive proposals for reforming the American military. These are by no means to be taken as perfect or definitive solutions. My original purpose in undertaking this book will be fulfilled if the public, informed and alerted, comes forward with its own determination of what should be done.

Peter Barnes
Point Reyes, California
March 1971

PART I

1. ILLEGITIMATE POWER

DRIVE THROUGH any small town in America and you are likely to find, in a central plaza or shaded park, a monument to the townspeople who have died in the service of their country. It is very peaceful around the monument. People read the local paper, full of local news, and the voices you hear are talking about matters of local interest. Yet the names of the battlefields etched onto the monument stone are strange, foreign-sounding: Chateau-Thierry, Guadalcanal, Inchon.

Just outside of Concord, Massachusetts, in another peaceful setting, stands another monument. It is a statue of the first modern guerrilla revolutionary: the American Minuteman. In one hand he holds a plow; in the other, a rifle. On the pedestal is a verse by Ralph Waldo Emerson commemorating the "embattled farmers" who, from this spot in April 1775, "fired the shot heard round the world."

The statue near Concord and the more recent monuments to wartime dead reflect a major historical change in the role of American fighting men. The impact of the Minutemen's shots may have been felt throughout the world, but the Minutemen themselves did not wander far from their Massachusetts homesteads; they were farmers first and soldiers second, part-time warriors who took to arms because their liberties were threatened by the proximity of British redcoats. They could hardly have dreamed that within two hundred years a powerful national government would be turning their descendants into disciplined full-time soldiers and sending them into battle— without their consent—against the farmers of a country called Vietnam.

The early Americans were not averse to fighting; they recognized that each male citizen owed a military obligation to his community. But they considered themselves to be citizen-soldiers, with emphasis on the word preceding the hyphen. A citizen-soldier did not give up his rights; indeed, it was those very rights he took up arms to defend. The citizen-soldier's obligation to serve his community, moreover, was strictly a local and defensive one; the government had no right to compel him to take part in far-off military adventures. That kind of work belonged to professional soldiers like the redcoats and was viewed with great disfavor by American settlers.

Wars, of course, were fought by Americans, and most were won. But invariably, after each major war, the nation demobilized with a frenzy. This was in consonance with the tradition of the citizen-soldier. Americans were quite prepared to train periodically and fight when the occasion demanded, but they were most reluctant to remain in uniform for extended periods of time, or to travel to distant battlefields in pursuit of ill-defined policy goals.

In the last twenty-odd years, however, all this has dramatically changed. America has become a nation of professionalized soldiers. The military obligation of male citizens has been transformed from a defensive obligation into an open-ended one. Those who bear arms for their country have been deprived of many of the rights guaranteed to all citizens by the Constitution. And, in the midst of a land that was once a haven for those fleeing the standing armies of Europe, there has been created the most powerful standing army of all time.

The American army [1] is an awesome institution. Each year hundreds of thousands of young men enter and leave it, making it the largest single processor of people in the Western Hemisphere. It is not its size alone, however, that makes the military awesome. It is also the way it operates within the larger society, and the power that it possesses over its members.

Modern sociologists have studied and analyzed what they call "total institutions"—places like mental hospitals, prisons, old age homes. Erving Goffman has described their principal characteristics as follows:

First, all aspects of life are conducted in the same place and under the same single authority. Second, each phase of the member's daily activity is carried on in the immediate company of a large batch of others, all of whom are treated alike and required to do the same thing together. Third, all phases of the day's activities are tightly scheduled, with one activity leading at a pre-arranged time into the next, the whole sequence of activities being imposed from above by a system of explicit formal rulings and a body of officials. Finally, the various enforced activities are brought together into a single rational plan purportedly designed to fulfill the official aims of the institution.[2]

The army, clearly, is the most enormous total institution in America. Soldiers must eat, work, play, and sleep in it. If they die, they are buried by it. For twenty-four hours a day, they live under its authority, moving to their assigned tasks like throngs of ants, never alone, always watched. Their time is controlled by it, and so are their appearance, behavior, and—to a degree—their thoughts.

As in other total institutions, a power structure is established to ensure that the inmates behave according to their guardians' plans. In the army, power is distributed according to a carefully designed pyramid, with those on the higher levels exercising

1. Henceforth in this book "Army," capitalized, refers to the U.S. Army, a branch of the American armed forces; "army," uncapitalized, refers to the military generally.

2. Erving Goffman: *Asylums* (New York: Doubleday Anchor; 1961), p. 6.

their power over those further down by the issuance and enforcement of directives, regulations, and orders. The nature of these rules is such that the men on the bottom can't beat them. There is rarely a recourse, almost never an appeal, and rulebreakers are nearly always punished.

The men at the base of the army pyramid, the enlisted men, have no power, not even over their own lives. Their powerlessness extends from matters of the most vital concern—like avoiding death—to the most trivial details of daily existence. They are told when to get up, what to wear, how to walk and talk, and ultimately, whether they must carry a rifle in the rice paddies or sit behind a desk in North Carolina. In terms of numbers and in terms of social conditions, these men—enlisted GI's—constitute a class that in many ways is now the most oppressed in America.

Of course, the extraordinary piece of social engineering that is the modern American army did not emerge from the mists of history purely for the sake of institutionalizing American citizens. It was constructed, and was tolerated, because it fulfilled, at least in theory, an ultimate purpose: the defense of the nation. The trouble is that today the function of the army is no longer solely to defend the nation; the military is also engaged in the conduct of what may fairly be called non-defensive foreign policy. And from this significant alteration of the military's function arises some serious doubt about the legitimacy of the powers that the army exercises over Americans.

A military officer would probably deny that there is any meaningful distinction between defending the nation and conducting a non-defensive foreign policy. The proper role of the army, he would straightforwardly explain, is to execute the orders of the Commander in Chief. Since the Commander in Chief—the President—is elected by the people, whatever the Commander in Chief tells the army to do is, by definition, legitimate and democratic.

There are, however, certain problems with this standard justification of the army's powers. In the first place, though the President *is* the Commander in Chief, he is not responsible by himself for the formulation and conduct of American foreign policy. Most particularly, he is not responsible, under the Constitution, for declaring war. It was the Founding Fathers' intention, and until recently the obtaining practice, for Congress to determine when the army would be used in a major way. The President could entangle and cajole, but he could not commit the army to large-scale combat. Indeed, until the 1940's, he scarcely had an army to commit.

Moreover, the relationship of the army to the carrying out of American foreign policy was not always what it is today. The tradition was for armies in America to be organized for specific purposes: the winning of independence from England, the annexation of Canadian and Mexican and Spanish territories, the repelling of German and Japanese aggression. Whatever the merits of the particular goals, the fact is that America chose its causes and then raised armies to fight for them.

Today the cart has placed itself in front of the horse. The American army no longer merely carries out predetermined foreign policy; it plays a major role in shaping that policy. It has 10,000 men in Turkey, 1,600 in Ethiopia, 24,000 scattered throughout Latin America—all told, more than a million men in thirty foreign countries. In Washington as well as abroad, it maintains a sprawling bureaucracy, its own private intelligence agencies, and a multimillion-dollar public relations program aimed at Congress and the American people. Collectively, it is the largest corporation in the world, vitally interested in its own preservation and expansion. When it comes to dazzling civilian leaders with slide-studded briefings, ready-made contingency plans, and confident predictions of victory, the U.S. military knows no equal.

Interservice rivalries add to the pressures on foreign policy. All four services were competing with each other in the early 1960's to build up forces in Vietnam. The Air Force was anxious to prove that bombing was effective against guerrilla insurgencies. The Navy wanted to show that offshore gunnery was still as important as in World War II. The Marine Corps was jealous of the Army's growing role in Southeast Asia; many of its officers feared that the Corps was in jeopardy unless it could justify its continued existence. After a U.S. Special

Forces camp at Pleiku was attacked in February 1965, the services virtually raced with each other to see who could get the biggest share of the action in Indochina.

In short, it is no longer possible to speak of the army obediently following the President, and the President in turn following the wishes of the people. In a very real sense, it is now the army that leads the President, and the President who commits the people.

How, then, are we to assess and justify the vast powers that the military has come to hold over millions of American citizens? Simply, the military's powers are legitimate to the extent—and *only* to the extent—that they are, in the first instance, consonant with contemporary standards of justice and humanity, and then only when the foreign policy which the military carries out is both (1) directly related to the defense of the nation or its closest democratic allies, *and* (2) determined in a constitutional manner by elected officials whose decisions are guided by the will of the people, as expressed through the political process.

A brief look at American history, however, reveals two divergent trends: as the military has steadily extended its powers over citizens, the legitimacy of those powers, as judged by the above criteria, has almost as steadily diminished.

II

IN THE beginning, America's armed forces had their roots in the needs and democratic spirit of its people. None of the colonies could afford to maintain a standing body of regular soldiers, and none had the slightest desire to do so. But there was a need for defense against Indian attack, and so all the colonies except Quaker Pennsylvania made provision for a popular militia.

Colonial militias were based upon the principle of universal male obligation. All men, usually between the ages of 16 and 60, were required to arm themselves and muster for drill about half a dozen times a year. New England militiamen elected their company officers; in Massachusetts, over-all command of the militia was vested in an elected official known as the sergeant major-general. Elsewhere militias were commanded by colonial governors, with the elected assemblies maintaining control of expenditures and close surveillance over all military operations.

In practice, the need never arose for the simultaneous service of every able-bodied male in a colony. Consequently, when a limited number of troops was required for a specific campaign, the legislatures assigned quotas to local militia districts. Local officers then called for volunteers; if a sufficient number did not step forward, they would draft men for the duration of the campaign. One very important limitation, however, applied to the use of militiamen except in special circumstances: they could not be sent against their will on expeditions outside the boundaries of their colony.

This form of military organization suited the new settlements well. As farmers, craftsmen, and traders, the colonists' prime concern was earning a living. To their way of thinking, it was neither necessary nor desirable to create a special class of full-time soldiers, separate from, supported by, and inherently dangerous to, the general body of citizens. Moreover, the system worked well in practice, at least in terms of local actions: in campaigns against the Pequots, Mipmucks, and Narragansetts of New England, the Yamasees of South Carolina, and various other Indian tribes, the militia emerged victorious.

Significantly, the militia did not fare well in the French and Indian War, an aggressive affair that reached far beyond the existing limits of colonial settlement. Few militiamen volunteered for active duty, and the colonial assemblies were unwilling to enforce a rigorous draft. Virginia Governor Robert Dinwiddie originally proposed to raise a regiment of two thousand volunteers. After a few weeks of fruitless recruiting, he lowered his request to eight hundred. When even that number failed to come forward, he asked the legislature to draft one in ten of the militia. The House of Burgesses refused. The experience in other colonies was similar. Although British regulars eventually managed to win control of French Canada and the Ohio Valley, they did so without much help from the colonists.

Within a decade, American militiamen were not merely ignoring British efforts to turn them into professionals; they were actively revolting against the Crown's misuse of its standing armies. Among the grievances listed against King George III in the Declaration of Independence were four pertaining to his abuse of military powers:

> He has kept among us, in times of peace, Standing Armies without the Consent of our legislatures. —He has affected to render the Military independent of and superior to the Civil Power . . .
> He is at this time transporting large armies of foreign mercenaries to complete the works of death, desolation and tyranny. . . . He has constrained our fellow Citizens taken Captive on the high seas to bear Arms against their country.

The Revolution spawned the first standing army of Americans. But despite the importance of the cause, the Continental Congress was almost as wary of its military creature as it was eager to expel the British. The last thing Congress wanted was a native Cromwell emerging from the ranks of the Continental Army, and though Washington had no such inclinations, Congress eyed him apprehensively nonetheless.

The "regulars" in the Continental Army consisted of militia regiments provided by the states, and Washington was hard-pressed to mold them into a disciplined force. For one thing, they kept returning to their farms when their short enlistments expired; for another, they were unused to the kind of formalized, European-style fighting that Washington felt was necessary to defeat the British redcoats and Hessian mercenaries.

At times during the eight-year struggle, it appeared as though Washington's army would completely disintegrate. Volunteers, food, and supplies were often perilously low. But Washington kept his band of regulars together and gradually began to instill in them the discipline he sought. Punishment for misconduct or infractions of regulations was harsh. Washington's favorite remedy for misbehavior was the lash; he persuaded Congress to raise the permitted number of strokes from thirty-nine to one hundred. He also approved on occasion the un-authorized punishment of running the gauntlet. With the invaluable aid of Baron von Steuben, fresh from the court of Frederick the Great, he drilled the Continentals with Prussian-like rigor.

In the end, it was Washington's main-force regiments, as-sisted by a fleet of French warships, that surrounded Corn-wallis at Yorktown and sealed the victory. Even so, local militia were essential throughout the Revolution, and it is un-likely that the war would have been won without them. Colonel Ethan Allen's Green Mountain Boys seized Fort Ticonderoga in 1775 and hauled its artillery to Boston in time to help the assembled New England militia fight the Battle of Bunker Hill. In the South, guerrilla forays conducted by partisan colonists under Colonel Francis Marion ("the Swamp Fox"), "Light Horse Harry" Lee, and others helped defeat superior British forces in Georgia and the Carolinas, pushing Cornwallis toward the sea and inspiring him to retreat to what he thought was the relative safety of Virginia.

No sooner had the British departed than Congress dismantled the army it had created. "Standing armies in time of peace are inconsistent with the principles of republican governments, dangerous to the liberties of a free people, and generally con-verted into destructive engines for establishing despotism," Congress resolved in 1783. It then directed that "the command-ing officer . . . discharge the troops now in the service of the United States, except twenty-five privates to guard the stores at Fort Pitt, and twenty-five to guard the stores at West Point and other magazines."

The men who gathered at Philadelphia four years later were more attentive to the need for a regular national army, but not by much. Many believed along with Sam Adams that "it is a very improbable supposition that any people can long remain free with a strong military power in the heart of their country, unless that military power is under the direction of the people, and even then it is dangerous."

As in so many other areas of controversy, the arrangement finally agreed upon by the drafters of the Constitution was a compromise. It provided for two different types of armies in America: a part-time citizens' militia controlled by the states, and a full-time regular army controlled by the national government. The understanding, however, was that by far the more numerous of the two would be the militia of citizen-soldiers. It was also understood that, to the extent that a universal military obligation would be continued in America, a citizen would only be obliged to serve in his local militia; the national army would be composed solely of volunteers. Most importantly, it was explicitly stipulated that the militia, whose officers would be appointed by the states, could be called into federal service only for three purposes: "to execute the laws of the Union, suppress insurrections and repel invasions." Citizen-soldiers, in other words, could be used to maintain internal order and to defend against attack, but they could not be employed for non-defensive purposes.

The granting to Congress of the power to raise a national army was undertaken with many qualms. Primarily, it was thought, the standing federal army would be needed to fight Indians and to quash domestic uprisings. (Shay's Rebellion of just a year before was much on the Framers' minds, though it had been successfully put down by the Massachusetts militia.) But while the federal government was empowered to raise a standing army, numerous safeguards were instituted to prevent such an army from accumulating unwarranted power over the citizenry.

First of all, it was established, or at least understood, that no citizen would be compelled to serve in the standing army or even to quarter its soldiers. Governor Edmund Randolph of Virginia undoubtedly expressed the prevailing sentiments among Convention delegates when he declared in his opening address that only "inlistments," not "draughts," were appropriate for raising a national force.[3] Although no outright ban on national conscription was written into the Constitution, a prohibition against the involuntary quartering of troops during

3. This and all subsequent quotations of statements by delegates to the Constitutional Convention are taken from James Madison's *Notes on Debates in the Federal Convention of 1787* (Ohio University Press; 1966).

peacetime—which was considered a much more palpable danger at the time than federal conscription—was incorporated in the Bill of Rights.

Secondly, it was anticipated by nearly everyone at the Convention that the standing national army would always remain small. Elbridge Gerry of Massachusetts at one point proposed a constitutional provision "that there shall not be kept up in time of peace more than ＿＿＿＿ thousand troops." His idea, according to Madison, "was that the blank should be filled in with two or three thousand." While Gerry's motion for a specific constitutional troop limitation was voted down, it was clear from the discussion that the Framers believed, as George Mason of Virginia put it, that "there would be no standing army in time of peace, unless it might be for a few garrisons."

To make sure that the army would stay small and not be enlarged by an ambitious executive, the power to appropriate funds for the military was vested in Congress. Moreover, even Congress was deterred from acting imprudently in its dispensing of military funds by a provision that "no appropriation [for the army] . . . shall be for a longer term than two years." In no other area of government was Congress's power of the purse thus limited. The limitation was patterned after the British Mutiny Act, which set forth the rules for administering the British army. Parliament took it upon itself to subject the Mutiny Act to annual renewal; if Parliament did not renew the law, the King's army, at least in theory, would disintegrate.

Thirdly, the Convention determined that the ultimate power to control this tiny federal force would lie with the legislature and not with the executive. The President, under the new Constitution, would be Commander in Chief of the armed forces when they were in the field, but the power to raise the armed forces, to make rules for their governance, and—most importantly—to inaugurate war, would rest exclusively with Congress.

The debate at the Convention also made clear the delegates' intention that Congress's power to "declare" war be truly the power to inaugurate war and not merely to issue a formal declaration that a state of hostilities existed. The original version of the war-making clause authorized Congress to "make" war. Madison moved that the word "make" be changed to "declare," so that the President might "repel sudden attacks"; this amendment was adopted by a vote of eight to one, with only New Hampshire in the negative. Thus, the President could defend the nation in the event that another country *suddenly* attacked America first, but could not otherwise embark upon a war. In this respect, as Alexander Hamilton pointed out in Essay Number 69 of *The Federalist*, the President's powers were considerably less than those of the British monarch, who could initiate wars purely on his own volition.

Thomas Jefferson did not attend the Convention, but was in full accord with the Framers' determination that the President should not have the power to initiate war. "We have already given in example one effectual check to the Dog of war," he wrote to Madison in 1789, "by transferring the power of letting him loose from the Executive to the Legislative body, from those who are to spend to those who are to pay."

Despite all these safeguards, there continued to be widespread aversion throughout the young republic to providing for any standing army at all. Fear of an uncontrollable military that might threaten the liberties of citizens was in fact a principal cause of opposition to the proposed new Constitution. Patrick Henry, for one, exclaimed before the Virginia ratifying convention:

Had we a standing army when the British invaded our peaceful shores? Was it a standing army that gained the battles of Lexington and Bunker Hill, and took the ill-fated Burgoyne? Is not a well regulated militia sufficient for every purpose of internal defense? And which of you, my fellow citizens, is afraid of any invasion from foreign powers that our brave militia would not be able immediately to repel?

To allay such fears, Madison and Hamilton argued in *The Federalist* that the people's liberties would be protected at three levels: first, at the level of the federal legislature, which would keep a wary eye on the executive; next, at the level of the states, which would guard against undue federal aggrandizements; and finally at the level of the people themselves, who if worst came to worst could fight off the national army with their own rifles. Thus, Hamilton pointed out in Number 24 that:

The legislature of the United States will be *obliged* . . . once at least in every two years, to deliberate upon the propriety of keeping a military force on foot; to come to a new resolution on the point; and to declare their sense of the matter, by a formal vote in the face of their constituents. They are not *at liberty* to vest in the executive department permanent funds for the support of an army, if they were even incautious enough to be willing to repose in it so improper a confidence. . . ,

Independent of parties in the national legislature itself, the State legislatures, who will always be not only vigilant but suspicious and jealous guardians of the rights of citizens against encroachments from the federal government, will constantly have their attention awake to the conduct of the national rulers, and will be ready enough, if any thing improper appears, to sound the alarm to the people, and not only to be the VOICE, but, if necessary, the ARM of their discontent.

Madison was even more explicit in Number 46.

Extravagant as the supposition is, let it however be made. Let a regular army, fully equal to the resources of the country, be formed; let it be entirely at the devotion of the federal government: still it would not be going too far to say that the State governments, with the people on their side, would be able to repel the danger. The highest number to which, according to the best computation, a standing army can be carried in any country, does not exceed one hundredth part of the whole number of souls; or one twenty-fifth part of the number able to bear arms. This proportion would not yield, in the United States, an army of more than twenty-five or thirty thousand men. To these would be opposed a militia amounting to near half a million of citizens with arms in their hands, officered by men chosen from among themselves, fighting for their common liberties, and united and conducted by governments possessing their affections and confidence. It may well be doubted, whether a militia thus circumstanced could ever be conquered by such a proportion of regular troops.

Such arguments as these helped carry the day for the Federalists. Even so, it is unlikely that the new Constitution would have been ratified had its advocates not agreed to support a Bill of Rights embodying, in the Second Amendment's guarantee of the right to bear arms, Madison's vision of an armed citizenry as the ultimate check against illegitimate federal power.

The early Congresses acted to reinforce the constitutional safeguards against a powerful standing army of professional soldiers. The second Congress under the new Constitution adopted the Militia Act of 1792. In doing so, it rejected the advice of Washington—who, as a professional, was not very fond of the militia. Instead of providing for federal arming and training of the state militia, as Washington had recommended, the law of 1792 simply instructed able-bodied males to equip themselves with rifles and report to their local company commander. It also restricted the period for which the President might call militiamen into national service to no more than three months per year. As for the standing army, its strength was limited under an earlier law to 1,216 enlisted volunteers, mostly privates whose pay was fixed at $3 a month.

The War of 1812 illustrated both the weaknesses and the advantages, depending upon one's viewpoint, of America's dual military system. The performance of the militia in defending against attack was mixed: at Bladensburg it stumbled badly, allowing an outnumbered British raiding party to sack the city of Washington, while at New Orleans, under Andrew Jackson, a motley assortment of militiamen, sailors, and free Negroes savagely routed an attacking force of eight thousand British regulars.

More interesting was the militia's performance as an offensive force. The first American undertaking of the war was an invasion of Canada. President Madison requested the New England state governors to deliver into federal service as many militiamen as General Henry Dearborn required. These governors, however, were opposed to the war, and they stalled on the grounds that no invasion of America had taken place. Eventually Dearborn was able to assemble a mixed force of regulars and militia, and he set out along Lake Champlain toward Montreal. Much to his chagrin, however, most of his militiamen refused to cross the border into Canada, insisting again that the Constitution required them only to repel invasion, and no invasion had occurred. Thus was America's first aggressive military plan thwarted. Significantly, after the New England coast *was* attacked by Britain in 1814, thousands of New Englanders volunteered for service in the regular army.

One other aspect of the War of 1812 deserves note. The early recalcitrance of New England, coupled with the disappointing number of volunteers elsewhere, caused Madison to propose America's first national conscription plan. Daniel Webster denounced the proposal as a sinister attempt to bypass the constitutional restrictions upon federal use of the citizen-soldier:

> This, then, Sir, is a bill for calling out the Militia, not according to its existing organization, but by draft from new created classes; —not merely for the purpose of "repelling invasion, suppressing insurrection, or executing the laws," but for the general objects of war—for defending ourselves, or invading others, as may be thought expedient;—not for a sudden emergency, or for a short time, but for long stated periods; for two years, if the proposition of the Senate should finally prevail; for one year, if the amendment in the House should be adopted. . . .
>
> The question is nothing less, than whether the most essential rights of personal liberty shall be surrendered, & despotism embraced in its worst form

Despite Webster's eloquence, the Senate approved a two-year draft, but the measure died in a conference committee in 1814 as the war drew to an end.

The years preceding the Civil War saw the regular army grow in size and professionalism. Though enlisted men tended to come from the poorest and least educated elements of society, the Military Academy at West Point began turning out a corps of skilled and dedicated officers, not a few of whom had political ambitions. The ranks of the Army swelled to six thousand by 1830 and twelve thousand by 1840, as the credo of Manifest Destiny impelled the nation westward into confrontation with the Plains Indians and, by 1845, with Mexico. The Mexican War was an important milestone in many ways. Not only did it give the Army a chance to test its mettle in a major foreign expedition; it also marked the first time that an American Commander in Chief exceeded the constitutional limits on the President's war-making powers.

Earlier Presidents had all carefully respected these constitutional boundaries. John Adams and Thomas Jefferson responded to international harassment of American commerce by turning to Congress for authority to defend ships at sea; and James Madison insisted in 1812 that the choice of whether or not to declare war against England was a responsibility "which the Constitution wisely confides in the legislative department of government."

James K. Polk, on the other hand, without authority from Congress, dispatched some four thousand American troops under Zachary Taylor into territory south of Corpus Christi that had always been considered part of Mexico. Taylor proceeded to build a fort on this Mexican soil and to block the Rio Grande to Mexican shipping.

The Mexicans, not surprisingly, attacked Taylor's forces, and Congress thereupon authorized further hostilities against Mexico. But two years later, in passing a resolution of thanks to General Taylor, the House of Representatives, by a vote of eighty-five to eighty-one, attached an amendment denouncing the war as having been "unnecessarily and unconstitutionally begun by the President of the United States."

As the Regular Army steadily grew in strength and prestige during the mid-nineteenth century, the militia correspondingly declined. States were notoriously lax in enforcing the universal male obligation, and were just as relaxed about providing effective training. Though some elite units voluntarily kept themselves in spiffy shape, most militia musterings were occasions for drink and merriment, not for serious drilling.

The federal government had little inclination to correct these shortcomings. Recalling Dearborn's troubles at the Canadian border, Polk realized the militias were not suited to his purposes; he got around the constitutional limitations on non-defensive use of citizen-soldiers by creating a new category of volunteers under Regular Army command. Later, because of sectional tensions, Congress was understandably reluctant to strengthen the state-controlled militias.

In 1861 the domestic insurrection that had been simmering for decades finally erupted. Nearly a third of the Regular Army's officers resigned to aid the Southern rebellion. Lincoln called out the Northern militias for three months' federal service until Congress could convene. They fought—not very well—at Bull Run, and the Civil War was on in earnest.

Both the Confederacy and the Union, once Congress assembled in July 1861, determined to build massive regular armies strengthened with long-term volunteers. Soon after Bull Run the Confederate Congress voted to raise 400,000 volunteers for three years. Not to be outdone, the Union Congress authorized a million-man army, though with the careful proviso that it be reduced to 25,000 as soon as peace was restored.

Initial enthusiasm was such that volunteers stepped forward faster than their armies could absorb them. In the North, the volunteer units, though legally distinct from the state militias, retained much of the militia spirit; uniforms were varied and colorful, discipline was lenient, company officers were usually elected by the men, while commanders were frequently political appointees.

As the war dragged on with no end in sight, it became apparent on both sides that the consuming need for manpower was exceeding the willingness of the male citizenry to volunteer. Large bounties were offered to spur enlistment, but to little avail. Casualties and desertions mounted. Soon the Confederacy and then the Union fell back upon the expedient that few of the Founders had thought possible: national conscription.

The Confederate conscription law of 1862 subjected to compulsory military service all white male citizens between the ages of 17 and 50. Men engaged in essential war industries could be exempted at executive discretion. Slaveowners or overseers were also exempted if they possessed or supervised fifteen slaves, which raised protests about class discrimination. By means of its draft law, the Confederacy provided directly or indirectly for some 300,000 soldiers, about a third of its total strength.

In the North, the Enrollment Act of 1863 imposed a federal military obligation upon all male citizens between the ages of 20 and 45. Military provost marshals were sent from door to door to register eligible males. The law had many loopholes, mostly favorable to the rich. For $300 a drafted citizen could purchase a commutation, or he could hire a substitute (if he could find one) for less.

Enactment of the conscription law provoked widespread resistance. Some state and local governments passed laws to buy general commutation for their residents. Anti-draft riots in New York City caused 1,200 deaths, and there were frequent protest demonstrations elsewhere. Draft evasion became so widespread that a new word—"skedaddling"—was coined to describe it. Enrolling marshals were lied to, avoided, even attacked. New towns sprang up across the Canadian border, populated by evaders from all parts of the country. Many fled to California or mining towns in the Rockies. In the end, only 249,259 persons were actually called up under the Enrollment Act, and of these 86,724 escaped by payment of commutation while another 116,188 sent substitutes.

Though the Civil War was uniquely an internal quarrel, it had a lasting effect upon the American military. The drift toward centralization of the armed forces was accentuated. Not only did the federal government resort, for the first time, to conscription; it also recruited directly from among the citizenry, instead of having the states provide troops to meet federal quotas. It also proposed, unsuccessfully for the moment, creation of a national army reserve that would have effectively supplanted the militias. Discipline, too, was tightened by the war, and though flogging in the Navy was abolished in 1861, bucking and gagging in the infantry and spread-eagling in the artillery were common punishments.

Nonetheless, by the end of Reconstruction, the United States Army had in fact been reduced in strength to within a few thousand of the 25,000 figure that Congress had earlier prescribed. Until the outbreak of the Spanish-American War in 1898, there wasn't much for the Army to do except fight Indians and break workers' strikes, and after the Battle of Wounded Knee in 1890 there weren't even any fighting Indians left. So the Army sulked, its increasingly professional officers biding their time, casting aspersions upon the militia and yearning for a more active role in the nation's destiny.

The two most influential military thinkers of this period were Captain Alfred Thayer Mahan, the prolific naval historian, and Major General Emory Upton, a West Pointer and a protégé of General William Tecumseh Sherman. While Mahan was whetting the public's appetite for American dominance of the oceans, Upton was quietly urging a more professional organization on dry land. In 1876 he departed on a round-the-world tour to study foreign armies; he returned with an unabashed affection for the German war machine with which Bismarck had recently humiliated France and Austria and forged the modern German state. In his report, entitled *The Armies of Asia and Europe*, Upton recommended that America abandon its dual military system and adopt a unitary professional army patterned after Germany's. In peace, the regular officers would prepare for war by attending a system of military schools; in war, the expanded army would consist entirely of forces led by these thoroughly trained professionals.

Upton's magnum opus was his unfinished book *The Military Policy of the United States*. In it he utterly condemned the militias—not only because they fought terribly, but also, he argued, because they lured the nation into thinking it was possible to be prepared for war without maintaining a first-rate standing army. If America's seemingly successful military history proved anything, Upton contended, it was that lack of preparedness in 1775, 1812, 1846, and 1861 had prevented the army from seizing quick victories, thus costing the nation dearly in lives and treasure. Another lesson, he wrote, was that the military suffered from too much civilian control.

Upton's arguments gained wide appeal among the officer corps, which then as now tended to the belief that the nation ought to adjust its institutions to fit the military's needs, and not the other way around. His most important convert, however, was a civilian: Elihu Root, the New York corporation lawyer who became President McKinley's Secretary of War in 1899, eighteen years after Upton's suicide. Like Theodore Roosevelt, whom he would later serve as Secretary of State, Root believed America should play a greater role in the world, and he set out to create an army suitable for an imperial power. A relative neophyte in military affairs, he turned to Upton's writings for guidance.

By 1903, Root had done much to advance the army toward European-style professionalism. A War College was opened in Washington, as Upton had recommended. A general staff system was established, based on the German model. The Militia Act of 1903 began the process of converting the state militias (by then generally referred to as the National Guard) into a reserve for the national army. The federal government was to issue arms and equipment to the Guard free of charge. In exchange, Guard units had to conduct at least twenty-four drills a year as well as an annual summer encampment of not less than five days. Regular Army officers would instruct the Guardsmen and periodically inspect their organizations. Guard units could be called into federal service for up to nine months, a tripling of the then-existing limit of three months. In 1908 the time limitation was dropped altogether, and National Guard units were explicitly authorized to serve "either within or without the territory of the United States."

Major General Leonard Wood, who became Chief of Staff in 1910, sought to extend Root's reforms. An energetic man with presidential ambitions, Wood wanted to make the American army a match for any potential European foe. Like Upton, he greatly admired the German army's ability to absorb great masses of conscripts under the direction of a highly trained professional cadre. He also possessed great faith in the ability of citizen-soldiers to become competent warriors with only brief, albeit intensive training. Wood hoped to establish a program of universal military training and a truly national reserve force, but realized that achievement of these aims required public support. So, with indefatigable zeal, he set out through speeches and publicity to condition the American people to the notion that a mass army of citizen-soldiers was not only necessary but democratic. His ideas failed to win acceptance during his tenure, but they were harbingers of things to come.

In 1916, Congress increased federal supervision of the National Guard, provided for forty-eight drills a year instead of twenty-four, and required Guardsmen to take an oath to obey the President and uphold the Constitution. At the same time Congress established a new national reserve, to be composed of veterans of the Regular Army, an Officers' Reserve Corps, and a Reserve Officers' Training Corps.

Within a year, America was at war with the Kaiser.

Though few persons could have foreseen it at the time, World War I was a major milestone on the road to the awesome military institution of today. The Selective Service Act of 1917, more than the Enrollment Act of 1863, was the precursor of the modern draft. It applied national conscription for the first time to the task of raising a foreign expeditionary force. It also did away with some of the more abrasive features of the 1863 law. Male citizens between the ages of 18 and 35 registered themselves; no provost marshals moved from house to house in search of them. Moreover, no substitutions or commutations were permitted. To administer the Selective Service System, thousands of civilian draft boards were established in localities throughout the country. The system worked so well that, for the first time, military strategists in Washington were able to make decisions without worrying too much about popular opinion.

World War I was a milestone in other ways. It was America's first major war of a truly nationalistic cast, with public emotions pumped up and orchestrated by skillful government propaganda. Most important, it marked the definitive transformation of the American citizen-soldier from the part-time defender of his homestead to the full-time legionnaire, trained and disciplined and equipped by the national government and sent to clash on distant battlefields with the greatest armies of the world. Leonard Wood and those who said that American citizens could hold their own against any warriors were proven right. The magic formula was strict discipline and professional leadership. The Army had learned the formula and would apply it again.

By the end of 1919, only 200,000 soldiers, mostly regulars, remained in uniform, compared to the 2½ million who had stood in arms barely twelve months earlier. But Chief of Staff General Peyton C. March came before Congress with a plan which would have made the peacetime Army resemble even more strikingly than it already did the forces of the very country it had just defeated—Germany. March proposed a permanent Regular Army of 500,000 men. Backing up the regulars would be a conscripted national reserve force, formed by subjecting every able-bodied male citizen to three months of military training. In the event of war, the reserves would be blended into an expanded national Army with regulars leading the way.

The National Defense Act of 1920 did not go as far as March and his planners had wanted. Universal military training was rejected. The size of the Regular Army was fixed at 280,000—substantially less than the half million asked for, but a hefty force nonetheless, considering there wasn't an enemy in sight. The act also provided for an Organized Reserve alongside the National Guard, the reserve to be primarily led by citizen-officers who would come from an enlarged ROTC program in the colleges.

The interwar years marked a significant change in the army's attitude toward the American people. Prior to World War I, the military had led an almost cloistered existence, tending to its garrisons and schools and fighting Indians or Latin Americans when called upon. Leonard Wood had begun to take the army out of its isolation and inject its views into the national consciousness; now this process was vastly intensified. Military spokesmen roamed the country, spreading the gospel of national preparedness and citizen training. With new reserve branches in almost every community, the War Department expressed the hope that reservists' views would be "felt among their neighbors until all our people come to appreciate the wisdom" of supporting a strong national defense. If Congress, through ROTC, was trying to democratize the military, the army would make the best of things by trying to militarize the democracy.

Within a generation after the Treaty of Versailles, the army found itself at war again, this time against two enemies on two vastly different fronts. Once again, national conscription was imposed, and the staggering total of fifteen million citizens were converted into soldiers. America proved again, as it had in World War I, that it could quickly mobilize both its manpower and its economy and that it could outlast and defeat the strongest armies in the world.

But the American army that fought World War II was not, despite ROTC, a democratic army, as millions of disgruntled enlisted men discovered. They could not understand why officers drank bourbon while they often could not get hold of Coke; why the best clubs in town were off limits to enlisted personnel; why military justice was such a one-edged sword, painfully sharp to them but sheathed for officers. If they were, indeed, citizen-soldiers, why were they treated like second-class citizens?

As soon as the fighting ended, a volcano of protest erupted. Veterans marched in the streets, wrote letters to editors, petitioned their Congressmen. The issue of army reform came alive. Hanson Baldwin of *The New York Times* called for an overhaul of the military's archaic legal system. The St. Louis *Globe-Democrat* editorialized: "A democratic people, now forced to have a standing Army, demands a democratic Army. That means radical change from present customs."

Brigadier General Herbert C. Holdridge, a retired West Pointer, suggested abolishing the officer corps, calling all GI's "soldiers," and ranking them according to skill and ability. On January 13, 1946, five hundred GI's, described by the *Times* as "orderly but angry," demonstrated in Paris in support of a three-page program they called the Enlisted Man's Magna Carta; it demanded an end to officers' messes and special officers' quarters, reform of court-martial juries to include enlisted men, and a requirement that all officers serve one year as enlisted men except in time of war. In April a Gallup poll revealed that eighty-six percent of former enlisted men favored eliminating officer privileges.

The Army responded by appointing a six-man board under Lieutenant General James H. Doolittle, hero of the first bombing raid over Tokyo, to study the problem of reform. The Doolittle board received both written and oral testimony from hundreds of active and former soldiers, from privates to generals. Its conclusions and recommendations were moderate. "Discipline and obedience can only be accomplished by creating rank and by giving necessary privileges to accompany increased responsibilities," it argued. But it acknowledged that "more definite protection from arbitrary acts of superiors is essential," and recommended that there be "definite equality of treatment of both enlisted and commissioned personnel in the administration of military justice."

The Army accepted some of the Doolittle board's suggestions. It abolished the difference between officers' and enlisted men's uniforms, except for insignia; it did away with OFF LIMITS TO ENLISTED PERSONNEL signs; it beefed up the Inspector General system for handling complaints. Old-time regulars grumbled that the Army would never be the same. A few handed in their resignations. Actually, however, the changes were more superficial than real—just enough to quiet the clamor for reform.

Military leaders, meanwhile, had more important things to worry about. There was first of all the question of demobilization: the nation, and especially the troops, wanted to demobilize as fast as possible, just as they had after previous wars. President Truman and the generals, on the other hand, were concerned about Soviet intentions, and they persuaded Congress to authorize a one-million-man peacetime Army, the largest in America's history.

Another problem was unification. This was resolved by the National Security Act of 1946, which created the office of Secretary of Defense and a confederation of the four services.

As always, the crucial problem was manpower procurement. General George C. Marshall recommended universal military training and a strong reserve system, and Truman backed him enthusiastically, as did a number of civilian educators, who felt it would make for a democratic army. But lawmakers were wary of militarizing the entire citizenry, especially since nuclear weapons seemed to make mass armies irrelevant. So Congress came up with a peacetime selective service system under which some men would be drafted while others would be deferred. The new law was perhaps less far-reaching than a universal training program would have been. But it surrendered to the President a virtual blank check over the lives of young people.

The new law came in handy in 1950, when Truman intervened in Korea. Draft calls were stepped up to replenish the Regular Army. Also, as in World War II, several National Guard units were federalized and shipped to the battlefront— any concept of the Guard as a defensive force, separate from the Regular Army, having by now quite disappeared.

It remained for Secretary of Defense Robert McNamara to put the finishing touches on today's prodigious military institution. McNamara's plans were keyed to the concept of "flexible response": the United States should be able to meet international threats without resorting to nuclear weapons. To achieve a capability for less-than-nuclear response, the size of the army was substantially increased; so was its training in counter-insurgency warfare.

Soon McNamara got a chance to test his theories in Southeast Asia. The trouble was that, although the standing army now had more power—save for during the two World Wars—

to turn American citizens into obedient executors of national policy than it had ever had before, that power had never been less legitimate.

III

THE SWEEP of American military history yields several important lessons. One is that too much preparedness in times of peace can be as dangerous as too little. Never before was America as prepared militarily for a war as it was for Vietnam; Emory Upton would have been quite pleased. Yet America's preparedness led to overconfidence, not to victory. In the past, America has proved that it can mobilize rapidly when the need is urgent; it has yet to show that it can minimize losses from adventures too eagerly entered into.

A second lesson is that professionalism—like preparedness, a cardinal tenet of modern American military dogma—is also a mixed blessing. Professionalism in its purest sense implies a high degree of training coupled with a selfless dedication to one's calling. In the military context, however, it takes on an added meaning: the professional soldier is one who stands ready, full-time, even during periods of peace, to plunge instantly and unquestioningly into battle when ordered. Professionalism thus produces soldiers who know how to fight well, which is good; but it also produces soldiers who are conditioned to fight anywhere, which is dangerous.

A third lesson is that the President of the United States has acquired more solitary power to embroil his nation in war than the leader of any other democratic country—and probably even more than the Soviet head of government. Thanks to the open-ended peacetime draft, it is incongruous but nonetheless true that if the President desires 20,000 men in February to be trained for deployment to Asia, he merely snaps his fingers; if he wants $20,000 to fight poverty in West Virginia, he must fight like hell for the appropriation.

The checks and balances designed by the Framers of the Constitution no longer seem to apply to the war-making power.

Congressional declarations of war have been labeled "outmoded" by presidential spokesmen. Congressional control of the purse strings has likewise become a merely vestigial power; when Presidents deploy troops first and then come to Congress for money to support "our boys," it is the rare politician who feels free to vote No. Nor are the state legislatures or the National Guard bulwarks against the President's army. Even the people's ultimate political protection against unwanted presidential wars—the quadrennial presidential election—was shown in 1964 and 1968 to be all but irrelevant.

A fourth lesson is that it is vitally important to distinguish among the different types of wars that America has been involved in in the past and is likely to become involved in in the future. Essentially these wars fall into three categories: internal rebellions, defensive wars, and non-defensive wars. The Civil War falls into the first category. The First and Second World Wars could aptly be described as defensive: both were provoked by direct attacks upon United States ships or installations preceded by invasions of close democratic friends, both were all-out efforts in which the nation's economy and manpower were mobilized to the fullest, both were declared by Congress in the proper constitutional manner, and both were unquestionably wars in which victory was essential. All the other wars that America has fought, at least since 1815, lacked at least one of these characteristics and can be classified as non-defensive.

The Framers of the Constitution made a similar sort of differentiation in order to limit the military obligations of citizens. The national government, they agreed, had the right to call upon citizen-soldiers (in those days, militiamen) only "to execute the laws of the Union, suppress insurrection, and repel invasions." The Framers granted to Congress the power to raise a small national army for unspecified purposes that presumably could include non-defensive warfare; but the understanding was that this army would be composed of voluntary professionals, not citizen-soldiers, and that it could not actually be deployed in non-defensive combat without prior approval by Congress.

The reason it is important once again to make such differentiations is that American citizens are now subject to military powers never imagined by the original settlers and for purposes glaringly at odds with the Constitution's intent. The imposition of military powers upon the citizenry is justified on the grounds that all wars that America fights are defensive. Yet this is simply not the case. On the contrary, America has become a nation almost perpetually at war, not because it is under attack but because it has become today's principal practitioner of *Realpolitik*, an approach to international relations in which war, as Clausewitz put it, is merely a continuation of politics by other means.

The Founders had not thought a standing army would be a problem for America because they expected that nearly everyone would be subject to a defensive obligation only. They were wrong. Over the past two hundred years, the militia have all but disappeared and nearly everyone has been obligated to become a professional—if not to think like one, at least to behave like one. The military today demands that citizens take to arms for long periods of time, at places far from their homes, to fight in wars that have not been declared by Congress. It has turned American citizens from willing defenders of their homes and liberties to helpless pawns on an international chessboard. By so doing, it has changed America from a country *to* which people fled into a country *from* which people flee.

PART II

PARIS IS ONLY ONE OF THE MANY
OVERSEAS MARINE CORPS POSTS OR INSTALLATIONS
WHERE YOU COULD BE STATIONED.

—*Marine Corps*
recruiting pamphlet, 1966

2. YOUR FRIENDLY
NEIGHBORHOOD RECRUITER

THE MOST fundamental of the military's prerogatives in any society is its right to procure young men for the job of soldiering.

Much has been written in recent years about the American system of conscription. The distastefulness of coercion, the inequity of deferments, the obtuseness of local draft boards—all this has been pointed out with passion and frequency. Little attention, on the other hand, has been paid to military recruiting, and the reason for this oversight is not hard to uncover. To the vocal, educated elements of society who define the issues that get debated, conscription is the danger, the force that threatens an otherwise comfortable and secure existence.

The fact is, however, that recruiting has always been, and remains, the military's primary source of manpower. The ranks of the Air Force and Navy in their entirety, over ninety percent of the Marine Corps, and nearly half the Army are filled at present with young men who signed up with their local recruiters, and the number is rising as President Nixon edges toward an all-volunteer military. These youths are the core of the military—the three- and four-year men who come, at least originally, in good faith. The trouble is that their faith is often sadly misplaced, for military recruiting today is an unacceptably deceptive business: it creates an image of the military for young people that is, like most advertising images, distorted, and it makes promises to induce enlistments that the army does not keep and is not even bound by law to keep. Worst of all, the victims of these deceptions are usually those who have already been most victimized by society—the poorer, less-educated segments of the population.

Private First Class Randy Williams was 17, very naïve, and very unsure of himself when he went to see his Marine Corps recruiter in Costa Mesa, California. His father had been killed while in the Navy, and as a sole surviving son, Williams was eligible to be deferred from military service altogether. But, as he relates it, "I got into a little trouble at high school, and I thought the Marine Corps would really be a good thing for me. I thought I would be doing a good thing for my country, too."

The way Williams remembers it, his recruiter assured him that as a sole surviving son, he would not be sent to Vietnam. This was fine with him; he wasn't that excited about the war. However, the recruiter also told him he would have to sign a waiver of his sole-surviving-son rights in order to be accepted by the Marines. Williams signed the papers and headed off to boot camp to begin a four-year stint.

Six months later, after advanced training as a teletype operator, he was ordered to Vietnam. He tried to complain, to get his superiors to understand about his recruiter's promise. It doesn't matter what your recruiter *said*, he was told; you signed a waiver and lost all your rights. Williams went to Vietnam with an infantry unit. Nine months later, he came back with two Purple Hearts, several pieces of shrapnel in his body—and a wide swath of raw burned skin on his right forearm, the remnants of an old tattoo. "It was the four big letters—you know, 'U.S.M.C.' I got it at the beginning when I was really gung-ho. Then—well, then came Vietnam. I swallowed a couple of reds [seconals] and burned it off with a cigarette lighter. I hate the Marine Corps now, man. They screwed me so bad . . ." There is no anger in his voice—just pain.

Private John Stephen Drake, 22, an articulate, sandy-haired soldier from San Antonio, Texas, is a fist-clenching member of the American Servicemen's Union, and he *is* angry. "These damn recruiters," he says. "They promise a guy the world—as long as it's not in writing. 'Choice, Not Chance,' they say. It's an absolute farce."

Two years ago, Drake was anything but an angry radical. The son of an Air Force captain, he was married and working for an airline. Like Randy Williams, he was a sole surviving son—his father was killed while on active duty in 1956—and so he didn't have to serve in the military. But he did want to fly helicopters. In Dallas, Drake enlisted for three years in the Army's popular Warrant Officer Flight Training program. After basic training he would go to flight school—if he passed a flight physical. What would happen if he failed the physical? In that case, his recruiter assured him, he'd get a discharge. The recruiting sergeant even gave Drake a little wallet-sized card which was headlined ENLISTMENT PROMISE and was supposed to be proof of the Army's commitment either to send him to flight school or to let him void the enlistment contract. If anything went wrong, Drake was told, all he had to do was follow the instructions on the card: "In the event the enlistment commitment stated on the reverse is not honored and cannot be resolved by your commander and personnel officer, write directly to: OPO-FPD, ATTN: EPPAS, Department of the Army, Washington, D.C."

Drake was pleased with his enlistment contract because he figured he couldn't lose: he'd either get the training he wanted or he'd get out. During basic at Fort Polk, Louisiana, he was a model soldier, really striving, looking forward to piloting helicopters. Then came the physical, and it turned out he had a minor vision defect in his left eye—flight school was out. Greatly disappointed, Drake applied for a discharge. He was in for another shock: according to some small print in his enlistment "understanding," the Army didn't have to discharge him after all. Anyone who failed to get into or dropped out of warrant officer training was required to serve out his term as an enlisted man. Drake took out the little card his recruiter had given him, showed it to everyone concerned, and even wrote to OPO-EPD, ATTN: EPPAS. It didn't help. Over one-third of the men who sign up to become warrant officer pilots, it turns out, don't make it; any promises from a recruiter about getting a discharge are worthless.

Private John S. Feild Jr. of Highland Springs, Virginia, accepted at face value one of the favorite poses of Army recruiters: that of the disinterested "career counselor." Intelligent and serious, Feild wanted very much to become a medical laboratory technician. He made several visits to the Army recruiting station in Richmond and explained in detail the career he wished to follow. Upon the advice of his recruiter, he enlisted for three years in Army Career Group 91—Medical Care and Treatment—expecting to attend the Army's medical services school at Fort Sam Houston, Texas, and from there go on to serve as a laboratory technician. He was aware that there were other assignments included under ACG 91, but the recruiter assured him he need have no fear of receiving any of these; they were, allegedly, extremely difficult to get even when they were requested.

When Feild completed basic, however, he found himself enrolled in a food inspection course in Chicago—precisely one of the assignments he had been assured he would not get. As Army jobs go, food inspection is not bad. But it was not what Feild had wanted or expected, and when he found out that laboratory technicians are not even included in ACG 91, and thus that his recruiter had known all along that he would never be one, he was enraged. He strongly protested his assignment to food inspection, so the Army assigned him to artillery instead. When, soon after, the orders came for Vietnam, Feild decided to desert. He is now living in a foreign country.

"I saw the eagerness with which my son enlisted and I know the future he looked forward to in the Army," says his mother,

Edna Feild. "I know how confident he was of receiving the training he desired and that this confidence was a direct result of his discussions at the recruiting office. I then saw him beaten down to a bitter, disillusioned, and frustrated young man. He feels he has been betrayed by the Army and by his country. I fully agree with him. Every effort to have his situation corrected was met with defeat or indifference. The standard Army answer seemed to be 'Tough luck.' Now my family has been split apart, and my only child can never come home again."

Private Ronald E. Stoker of Lorton, Virginia, had the toughest luck of all. Stoker dropped out of high school and signed up for the Army when he was only seventeen. His recruiter assured him that, because he was seventeen and enlisting for only two years, he would not be sent into combat. It *is* Army policy not to send seventeen-year-olds to Vietnam; but Stoker turned eighteen in November 1968, and a few weeks later, he was in Southeast Asia as an infantryman. On January 20, 1969, he was killed by a mortar blast. The Army denies that Stoker's recruiter promised he would not be sent into combat, but Stoker's father, who accompanied his son to the recruiting station, swears to it.

These soldiers' stories could be supplemented with many others, they are not at all unusual or atypical. Lloyd McMurray, a San Francisco attorney who has represented several servicemen in enlistment contract cases, is blunt in his characterization of the recruiting system: "Fraud is not too strong a word. . . . My experience is that recruiters do not scruple to make promises they have no authority to make, and which the armed services are in no position to honor."

Whether "fraud" is the appropriate word or not, there is no question that recruiters oversell. Like all salesmen, they make promises, and statements that sound like promises, in their zeal to nail down a deal. When these promises are in the form of written guarantees, the army does, in the majority of instances, live up to them. But when the promises are in the form of verbal assurances, as is usually the case, there isn't a thing that can be done to enforce them.

II

THE AVERAGE Army recruiter is 36 years old, married, has been in the service 15 years, and has two children. He has been trained in sales and public relations techniques at Fort Benjamin Harrison, Indiana, and he works hard: fifty-three hours a week, according to Army time sheets, plus twelve additional hours of traveling. Each month he drives one thousand miles, personally contacts at least one hundred prospects, and signs up an average of 8.3 enlistees.

Recruiters are rated on how successfully they fulfill their monthly quotas. If they fail to meet their quotas, they have some hard explaining to do to their superiors; if they regularly meet or exceed their quotas, they receive the kind of recognition that really counts for men in the military: "Recruiter of the Year" plaques, certificates of achievement, and promotion. "If three or four guys are after that certificate," says Sergeant John D. Currie, head of the Army recruiting station in Oakland, California, "a difference of one recruit per month can make the difference. It can get pretty hairy."

The key to success in recruiting is what the army calls "prospecting." This means just what it sounds like—getting out into the countryside and scouring for gold in the form of fresh young bodies. The notion of recruiters sitting passively behind desks, waiting for eager volunteers to walk through the doors, is grossly inaccurate.

There are many tricks of the trade in the business of military prospecting. There is, first of all, the primary requirement: establishing good relations with the adult community. Recruiters, when they move into a town, become outstanding citizens. They join the PTA, support the Boy Scouts and the Little League, speak whenever possible before the Lions, Kiwanis, and Rotary. This is essential for establishing credibility with parents, who are often harder to sell on the military than are their sons.

Next, a recruiter gets to know the local media people: newspaper editors, TV programmers, popular disc jockeys. These are the people who will publish his press releases ("Joe Wilson, star halfback for Central High School last year, was awarded the Silver Star for distinguished service with the Americal Division, U.S. Army, in the Republic of Vietnam") and broadcast his radio and TV spots. The recruiter also touches base with local educators: the high school principal from whom he will seek the senior class list and permission to address the students on Career Day, the guidance counselors, the gym and shop teachers who have influence over the boys most likely to join the army. And he makes sure to drop off some literature at the unemployment office. Finally, the recruiter looks for ways to establish direct contact with his market. He does this primarily by getting names.

Names come from three main sources: so-called "centers of influence," the high school senior list, and the pre-induction physical (PIP) list. A "center of influence" is any person who comes in contact with large numbers of young men. He might be a barber, a dentist, or a neighborhood ringleader who turns on his buddies to the army. If an active-duty soldier provides the name of a friend who then enlists, the soldier is rewarded with five days extra leave. ("It's ironic," says a GI who did this. "You get another guy to come in, and *you* get a chance to get out.")

When recruiters can get a senior list early in the year (not all high schools are so cooperative), they like to mail out form letters urging the young men to stay in school. This establishes contact with hundreds of prospects and can be used as evidence that the military has their best interests at heart. As graduation approaches, recruiters send out another postage-free mailing urging students to "fill out the enclosed card today." Every nibble is vigorously followed up by a telephone call and, wherever possible, a personal visit. Many recruiters conduct a telephone canvass of the entire senior list immediately after graduation.

PIP lists are another important prospecting device, and, like the senior list, a valuable tool for direct mail and telephone canvassing. These are weekly or twice-weekly rosters provided by the nearest induction center of all persons who have taken their pre-induction physical and written examinations. Everyone on such a list knows he is on the verge of being drafted; thus the recruiter has an automatic leg up. As soon as the list comes out, the recruiter selects from it the names of young men in his area. He then writes to them, or more likely telephones them at once. Sometimes he drives out to a PIP fellow's house without an appointment, knocks on the door, politely introduces himself to whoever is at home, and begins a sales pitch on the advantages of enlisting over being drafted.

Prospecting is the art and science of *locating* potential enlistees; but the ultimate test of a recruiter's mettle is his ability to "close the deal." Here is where salesmanship becomes all-important, where the recruiter must smell out the real motives, desires, and fears of each prospect and come up with just the right assurances to cover them.

The recruiter knows that when a young man walks into his office, the battle to sign him up is half won. The kid is there for a reason: maybe he's facing the draft, maybe he's having a hard time in school, maybe he wants to get away from his parents or a difficult family situation. He might also have gotten his girlfriend pregnant, be out of a job and in need of money, or in trouble with the law. Though he tries not to show it, his state of mind is anxious. He is vulnerable and within the recruiter's grasp.

At this point the recruiter has two immediate goals: to persuade the prospect to take the physical and the Armed Forces Qualifying Test, and to dissuade him from joining any other branch of the military. Taking the AFQT is a little like test-driving an automobile; it brings the customer one step closer to the final sale. It also has another, more subtle effect: with AFQT and Army Qualification Battery scores in hand, the recruiter can talk about the army in terms of the many training opportunities that are ostensibly fitted to the prospect's newly established aptitudes. The recruiter knows, in many cases, that he is in no position to make a specific guarantee, but his words about training schools and aptitude scores weave a spell. The prospect feels that he is involved in a highly scientific process, that his scores must somehow be related to the assignment he'll get, that they wouldn't have bothered to test him if they weren't going to use his abilities wisely and well. Without knowing exactly why, he feels a little more secure about his future, a little less unwilling to sign a contract.

As the moment of decision nears, the recruiter pleasantly, convincingly puts forward the arguments best calculated to win the sale. For every question, there is a ready answer. Is the prospect, a black youth, concerned about discrimination? Don't worry, it's worse in civilian life. Is he interested in continuing his academic education? No problem, almost every base has a college right next door.

One topic that is decidedly not a selling point is Vietnam; recruiters don't discuss it unless the prospect himself brings it up. When the subject does arise, the recruiter often handles it as did Staff Sergeant Jack A. Kralevich, a Marine Corps recruiter in San Mateo, California, in this tape-recorded conversation with one 18-year-old youth:

PROSPECT: What are the odds of going to Vietnam if I join the Marines?

RECRUITER: This I cannot tell you. I've been trying for two years now, and I can't get over. (*A masterful response: it not only conveys the notion that the proper attitude is to desire to go to Vietnam, it also implies, while evading the question, that most Marines don't get there.*)

PROSPECT: Would you say there are advantages in going to Vietnam?

RECRUITER: Definitely. I saved a heck of a lot of money while I was there. (*Kralevich has already served one tour in Vietnam.*) You don't spend it. I was in Taiwan, Hong Kong, Bangkok. You can go there and for $20 or $30 spend a whole week. You talk about your camera. I got Minoltas, Yashicas, three movie cameras, four thirty-five millimeter cameras. Cost me $2,000, but if I was buying them over here, it would cost me $7,000 or $8,000.

PROSPECT: How do the people overseas treat you? The civilian people?

RECRUITER: I'm treated better over there than I am in this country. No matter where you go in the Marine Corps, people are going to respect you.

PROSPECT: Why is that?

RECRUITER: Well, they realize the things that you've done, the places you've been, and they know it isn't easy. They know that if anything happens, we will be the first ones to be there and the last ones to leave. Now, you talk about Vietnam and the Green Berets and all this other stuff. Well, I don't care if you get the best Green Beret in the world, he can't get into the Marine Corps without going through boot camp. While I can go right up there (*motions toward the Army recruiting station a block away*) and go right up into the Green Berets and teach those guys.

PROSPECT: The Marine is basically like that—the true professional soldier. Is that right?

RECRUITER: Right. I'd say eighty percent of Marines stay in the Marine Corps. Seventy-five or eighty percent. (*The actual Marine Corps re-enlistment rate for fiscal 1970 was twelve percent, and for first-term enlisted men it was five percent.*)

PROSPECT: What would be the odds on getting killed if I went into the Marines and got sent to Vietnam?

RECRUITER: Well, I stayed four years in Vietnam.

PROSPECT: But in all probability . . .

RECRUITER: That's why I say, go into aviation. You're not going to get into any hand-to-hand combat. You're not even going to be carrying a weapon around. You're going to be so far behind the firing lines you won't even have to worry about it.

PROSPECT: Hmmm. One thing that kind of scares me are these massacre deals. I wouldn't want to get involved in anything like that.

RECRUITER: I came back from Vietnam in January of '68. Walked into San Francisco, and this guy is standing by a lamppost, and the guy says, "You're a killer." Just like that. I say, "What are you doing, calling me a killer?" He says, "What do you expect me to call you when I see these pictures of people being murdered in Vietnam?" I say, "Did you see [the originals of] those pictures?" "No." "Well, do you know anything about photography?" It was trick photography. *I* could see it. But you show it to the general public, and that's what they're going to believe. This is what they see. How many people know anything about trick photography?

PROSPECT: Well, I've done some trick photography. But that would be slander against the United States.

RECRUITER: These people work this way. This is what they want.

Much of the time, recruiters do actually believe what they say to their prospects. Most are aware, however, that they stretch—or bypass—the truth rather frequently. "Just like car salesmen," says the Army's Sergeant Currie. "You don't sell cars by talking about the defects. I couldn't sell an Oldsmobile if I told the guy we had to recall 100,000 last year because of a bad transmission."

Are recruiters bothered by the thought that they might not be telling it straight? Less so, it seems, than they might be. Most view the need to stretch the truth as simply part of the job, while some even see it as a public service. To be a recruiter, a soldier must genuinely believe in the military; he could not sell it very effectively if he didn't. Most recruiters remember when they were 18 and, just like the kids they are dealing with, were confused about life, running away, trying to get a new start. For them, the military *was* the answer. They *did* make it. If, in order to sign up another confused or disadvantaged adolescent, they have to exaggerate here and there or mislead just a little bit, well, it's all for the kid's own good.

III

IN RECENT years the military has made a special effort to enlist prospects from urban minority groups. This effort began in 1966 as part of a program called Project 100,000. Prior to

1966, the minimum passing score on the AFQT was 31 out of 100; under Project 100,000, badly educated youths who scored as low as 10 on the test were taken into the military if they lived in specially designated "poverty areas."

To help fill the 100,000 slots allocated to below-standard men, higher recruiting quotas were established for low-income urban neighborhoods, and recruiters intensified their prospecting in these areas. Temporary offices were set up in ghettos, mobile recruiting vans were sent out, and care was taken to assign black recruiters to black neighborhoods. Working through Boys Clubs, Youth Opportunity Centers, and unemployment offices, recruiters strove to get across to dropouts and drifters that there *was* a place for them in the military.

As it turned out, the stepped-up quotas for underprivileged youngsters were filled quite easily; in many cities, in fact, the excess from poverty areas was used to compensate for the decline in volunteers from more affluent neighborhoods. "President Johnson wanted these guys off the street," recalls Colonel William Cole of the Army's Sixth Recruiting District, headquartered in San Francisco. "The Defense Department gave us an objective. We never had any problem. We got more than one hundred percent every time."

Across San Francisco Bay, Marine Corps statistics tell the same story. In fiscal year 1969, the Marines enlisted one resident of Piedmont (white middle and upper middle class), four from Berkeley (also white middle and upper middle class, with some black middle class), and 120 from Oakland (black and white lower and lower-middle class). Of the Oakland volunteers, nearly ninety percent scored under 31 on the AFQT, almost all had police records, and more than seventy percent were black or Mexican-American.

Of the four Marine recruiters in Oakland, two—Gunnery Sergeant Val Rideout and Sergeant Ray LeBlanc—are black. Often they work as a team, going around to street corners, hamburger joints, and basketball courts to "rap with the brothers." If the black youths become hostile, Rideout and LeBlanc are adept at dealing with them. "You get so you can put on almost any kind of personality," says Rideout. "I'll put on one kind of personality, and if that doesn't hit it off, Ray will come by and try another. He'll tell the fellows, 'Don't pay any attention to that other sergeant. Listen to *me*.' "

"We use their language," notes Sergeant Paul Conti, the hard-working white NCO who's in charge of the Marines' Oakland station. "You know, we say 'man.' We even call the cops 'pigs.' " And Staff Sergeant Pascal Thigben, the other white recruiter in the office, adds: "A really big selling point is that everybody starts out *even* at boot camp. Then it's up to you, as a man, to make it on your own. Man to man." The street-toughened dropout gets the message: in the Marine Corps, he can get the better of those smart-ass college kids.

The influence of the Black Panthers in Oakland has somewhat hampered recruiters there in using the high schools as a base of operations. Once, when a Marine Corps band was brought to a predominantly black high school and started to play the national anthem, there was, in Conti's words, "a near-riot." So recruiters devote particular attention to other prospecting techniques.

Several days a week, Sergeant LeBlanc sets out in a red Econoline van to visit the homes of men whose names are on the PIP list. As he drives around the shabby wood-frame slums of East Oakland, he waves to the ladies and stops to chat with an occasional teenager. He arrives at an address on the PIP list. It is afternoon, and not unexpectedly, the son is out; only the mother and a daughter are at home. This is just as well. LeBlanc explains to the mother that if her son is drafted, nine times out of ten he won't get the job he wants. On the other hand, if he enlists in the Marines, he can receive valuable training. He asks the mother to talk it over with her son, and leaves her a forty-page brochure, "Occupational Opportunities, United States Marine Corps."

Of course, LeBlanc realizes from the absent boy's low AFQT score that he wouldn't be likely to be trained as anything but a combat infantryman.[1] But there is always that slim chance,

1. The Project 100,000 men taken into the armed forces from the Oakland ghetto and throughout the country share some interesting characteristics. A 1970 Defense Department study disclosed that forty-one per-

probably a better chance than he'd have on the street. "The Marine Corps isn't all blood and guts," LeBlanc says later. "There *are* many skills that kids can learn. And if they've got a police record, the military gives them a chance to overcome it. When they go for a job, they've got their honorable discharge, and that can overshadow their police record."

Only Sergeant Conti, back at the station, voices a degree of skepticism: "The theory behind this program was to give the men some training after their service in the infantry. But somebody let the ball down. It's sad. There's nothing wrong with these kids except they lack education. If the service had the time . . ." Conti's voice trails off. It is the end of the day; he is physically and emotionally exhausted.

IV

DECEPTION IN the recruiting process does not begin with the hard-pressed neighborhood recruiter struggling to meet his quota. It starts at a much higher level, where policy decisions are made and where advertising themes are developed and approved.

As Senator J. William Fulbright and others have pointed out, the Defense Department operates a publicity apparatus that spends, conservatively, $40 million a year and is manned by a public relations force of thousands. The work of these military publicists includes such activities as a continuing program of junkets for friendly opinion-makers; a constant stream of films and radio and TV programs distributed free of charge; a series of touring exhibits; and a speakers bureau that dispatches hun-

---

cent of the Project 100,000 men are black, compared with twelve percent in the armed forces as a whole. Forty-nine percent come from the South, compared to twenty-eight percent in a random control group. Forty percent are trained for combat, compared with twenty-five percent for the services generally, and half the Project 100,000 men in the Army and Marine Corps go to Vietnam. One does not have to be a statistical wizard to recognize that Project 100,000 serves as a vehicle for channeling poor, mostly Southern and Negro youths to the front lines in Indochina.

dreds of military officers to conventions, Rotary luncheons, and other available pulpits. The purpose of all this feverish activity is not to provide the public with unvarnished facts, but, as Senator Fulbright has stated, to persuade it "that the programs and weapons systems of the Army, Navy, or Air Force . . . should have the first claim on public funds and are the key to peace."

There is a second military public relations apparatus, however, that has thus far been little commented upon. This particular operation is not concerned with matters of military or foreign policy; indeed, it intentionally avoids such subjects. Nor is it primarily interested in what adults are thinking; its special target is young American males. And its single-minded purpose is to stimulate them to take one decisive personal action: to go down to their local recruiter and enlist.

Armies, of course, have always proclaimed their desire for recruits. But in the pre-electronic era such proclamations were limited to wall posters that emphasized facts much more than images. These facts usually pertained to such matters as pay and bounties, allowances for food and clothing, and the time and place where volunteers could sign up. Early American recruitment posters also invariably wound up with a plea for the cause at hand—"God Save the Union!" or some other such timely exhortation.

By the outbreak of World War I, however, recruiting, and war propaganda in general, had become a highly developed art form. Liberty Loan posters abounded in such jingoistic slogans as "Beat Back the Hun!," and gruesome portrayals of German soldiers as saber-toothed, cannibalistic monsters. Recruiting posters were generally more restrained, but exhibited great advances in motivational psychology. A 1917 Navy poster, for example, shows a seductive young lass in a sailor's cap and blouse, well ventilated at the neck, with an alluring twinkle in her eyes. "Gee! I wish I were a *man*," she is saying. "*I'd* join the Navy." A Marine Corps poster of the same year depicts a jut-jawed, virile-looking young man stripping off his suit jacket as if about to engage in a street fight. At his feet is a newspaper with the banner headline HUNS KILL WOMEN AND CHILDREN!

The poster proclaims, "Tell That to the Marines!—at 24 East 23rd Street."

Recruiting efforts were halted during World War II, since conscription made them unnecessary. When they came back after the war, it was with new energy and new assistance. For the first time, the services retained their own civilian ad agencies, and soon the media were flooded with enticing images of fun, travel, and adventure, army style. Today the beat goes on: Madison Avenue and the Pentagon have become lasting partners, well practiced at gauging and appealing to the unique motivations of their buying market: male, non-college-bound, late adolescents.

Thus, a 17-, 18-, or 19-year-old boy is at a point in his life where he is very much concerned about "becoming a man." He wants to become a man in a physical, bodily way, but also in a social and psychological way; he sees over the horizon the looming responsibilities of adulthood, and doesn't know quite what to do about them. Army advertising assuages his uncertainties: by joining the military, he *will* become a man—in body, mind, and spirit.

Boys in their late teens also very often want to get away from home; they are weary of their families, bored with small-town life, or yearn to strike out on their own. To these youths, the military presents itself as a good way to leave home without losing respect, to travel without admitting that they're running away.

Another characteristic of American late adolescents is a general fascination with machinery. For whatever reason, teen-age boys are greatly attracted by motorcycles, racing cars, and other shiny metal objects that move fast. Here, too, the advertising message strikes home: come with us and get a chance to play with some *really* sleek and powerful machines.

Young bucks also like to have fun, to meet girls, loll on tropical beaches and really be part of the action. This is a push-over for the admen: there's no easier way to become a member of the Pepsi generation—their posters and commercials guarantee you—than by enlisting in the U.S. army.

In addition to transmitting positive appeals, recruitment ads also seek to combat the negative images associated in young people's minds with the military. Of the four services, the Army and the Marine Corps have the poorest images—the Marine Corps because it is thought to be the most dangerous of the services, the Army because it is viewed as the least glamorous. A confidential study in 1969 by Audits and Surveys, Inc., a New York market analysis firm, found that the Army "is seen as the stepchild of authority, made to work hardest while others live better; made to walk while others ride." On the other hand, young people "hear the Navy message as 'see the world,' the Air Force as 'high-toned and technical.' "

To spruce up its Sad Sack image, the Army focuses heavily in its advertising on modern technology: helicopters, electronics, missiles, "precision" maintenance. It promotes the image of a new "Action Army" in which there seemingly are no foot soldiers: men work with advanced equipment, develop their bodies and leadership abilities, study and prepare for future success.

Although Indochina is never mentioned in Army advertising, the war *has* caused some changes in approach. In pre-Vietnam days, the Army's slogan was "If you're good enough," a low-key challenge to a young man's self-esteem that was followed by the customary appeals to his underlying desires. One typical early-sixties brochure shows a youth standing lazily over a broom; he is working as a gas station attendant and looks terribly bored. "*Some young men* don't mind killing time," says the caption. "It's easy for them to let day after day roll by." The next picture, by contrast, shows a group of junior John Waynes plunging into combat, guns at the ready, shells exploding overhead. "*An 'action guy'* can't just wait for things to happen . . . he *makes* them happen," reads the copy. "Routine plugging along just isn't for him. He's too much of a man for that." The next several pages explain with gritty pictures and text "why it takes a man—a big man—to carve a career out of the blued steel of combat soldiering."

With the onset of the Vietnam War, however, even the most unsophisticated farm boy began to realize that it didn't take much to be "good enough" for the U.S. Army. The slogan

was changed to "Your future . . . your decision . . . choose
Army." Combat and travel were de-emphasized, and the stress
in advertising was placed on education and Stateside fun. The
Army's agency, N. W. Ayer & Son, Inc., developed a series
of one-minute TV spots keyed to the theme, "Our man in . . ."
"Our man," needless to say, was never in Saigon or Da Nang, but
always in sunny American posts, happily water-skiing or
woman-chasing during his many hours of leisure. A new brochure carried a cover photo of an Army private, wearing an
infantry pin, intently reading a book in what was obviously a
library. "Study . . . Learn . . . Build . . . for your future," was
the headline. No guns, no violence, no war.

Early in 1971, Ayer unveiled a new series of radio and TV
ads keyed to the catchy slogan "Today's Army wants to join
you." Rock, soul, and country-and-Western songs urged kids
to "come on and dig" the Army. None of the ads made reference to Vietnam; the emphasis was on how well attuned the
"new" Army was to young people's style of living.

Marine Corps ads have also undergone notable changes over
the years. In 1950, J. Walter Thompson, the Corps's agency,
conducted a survey which showed that travel and adventure
were its best selling points. There subsequently followed a
series of posters that could have doubled as publicity for Trans
World Airlines, with handsome young Marines standing in
front of the Eiffel Tower, the Colosseum, and other tourist
splendors. A brochure depicted life at Marine boot camp—
one of the most terrifying experiences an American can go
through—as something akin to summer camp: smiling kids doing exercises and receiving instruction from friendly, attentive
drill sergeants.

Toward the end of the fifties a new theme came in: "The
Marine Corps Builds Men!" (This was later modified slightly
to "The Marine Corps Builds Men—Body, Mind and Spirit,"
in order to get away from the notion of the Marine as sheerly
a physical brute.) The emphasis was no longer on pleasant,
interesting experiences but on how tough the Marine Corps
was, and how tough it could make *you.* This change in approach may have been inspired by the surprising fact that,

following the nationwide publicity which surrounded the death by drowning of six Parris Island recruits in 1956, enlistments in the Marine Corps actually increased.

With the escalation of the war in Vietnam, the Marines decided to adopt a more innocuous slogan, "Ask a Marine." But the old appeals were still there, as in this 1970 radio commercial:

Young man, if you will be graduating from high school in the near future, you should know about an eight-week course that could be one of the biggest turning points in your life. It's the eight weeks new Marines spend in Marine Corps basic training. Eight weeks that mold them in body, mind and spirit—into *men* the Marine Corps is proud to call its own. And the Corps is not the only one who is proud—*you* will be too. In your proud uniform, you are a new man with muscles that respond instantly, and new self-confidence that will last the rest of your life. Now, you stand ready to handle any situation—overcome any obstacle—because Marine training has brought out the best in you. The way for you to find out how you can become a part of this elite military organization is to *ask a Marine*. A good one to ask is your nearby Marine Corps representative. See him today.

As befits a major Madison Avenue campaign, the military's recruitment publicity program utilizes all the available media. Posters—the old historic medium—are still widely displayed in front of federal buildings and on large twenty-four-sheet billboards which are made available, free of charge, by outdoor-advertising companies. Brochures are distributed through schools, youth clubs, job agencies, and direct mailing. Magazine ads, usually full-page, are purchased at regular space rates in such youth-market periodicals as *Senior Scholastic, Hot Rod*, and *Surfing*, as well as in *Playboy* and *Life*.

By far the biggest impact today, however, is made through radio and television. Radio commercials in the form of ten-, twenty-, thirty-, and sixty-second spots are professionally produced by the military's ad agencies. These ads feature endorsements by big-name celebrities (Ed McMahon, Jack Webb, Art Buchwald, and former Senator Paul Douglas plug the Marine Corps, for example) and attention-catching musical jingles.

Pre-recorded spots are distributed on long-playing records to
more than five thousand radio stations who broadcast them free
of charge. Reading copy is also sent out for the benefit of disc
jockeys and announcers. DJ's on soul stations doing recruitment ads in their own style are perhaps the military's best
means of communicating with street blacks.

Television ads are of high commercial quality—N. W. Ayer
spends up to $25,000 on production of a sixty-second Army
spot. The ads are distributed to some 730 television stations
who broadcast them, like the radio spots, as free public service
announcements. Such generosity on the part of the media—
designed to impress the Federal Communications Commission
—enables the Defense Department to stretch its advertising
budget considerably. In 1969, for example, the Army's advertising budget of $3 million was devoted almost entirely to
the production and distribution of ads. Air time—usually the
most expensive chunk of any advertising campaign—was do-
nated free to the Army by radio and TV stations to the tune
of $7 million. For all four services the donated air time was
worth nearly $25 million that year. In 1971 when Ayer came
up with its new "Today's Army wants to join *you*" commercials, the Army (though not the other services) began for the
first time to *pay* for air time, allocating $10 million for a four-
month blitz during which TV recruitment messages appeared
on "Gunsmoke," "Mission: Impossible," "The Bold Ones," and
other prime-time thrillers with large audiences in the 17-to-21
age range.

If this seems like a lot of military advertising on the airwaves,
it is nothing compared to what would happen if Congress and
the President decide to maintain, or try to maintain, a two- to
three-million man army without reliance upon the draft. For
such an all-volunteer situation, the military has drawn up plans
to advertise heavily during prime evening hours, when rates
run as high as $40,000 for a minute of network time. A special
Army study on converting to an all-volunteer system recommended in 1970 that "to sell and improve the Army image, the

USAREC [Army Recruiting Command] advertising budget should be increased . . . to $36 million annually." If the other services similarly increased their publicity expenditures, recruitment advertising would become a more than $100 million-a-year operation. The Army alone, with a budget of $36 million, would be America's fifteenth-largest advertiser, just behind General Mills and Gillette and just ahead of Chrysler. It would be spending over three times as much on advertising as Coca-Cola and more than four times as much as Anheuser-Busch (Budweiser). It would be sponsoring nighttime entertainment shows and, perhaps, running ads during Walter Cronkite's news. In a word, it would be all over the place.

V

THE OBJECTIVE of all the words and images brandished by admen and recruiting sergeants is to induce young men to sign up—specifically, to sign DD Form 4, a two-page standard form used by all branches of the military. At the very top, in capital letters, are printed the words ENLISTMENT CONTRACT: ARMED FORCES OF THE UNITED STATES.

A contract, according to Webster, is "an agreement that is legally enforceable." What happens, however, if the signing of a contract is fraudulently induced? What, in the case of an enlistment contract, can a young man do if, once he's in the army, he finds out that things are not the way the ads, brochures, and recruiters had led him to think they were?

According to law, there are two basic types of contract: commercial contracts, in which, for example, one party agrees to provide services to the other in return for money; and contracts which change the status of the signers, such as marriage contracts. The singular feature of the latter is that they are quite secure against breaches. Thus, if a businessman fails to provide a contracted service, he has breached his contract and the other party need not fulfill his side of the deal. But if a husband fails to support his wife, the marriage nevertheless remains in force; his status is still that of a husband and hers still that of a wife, and both remain legally bound to fulfill their marital responsibilities.

Enlistment contracts, according to an 1890 Supreme Court decision, *In re Grimley*, are of the marriage contract type. They are, consequently, difficult to terminate: if a soldier absents himself from duty, he remains a soldier and is still subject to military authority. But they are, nevertheless, contracts, and as such they are, or should be, governed by certain principles that apply to all contracts. In particular, they are, or should be, voidable when fraudulently induced, just as marriages can, on similar grounds, be annulled.

The United States government, however, does not see things this way. Rather, it entertains the quite extraordinary view that the enlistment contract is binding *only on the enlistee*. One party—the government—may alter, ignore, or terminate the contract as it sees fit; the other party—the citizen—can do none of these things. He lacks, like the slave Dred Scott, even the standing to sue.

Not only can the government alter at will, *post facto*, the enlistment contract; it can, with impunity, commit fraud to induce it—a striking deviation from the standard law of contracts, as well as from broad congressional policy. Congress claims to be an opponent of fraud. It long ago created the Federal Trade Commission to watch out for deceptive practices among businessmen, and has come out more recently for truth in packaging and truth in lending. Congress is for truth in recruiting too—but only if the *soldier* lies. Article 83 of the Uniform Code of Military Justice declares: "Any person who procures his own enlistment or appointment in the armed forces by knowingly false representation or deliberate concealment as to his qualifications . . . shall be punished as a court-martial may direct." This is a firm warning to 15-year-olds not to lie about their age. One searches in vain for the other half of this provision; it is not there. Volunteers must tell the truth. Recruiters? Well, it's up to them.

One man who fought—and lost—a battle against the Army's right to defraud him is Sergeant Ronald A. Gausmann. His case is an illuminating example of how hopelessly the cards are stacked against the innocent volunteer.

Gausmann was 19 when he visited the Army recruiting station in Hayward, California, with a couple of friends. He had completed two years of high school, then dropped out. He had already been called for his pre-induction physical and was looking for a better deal than the draft. It was November 1965, and President Johnson had begun the massive build-up of American forces in Vietnam; Gausmann didn't want to join their ranks.

Sergeant First Class James A. Ball was the recruiting officer who spoke with Gausmann and his friends. Ball sympathized with their desire to serve somewhere other than Vietnam. As a matter of fact, he pointed out, the Army had a deal that would assure just that. If Gausmann would sign up for four years, Ball would guarantee that he'd be stationed for three of those years in Europe. The first year would be spent in training in the United States.

Gausmann talked it over with his friends and they agreed it sounded good. On November 15, 1965, they all returned to the recruiting station to sign up.

At the bottom of page 1 of DD Form 4 is a clause which reads: "I have had this contract fully explained to me, I understand it, and certify that no promise of any kind has been made to me concerning assignment to duty, geographical area, schooling, special programs, assignment to government quarters, or transportation of dependents, except as indicated: _____." This is one escape clause by which the Army gets off the hook for any promises its recruiters make verbally. The recruit asks what to write in the blank space, and the recruiter usually tells him to write "None."

When Gausmann came to the blank space, Sergeant Ball told him to write "U.S. Army, Europe, Term of Enlistment Four Years." This was the authorized language to indicate a guarantee of *initial* assignment to Europe. Then Gausmann came to a separate sheet of paper entitled "Statement of Understanding." There was a blank space on that page, too, and Ball had Gausmann fill it again with "U.S. Army, Europe, Term of Enlistment Four Years." Gausmann asked what the sheet of paper was. "That's your guarantee," replied Ball, and Gausmann signed it.

The following week a photograph appeared in the local newspaper showing Gausmann and six friends standing with a smiling Sergeant Ball in front of the recruiting station. One of the boys was holding up a sign saying EUROPE.

After going through training at Fort Ord, Gausmann was, as promised, sent to an Army post in Germany. There he performed his duties well and rose to the rank of sergeant. Then, a year later, came the inevitable levy of men for Vietnam—and it included Gausmann. The young soldier unsuccessfully appealed the order through Army channels. He was already in the Oakland Overseas Replacement Center when he got a lawyer and petitioned for habeas corpus, arguing that his enlistment contract should be voided because it had been obtained through false representations.

The facts of Gausmann's case were as solid as they could ever be in a lawsuit of this type. Both Gausmann and a friend who had gone to the recruiting station with him testified under oath that Sergeant Ball had expressly guaranteed them three years in Europe, barring only a declaration of war somewhere else. Sergeant Ball, also called as a witness, could not remember exactly what he had told Gausmann back in 1965, but he explained his usual procedure. "I would indicate to an individual on this option, trying to explain it down to the 17- and 18-year level, people who had no concept of what military service was like, just what might happen to them. I would explain the normal tour [in Europe] is three years. If I went over, I would expect to stay three years. No one was moving out of the command at the time."

The government opposed Gausmann vigorously, not on the facts, which were against it, but on grounds of law. Its arguments were interesting revelations of the state of the government's mind as well as the state of the law.

In the first place, the government contended, the army can never breach an enlistment contract. This is clearly spelled out in the "Statement of Understanding" which Ball had said was

Gausmann's "guarantee." That statement, which all volunteers receiving a written guarantee are made to sign, contains a paragraph which provides that "military necessity may make it necessary to effect my reassignment at any time." This is another escape clause that can get the army out of anything. What is "military necessity"? Only the army knows for sure.

As its second major point, the government argued that recruiters are not authorized to guarantee three years in Europe; therefore the Army can't be held accountable for any such promise. The implication of this argument is that 19-year-olds, totally ignorant of military ways, must not only analyze everything their recruiter *says*; they must also possess knowledge of everything their recruiter is *authorized* to say—quite a burden for youths being asked to trust in the government for which, in good faith, they are about to fight.

Thirdly, the government asserted that, as a sovereign power, it could not be sued without its consent. Since it certainly wasn't consenting to be sued by Gausmann, the judge had no business even listening to the case.

As a clincher, the government contended that even if the judge insisted on hearing the case, he was powerless to rule in Gausmann's favor. An enlistment contract, however induced, could be voided only by the Secretary of the Army. The federal courts, said Assistant U.S. Attorney John Bartko, have not been delegated the power to direct military discharges.

Albert C. Wollenberg of the Northern California District, the respected liberal judge who heard the case, expressed shock that the Army might mislead young men in order to enlist them. Nevertheless, he ruled, the "military necessity" clause allowed the Army to assign Gausmann anywhere, regardless of how his enlistment might have been induced. "The Army's assignment of the petitioner to the Oakland military base in Oakland, California, for transfer to Vietnam is such a determination [of military necessity] which should not be reviewed by the Civil Courts." Petition for habeas corpus denied. On appeal, the Ninth Circuit affirmed without comment.

Gausmann's case is not noteworthy because it reveals great evil on the part of Sergeant Ball, who was only doing his job, or vileness on the part of the government. Rather it is indicative of the enormous and unrestrainable power that the army acquires over people, not only after they sign their enlistment contracts, but even before. From the moment a young man comes into contact with the army, from the first ad he sees, from the first visit he makes to a recruiter, he is being manipulated for the military's ultimate purposes, and his chances of protecting himself are slim indeed. Control of information is a major part of that manipulation. The soldier may learn that he has been lied to; he may find out that he has been given bad advice. But invariably, when he does find out, it is too late to do anything about it. Like Gausmann, the soldier who struggles against the army will sooner or later discover "Catch-22," the one universal truth about the military: no matter how much justice, humanity, or simple logic may be on your side, you can't beat the system.

IN WORLD WAR II, THE KIDS HAD MOTIVATION.
IN THIS WAR THEY DON'T.
OUR ARMY FIGHTS ONLY BECAUSE OF DISCIPLINE.
THAT'S WHY IT WORKS SO HARD AT DISCIPLINE.

Rear Admiral
Arnold E. True (ret.)

3. REMAKING THE CIVILIAN

THE PURPOSE of basic training, according to Army Regulation 350–1, is to convert "non-prior service enlisted personnel [the Army's circumlocution for civilians] . . . into well disciplined, highly motivated, and physically conditioned soldiers, who are qualified in their basic weapon and drilled in the fundamentals of soldiery."

Of the three prime objectives—discipline, motivation, and weapons skills—the simplest for the army to deal with is the last. Motivation and discipline are harder. They involve the spirit and the heart, the way men think and the way they behave.

High motivation and good discipline are important in warfare for two rather obvious reasons: (1) it is not natural under ordinary circumstances for men to advance into a line of hostile and possibly lethal fire; (2) when men do advance or hold against an enemy, they have a much better chance of surviving, not to speak of winning, if they operate together. But the nature of America's role in the world today raises some important questions: *Should* motivation and discipline be imposed where they are voluntarily lacking? If so, *what kind* of motivation and discipline? And *how* should they be imposed?

Americans have been brought up on the notion that their country goes to war only for good cause. The corollary of this is that American soldiers are motivated by a belief in the cause for which America is fighting. Democratic theory supports this notion: war cannot be entered into without prior national assent expressed through a congressional declaration; therefore, if the people support a war before entering into it, the soldiers will believe in it once entered.

At times in America's turbulent history, the motivation to risk death *has* derived from strong belief in a cause: in the Revolution, when "embattled farmers" lifted their rifles in revolt against arbitrary British rule; on the frontier, among both Indians and white men; in labor struggles and in the civil rights movement. Such motivation exists today among the Israelis and the Viet Cong.

In most of America's wars, however, as in most wars of other nations, there has been a blending of affirmative and negative motivations. Even if soldiers have understood the cause, it hasn't meant that much to them personally, and the government has therefore had to nudge, push, or coerce them into battle, depending on the nature of the war. In short, it has had to move its soldiers more through discipline than through motivation.

Discipline differs from motivation in that it is an external phenomenon, a measure of a man's behavior in the company of others. Groups or individuals are said to be well or poorly disciplined depending on how they behave. As a child is well disciplined if he adheres to the behavioral norms established by his parents, so a soldier is well disciplined if he adheres to the behavioral norms established by his superiors.

Until the advent of modern weaponry, a high degree of discipline was absolutely essential for successful armies. Soldiers had to be trained to move together into combat in such tight formations as the phalanx, the cavalry charge, or the fixed line. When muskets could fire only a single round without reloading, it was imperative that riflemen shoot only upon command and maintain their line so that a massive volley could be formed by firing in unison. Holding formation was even more important after the muskets were emptied and effective use of the bayonet meant the difference between defeat and victory.

Modern air power, armor, and automatic weapons have made such finely honed coordination in ground combat unnecessary. Today, discipline means essentially one thing: unquestioning obedience to orders, whether on the battlefield or off. Soldiers are taught close-order drill, not because it is useful in combat, but because it is thought to instill obedience and martial spirit. The same is true of saluting and other customs inherited from the military past.

Coordination and teamwork still remain essential, of course, even under modern conditions, but the need for blind obedience is greatly overrated. Except for battles in which men must be ordered to do things that are pointlessly suicidal (as, for example, at Hamburger Hill), soldiers engaged in combat have a pretty good common-sense understanding of what needs to be done, and a general readiness to do it. They appreciate the notion that, if the group is to survive, it is best that one man be the leader and that the leader's word be final. If the leader is the kind of person who listens to his men, possesses a real concern for their welfare, and leads by example as well as by command, his soldiers are not likely to endanger themselves or their comrades by departing from the concerted action of the group.

Obedience in today's army is much less assured out of battle than in. This is particularly true where affirmative motivation is lacking and men begin wondering why they are being told to fight. Soldiers tend to get weary of combat, especially when there is little in it for them. Thus the need in 1970 for discipline —instinctive obedience—to supplement affirmative motivation, and at times to replace it completely.

II

BASIC TRAINING systems differ slightly among the four military services; the Marine Corps' is the most rigorous and brutal, the Air Force's the least. The Army, which trains the most recruits, has lately begun an effort to reduce brutality to a minimum. In all services, however, the process is the same: first break down the recruit's individuality, then rebuild him as an obedient cog in the military machine, eager, or at least willing, to kill upon command.

Marine Corps boot camp is basic training in its most pristine, albeit extreme, form. It begins as recruits trickle in from all over the country to Parris Island, South Carolina, or the Marine Corps Recruit Depot, San Diego, California.[1]

"All right, you shitheads, you have ten seconds to get off this bus and five of them are gone."

The voice is booming, frightening, overpowering. It is coming from a strange-looking man in a Smokey-the-Bear hat, but the funny uniform is not a joke. This is the real thing; the guy is definitely not playing around. He is a Marine Corps drill instructor, and he is dead serious.

"Shut up and spit out any gum that you're chewing. When you get off the bus you are to stand at attention on the yellow footprints. You know what attention means? It means stand up straight! I catch any of you maggots farting around and I'll kick the shit out of you right here. Now move!"

The young Marine recruits stumble out of the bus and onto the yellow footprints that are painted on the pavement outside the reception station. Sometimes they stand there for hours until enough trainees arrive to make up a platoon—about eighty men. Then their heads are shaved, moles and all, in about forty seconds apiece.

1. The quotations and descriptions in this section are based on interviews with several dozen boot camp graduates and Marine Corps training officers, and on personal observations by the author at MCRD San Diego.

From the barber's chair the panicked recruits run to a counter where a corporal throws some clothes at them. Next they run or stumble into a large room with wooden desks on which everyone puts his clothes and waits.

"Move your ass, shithead," booms that voice again. Soon it is explaining how to send civilian clothes home, how to tear up draft cards ("You won't be needing *them* anymore"), how to do everything just the way it tells you.

"Why are you so stupid?" it shouts. Everyone is a moron. One guy faints from fright: the voice of the drill instructor is more than he can take.

Into the shower. "Pull your dick back and wash behind your balls. What the hell is so funny, faggot? You queer?" Back into the large room with desks. Put on military clothes, none of which fit.

Now the recruits grab seabags, get in formation, and meet another drill instructor—the senior DI who will be with them until they graduate from boot camp. His voice is even louder than the other's. "From here on," he bellows, "the first word out of your mouth will be the word 'Sir.' "

"Yes, sir!" the recruits shout back, overlooking the inconsistency.

"Louder!" demands the DI. "YES, SIR!" scream the recruits.

"All you have to do, privates, is exactly as you're goddam told. Is that clear?"

"YES, SIR!"

The attack upon the recruits' personalities has begun.

This attack takes many forms. It seeks to demolish, first of all, the recruit's concept of himself as an individual. Thus, he is made to look exactly like all the other recruits; he may abhor his appearance, but can do nothing about it. He is never called by his name; he is called "shithead," "turd," "maggot," "punk," "fatso," "Private Nigger," or "beanbag" (an epithet for Chicano), depending on the DI's vocabulary and the recruit's physical or racial characteristics.[2]

---

2. One 22-year-old recruit from New York, a graduate of the University of Pennsylvania and Wharton Business School, was told to step front

In turn, the recruit must learn never to use the first person when addressing his drill instructor. "Sir," he must say, "the private requests permission to speak to the Senior Drill Instructor, Staff Sergeant Wilcox," who may grant or deny the permission. If permission is granted, the recruit must continue to refer to himself as "the private." Nor can he use the first person plural: it is always "the other privates," "the platoon," never "we."

All contact with the outside world—with the recruit's friends and family and every other link with his previous identity—is cut off, except for a few minutes a day when he may receive or write letters. No telephoning is allowed. There are no TV sets or radios or newspapers.

Even access to the mails is at the mercy of the drill instructor. During mail call in the evening, every recruit must stand at attention in front of his bunk. The DI sits in the center of the squad bay and calls out the names of those with mail. As his name is called, the recruit runs to the DI and snaps to attention. The DI takes his letter, holds it outstretched in front of him, then drops it toward the floor. The recruit must clap his hands, catching the letter with the clap before it touches the floor. If he misses, too bad; he can try again the next day. No books, magazines, food, or other gifts may be received through the mail. One recruit at Parris Island received a tube of chapstick; the DI made him eat it.

Writing letters can be as harrowing as receiving them. Recruits are supposed to receive an hour of free time in the

---

and center by his DI at Parris Island. "Are you a Jew?" the DI demanded. "Yes, sir," shouted the terrified recruit. "Are you an old-fashioned Jew?" "No, sir." "O.K., then you can go back into line." Thereafter the DI called the recruit "Jewboy" and "bagel" and at one point painted a Star of David on his forehead. Another DI, of German extraction, told him, "You know what we Germans think of you Jews." The recruit began to have delusions, thinking he was in a concentration camp. After 7½ weeks he completely cracked up and was given a psychiatric discharge. Congressman Mario Biaggi of New York, who investigated the case, charged that "in many respects the recruit *was* treated like a prisoner in a concentration camp."

evening, between eight o'clock and taps at nine. Whether they get it or not depends on the DI, who can take it away as punishment, or see to it that almost all the time is taken up shining boots and performing other chores.

The assault on the recruit seeks to convey to him that he is wholly worthless as a person, that he is a dumb, flabby civilian, possibly a queer, at any rate not a man, and certainly not worthy of being called a Marine. To this end, the recruit is constantly told that he is stupid; he can do nothing right, nothing fast enough. College kids are ridiculed as "pussies," high school dropouts as "dum-dums." "I've never seen such a sorry group of people in all my life," the DI tells the platoon. "I've always had honor platoons and now, look at this bunch of cruds and sluts. You're lower than whale shit, and that's at the bottom of the ocean." His voice oozes with disgust.

Lack of masculinity is a constant theme. Recruits are collectively referred to as "girls" or "ladies," individually as "sweetheart" or "queer." A platoon at San Diego wasn't clicking its heels loud enough during close-order drill. "You want to march on your toes like you have a bunch of high heels on?" intoned the DI. "O.K., ladies, that's just fine. Put your right arm up like you're holding a purse. Now get on your toes and repeat after me [switching to a high falsetto]: 'We're a bunch of girls and we can't march.'" The entire process of breaking down the civilian and constructing the new soldier becomes one of emasculation, eventually followed by conferral of manhood.

When the recruits aren't females, they are often subhuman, animals. Platoons are often exercised in sand, then made to grovel on their backs like pigs in a sty, growling and oinking and making similar animal noises.

Psychological degradation is compounded and reinforced by physical punishment. A platoon is too slow getting back to the barracks? That's one hundred push-ups for everyone. And one hundred more. And one hundred more. A recruit scratches his head in formation? Rifle up and over shoulders one thousand times. Somebody talks in the shower? The platoon is made to roll around in the sand, exercise for an hour, then go to bed caked in mud and sweat. "We were going to be easy with you," says the DI, sneering. "But now we're going to have to get hard. The harder you are, the easier we are. The easier you get, the harder we get."

Individual disciplining of recruits by DI's can be even more terrifying than group punishment. Although Marine Corps regulations flatly prohibit "maltreatment, oppression or cruelty towards recruits," striking a trainee—or "thumping," as it's called—is second nature to the lion's share of DI's and as indigenous to the Marine Corps as fish to the sea. Recruits who displease a DI are told to report to the duty hut, the DI's private quarters. Here they are tongue-lashed and frequently "thumped." Often punishments are inflicted in bizarre and imaginative ways. Making recruits exercise inside wall lockers is a favorite penalty, as is placing a bucket on the head—this last a common punishment for recruits caught smoking. Another practice, also punishment for unauthorized smoking, is to make recruits eat cigarette butts or drink water from canteens in which ashes have been dumped. One Congressman was informed about recruits who had been locked in "Dempsey Dumpsters," which are garbage containers about four feet wide and six feet high. The "Dempsey Dumpsters" were pounded with baseball bats while the recruits were trapped inside. Recruits subjected to such treatment rarely complain, because the threat of retaliation is so thoroughly believable.

After a few days it begins to dawn on the recruit that he is trapped in some kind of nightmarish experiment. The whole recruit depot is an enormous Skinner box, a totally controlled environment from which there is no escape. The recruits run, run, run, always asshole to bellybutton, completely lost in the maze, responding to stimuli, reacting to punishments, not knowing the meaning of it all but getting conditioned like rats. There is no time to think, only time to jump at that voice, to exercise, to look straight ahead, to shout, to obey.

It also begins to dawn on the recruit that there are some unwritten rules in this rat race and that he had better learn them.

Rule No. 1: There's only one way out—go along. Escape is impossible; don't even dream about it. You are always watched.

Rule No. 2: The DI is lord of the Skinner box. He is omnipresent, superhuman, sees all and knows all. If he scorns you, you deserve it. If he hits you, it's for your own good.

Rule No. 3: Keep your mouth shut. Don't write horror stories to your parents; you'll only worry them needlessly. Forget about your Congressman. Remember that everyone who talks is caught, and they regret it.

Rule No. 4: If you screw up, it only gets worse. One false move too many, and you go to the Motivation Platoon. You don't want to go to the Motivation Platoon; you don't want to go to Correctional Custody; you don't want to go to the brig. It's worse, much worse. And you have to come back to the program anyway. So don't screw up. It only prolongs the agony.

The recruit absorbs these rules because his very survival seems in danger. He is constantly hungry and tired. For the first two or three weeks he knows no one's name. He doesn't talk to his bunkmate; he keeps to himself and gets to sleep as quickly as possible. And as his mental and emotional resistance is worn down, he is slowly, steadily conditioned into instant obedience to even the most trivial rules and commands.

Everything is endlessly repeated and reinforced. Even eating, excreting, and smoking are used as conditioning tools. Recruits are marched to the food counters with their trays directly in front of their faces. They sidestep through the chow line clicking their heels, then go to long tables where they stand until their table fills up. At the command of, "Ready, seat!" they must sit down and cross their arms in front of them. They must do so precisely in unison or hear the DI's scolding voice give them another Marine Corps lesson: "Oh, oh. Somebody's too slow. We'll have to do it again until we do it right. No sense doing something unless you're going to do it right. Ready, stand! Ready, seat!" Obedience is the price of food. Finally comes the command: "Eat." No one speaks. The recruits gulp down their food and run back to formation in seven minutes.

Toilet training is much the same. The squad bay in the barracks is divided into left and right sides. The DI announces, "Starboard side, make a head call." The right side shouts back the order: "Aye, aye, sir. Starboard side, make a head call." But the DI isn't satisfied: "Oh, starboard side, you're not very loud this morning. Port side, make a head call." Port side repeats the order more loudly than starboard, and port side goes. The platoon has learned another lesson.

Three times a day, unless the DI decrees otherwise, the platoon is allowed a brief cigarette break. The smokers fall out, form a group away from the nonsmokers, and shout together: "The smoking circle for Platoon 231 is now formed, sir." Upon command, the recruits light up, inhale and exhale, all in unison. When not inhaling, they must hold their cigarettes straight-armed in front of them; to inhale they must bend the elbow while keeping the upper arm stiff.

Despite the rigidity of the ritual, recruits look forward anxiously to their cigarette break. It is thus a natural privilege for the DI to withhold. "Well, ladies, I was going to give you a smoking break, but we can't have cigarettes because Richards here won't do his push-ups." This does not endear Richards to his peers. He may be beaten in the shower that night. The next day he is better motivated to do his push-ups, and perhaps the platoon will get a smoking break.

The one thing the recruit most desperately seeks to avoid is getting dropped from his platoon. Whatever the humiliations, whatever the punishments meted out by his drill instructors, the recruit has one certitude to hold on to: the fact that, if he stays with his original platoon, he will graduate in eight weeks. At first, graduation appears to be a millennium away; it does not seem possible to survive that long. But imperceptibly, as days blend into one another, time advances; milestones are passed and the recruit starts counting, first the weeks and then the days, until cessation, liberation, emancipation. What he dreads most of all is the abyss of uncertainty into which he will plunge if he is separated from his platoon. This is the DI's ultimate weapon; the young recruit knows it and lives in fear of it.

It is easy for the DI to take recruits out of their platoons. At both Parris Island and MCRD San Diego there is the innocuously named Special Training Branch, or STB.

Within the STB are five platoons, each designed to deal with its own particular brand of misfit (of whom there are plenty—one out of every four recruits passed through an STB platoon in 1969). There is the two-section Physical Proficiency Platoon, filled with weak bodies that can't take the strenuous pace—one section, the "fat farm," for overweight recruits, the other for skinny ones. There is the Academic Proficiency Platoon, where a handful of functional illiterates are taught something about reading. There is the Medical Rehabilitation Platoon, where recruits who get sick or break legs are held until they mend. And finally, there are the two most dreaded platoons, Motivation and Correctional Custody. Here is where the bad boys go, the ones who resist the program. Here they suffer for their sins, until, like spirits rising into Purgatory from the descending circles of Dante's Hell, they are deemed ready to return to a regular platoon, and, if they are lucky, to graduate from boot camp.

Motivation begins with a one-day ordeal on a Sunday. The DI's have picked out the recruits who don't look sharp, who fall behind in the runs, or are caught "eye-fucking." ("Eye-fucking" is a heinous crime in Marine Corps boot camp. It consists of moving one's eyeballs to the side while standing at attention.)

The errant recruits are started off with a ten-mile forced march around the base, punctuated by patriotic pep talks and denunciations of draft-card burners. They watch the American flag go up at eight o'clock, then march past the brig and the Commanding General's house. Laggards are slapped, pushed, kicked, or dragged along. Next comes an inspirational movie— at Parris Island it was at one time a film showing President Johnson awarding the Medal of Honor to a Marine post- humously. Then more running, more exercising, more re- minders from the Motivation sergeant that he doesn't have to return the recruits to their platoon, that if they want to get out of Motivation they had better shape up.

Finally there is a 225-yard infiltration course of ditches, obstacles, and mud. The recruit must carry a twenty-five-pound sand-filled ammunition box over, under, and through the course. He is thinking as he does this that he is going to collapse, drown, or die of heat prostration. He hears the sergeant yelling, "If you don't make it this time, we'll just stay here until you do." Soaked to the bone, enveloped in mud, gasping for breath as if it were life itself, the recruit survives. If he is lucky, he is returned to his platoon and can graduate with his buddies. If he is unlucky, he stays in Motivation for an additional week, sometimes for two.

Those who are kept in Motivation are divided into two sections: Incentive and Achievement. "Incentive is for the mama's boy, the cry-baby who's never been in a fight," explains Colonel William C. Joslyn, commander of training at MCRD San Diego. "Achievement is for the hard-nosed kid, the rebel who doesn't want to be a member of the team." Assignment to one of the two sections is made by a sergeant who briefly interviews each of the recruits as they arrive at the Motivation barracks.

Recruits slotted into Achievement are treated to a version of reverse psychology. They are not screamed at; in fact, except for a series of war films they must sit through, they are pretty much ignored. The theory is that the tough-guy types who are assigned to Achievement will resent this sudden lack of attention and yearn for the fatherly concern of their regular DI's—or that, motivated by the films and bored by inaction, they will want to return to the path that leads to the excitement of battle.

Recruits assigned to the Incentive section are in for tougher going. Here there is intense physical activity, constant punishment, and high mental stress. Recruits perform thousands of up-and-on shoulder lifts with a ten-pound rifle, "sounding off" all the time. They engage in such Sisyphean exercises as digging ditches and filling them up again, and the sand-and-bucket drill, in which buckets are repeatedly filled and emptied.

The theory of the Incentive section is that if boot camp doesn't work, give them more boot camp—prove to the recruits that they can take it, and get them mad enough to want to rejoin the program. Most of the time it works. Says a corporal who went through it: "Guys either come out with laryngitis, because they're completely hoarse from screaming all the time, or they come out like vegetables—completely passive from being buffeted back and forth, ready to take orders from anyone."

Compared to Correctional Custody, however, Motivation is like a paid vacation. Correctional Custody, or CC, is where the serious violators are sent: the guys who talk back to a DI, who break the no-smoking rule, who are caught trying to escape. Among them are many recruits who have decided that the Marine Corps is absurd and are determined to get out. Some of these can be quite strong-willed; they are treated accordingly.

Recruits refer to CC as a "Marine Corps chain gang"—only a partially accurate description, for it fails to convey the near-medieval bizarreness of the institution.

Outside the CC barracks at San Diego is a sign on which is painted the guiding philosophy of Correctional Custody: DISCIPLINE, DISCIPLINE, DISCIPLINE THE HARD WAY. The recruit arriving at CC is escorted past this sign; then he is placed inside a red circle on the floor and is ordered to do front-straddle hops, sounding off after each one. The DI's, in their loudest, most sarcastic voices, tell him he is doing the exercise all wrong. Other trainees are brought in and made to do straddle hops outside the circle. The trainees now join the DI's in mocking the new recruit. "If the guy in the circle goes berserk," explains the gunnery sergeant in charge, "we let him go for a while, because most of the time it's a phony act."

Soon after this initiation, the recruit is handed a list of the unusual regulations of his new platoon. These are as follows:

1. Breaking custody, that is, unauthorized absence or escaping, is a very serious offense which could lead to additional days in Correctional Custody or one year at hard labor (by court-martial).

2. No Talking: There will be absolutely no talking while in Correctional Custody. You will not talk to other privates either inside or outside of Building 119. The only time you will talk to anyone is when directed by the Drill Instructor or persons of higher authority.

3. No Smoking: There will be absolutely no smoking while in Correctional Custody. This means inside or outside of Building 119.

4. Contraband: At no time will you have contraband articles in your possession. Some of the contraband articles are: cigarettes, lighters, matches, razor blades, ammunition, knives, magazines, pocket books, food stuffs, any form of narcotics, or alcoholic beverages or any other article the Platoon Commander, Assistant Platoon Commander, NCO in Charge or Drill Instructor deems contraband.

5. Malingering: Malingering will not be tolerated at any time. Malingering is intentional avoiding of work, duty or service. Any form of malingering (such as laziness) will be cause for disciplinary action, which could result in the awarding of additional days in Correctional Custody.

6. Double Time: Whenever you are moving from place to place, you will move at double time. You will be required to move from place to place frequently at double time until the desired rate of speed and execution is acquired. At no time will you walk unless being marched by a Drill Instructor.

7. Racks: At no time will you sit, stand, lay or put your feet on your rack. Your rack will be made up neat and tight at all times. You may be required to make up your rack repeatedly until the Drill Instructor feels that the desired rate of speed and proficiency has been attained.

8. Clothing: All clothing will be folded and displayed as prescribed by the Drill Instructor. You will be required to fold your clothing repeatedly to attain the desired proficiency in speed and neatness and correctness in display. At no time will dirty clothing be displayed on the rack. All dirty clothing will be in a clean, clearly marked, serviceable,

laundry bag and secured to your rack as prescribed by the
Drill Instructor.

9. Head Calls: All head calls, use of drinking fountain and
showers are authorized and controlled by the Drill Instructor. At no time will you make a head call, use the
drinking fountain or take a shower unless authorized by the
Drill Instructor.

10. At no time will you cross a red line unless instructed to do
so by a Drill Instructor.

The tenth regulation prescribes a practice that used to prevail
in many Marine Corps brigs. The floor in the CC barracks is
crossed by a number of red lines, approximately twenty feet
apart. Every time a recruit comes to a red line, he must stop
and shout out, "Sir, the private requests permission to speak to
the Drill Instructor, Staff Sergeant Cox." If he receives permission to speak, he then must shout, "Sir, the private requests
permission to cross the red line." Permission may be granted or
denied.

The daily routine at CC consists of harassment, exercising,
more harassment and more exercising. For variety, recruits are
sent jogging around the base carrying sixteen-pound sledge
hammers. Sometimes they break up rocks with the sledge
hammers and put the little fragments into piles. Then they
move the piles from one spot to another, fragment by fragment. When they have finished, they may be sent back to the
barracks to spend several more hours shining buckets and
sanding down desks.

Meanwhile, the message of CC is hammered home day and
night by the DI's: You could have learned discipline the easy
way, but no, you chose to learn it the hard way. Don't think
you can get a discharge, because you can't. Nobody can.
There's only one way out of here, and that's to go along with
the program. Either that or a court-martial, which would mean
years in the brig.

Recruits remain in CC for up to thirty days or until the DI
decides that they are "squared away." Some recruits refuse to

get squared away; they want no part of the Marine Corps and will take any amount of punishment to prove it. In these cases, a real confrontation of wills develops. The recruit is determined that he will never go back to training; the DI's are equally determined that he will—and they have extraordinary methods for getting their way.

Painted on the floor in one corner of the CC barracks is a pair of yellow footprints identical to the footprints outside the reception station. The stubborn recruit is made to stand at attention on the footprints, staring at the wall, for five or eight hours a day. If, after a couple of days, he still refuses to train, the DI places him on a restricted diet—2,100 to 2,700 calories a day, three-ounce portions of meat without gravy, and skimmed milk only. If that doesn't work, there is the ultimate torture: the full-length mirror, just a few feet away from the yellow footprints.

Until 1969, recruits who reached this pinnacle of non-cooperation were handcuffed, naked, to the mirror and forced to stare at themselves for up to ten hours a day. One recruit, a Private Fores, was placed in front of the mirror on and off for twenty-one days, sometimes for twenty hours a day. In 1969, the handcuffing was discontinued; recruits now stand at attention, and they are dressed in at least shorts and a T-shirt. Colonel Joslyn, the commander of recruit training at MCRD, explained the mirror by saying, "We give them a chance for a little bit of self-appraisal."

Joslyn is proud of the Marines' high "salvage" rate. Between September 1968 and October 1969, twenty-one recruits underwent this version of self-appraisal at San Diego. Of these, fourteen agreed to return to training, while additional disciplinary action, including courts-martial, had to be taken against the other seven.

Breaking down the young recruit through degradation, harrassment, and brutality is only half of the basic training process. The other half is the creation of the soldier, the building of a new personality characterized by unquestioning obedience to higher military authority and a capacity for cold-blooded slaughter of any designated enemy.

This rebuilding process begins in earnest at about the fourth week, when the platoon moves to the rifle range. Here, for the first time, the recruit feels that he is being given something useful to do, that he is acquiring a skill that is of some interest and value. The anxiety and rage that develop during the first weeks of training now have an outlet. The recruit no longer merely absorbs punishment; he has an opportunity to perform, an opportunity to be aggressive as well as passive. He is tested on his proficiency with the rifle and he passes the test. Suddenly, he is no longer a worthless human being; he has a worth-while skill for which he is rewarded by a lessening of harassment.

The recruit acquires other skills and discovers hidden abilities that surprise and gratify him. He can run three miles in twenty-one minutes, climb a two-story rope in eighteen seconds, do a hundred push-ups without tiring. His new pride in his body makes him more confident, less afraid to meet the enemy, almost anxious to test his manliness against a foe.

The recruit also begins to develop a loyalty to his group. At the start of boot camp he had spoken to no one, known no one's first name or anything about them. Now he is able to make friends, and the anxiously shared experiences of training provide a natural bond. Those infuriating days when the entire unit would be punished for the shortcomings of one of its members also begin to bear fruit. Everyone falls into line; the better recruits encourage and assist the slower ones; the platoon begins to look sharp. Soon the DI is comparing it with other platoons, and the recruits want to make theirs the best. Trivial things like having the highest inspection marks and crisply executing the maneuvers of close-order drill take on new importance as the competition between platoons increases.

Most ironically of all, the recruit becomes strangely attracted to his drill instructor, that he-man in an ever-perfect uniform whose stentorian voice never quavers, never breaks, and has the penetrating power of an electric shock. The young recruit begins to look at his DI with a mixture of hate and respect, of fear and awe—a combination that works effectively to produce loyalty and emulation. Many recruits not only adopt the attitudes and behavioral patterns demanded of them by their DI; they genuinely come to believe that the humiliations, the punishments, even the beatings he metes out are well intentioned and beneficial.

As the eight-week period nears its end, the DI's scorn turns magically to paternal approbation. The platoon is O.K.; it might even be an honor platoon if it pulls together and drills hard. Miller has learned the rifle; he's not so dumb after all. The degrading epithets are forgotten; it's "Private Miller" now. Jones is no longer a queer; he's a real, rugged man. The DI begins to confide in his men some of the secrets of the fraternity into which their initiation is almost completed. "To be a Marine, you must be part animal," a San Diego DI tells his recruits. "To be a Marine in public, you must be able to conceal the animal within you."

Soon the recruits will be guardians of such secrets; soon they will be *Semper Fidelis*, always loyal to the Corps.

III

IN MOST important respects, Army basic training is closely akin to the Marines'. The verbal abuse, harassments, and constant repetition of simple-minded routines are much the same as at Marine Corps boot camp. The training cycle lasts eight weeks and adheres to the same psychological trajectory: degradation and emasculation, followed by a kindling of group *esprit* and the infusion of a new sense of military manhood. The dominating role and even the uniform of the Army drill instructor are consciously patterned after that of the Marine Corps.

Still, there are notable differences. The Army has nothing analogous to the Motivation and Correctional Custody platoons, and its drill instructors are markedly less brutal than the Marines'.[3] Beyond this, the Army relies somewhat less than the

3. Although there are always aberrations. In 1969, for example, an Army drill instructor at Fort Ord decided to scare his new trainees by

Marine Corps upon sheer behavioral conditioning in the making of its soldiers, and slightly more upon the instillation of abstract ideas and attitudes. It seeks, in other words, to sweeten the bitter pill of discipline with a few dollops of motivation.

The Army's concept of motivation (like that of the other services) is a rather simple one. It encompasses three major themes: anti-Communism, respect for authority, and the wisdom of "going along." It does not include such notions as individual responsibility, citizens' rights in a democracy, or the distinction between defensive and non-defensive wars.

Trainees are indoctrinated—this is the word the Army itself uses—in a variety of ways. They are shown the standard Defense Department films, lectured by officers, and constantly exposed to the views and attitudes of their drill instructors. *The Anatomy of Aggression,* for example, an outdated black-and-white Defense Department "documentary" about Communism, begins with Russian and American soldiers fraternizing on the banks of the Elbe at the close of World War II. Then Stalin ignores Yalta by fomenting a Communist revolution in Greece; tearful Greek widows and children are shown as the narrator tells about Communist terrorism. Next a map of Europe appears on the screen; drums roll ominously on the sound track. "The Soviet empire is not large enough for its ambitious leaders," the narrator intones. A hammer and sickle appear over Iran. There is footage of the Berlin airlift, the Communist seizure of power in Czechoslovakia, the invasion of South Korea. Then Guatemala, Southeast Asia, and the Philippines, where "Communist agents, serving an international conspiracy, had to be suppressed." Quick flash to Che Guevara

---

giving them a "square needle in the left testicle." The DI, Sergeant Daniel Rivera, arranged for a medic, Specialist Fourth Class Morris Keaton, to inject the trainees in the scrotum with the largest hypodermic needle he could find. Keaton put sterile water in a syringe and injected about a dozen recruits before he was stopped. Both men were court-martialed; Rivera was acquitted, and Keaton was sentenced to six months confinement.

and Khrushchev at the United Nations; more Communist treachery in East Germany, Hungary, and Tibet. The movie closes with John F. Kennedy addressing the nation on the Berlin crisis and promising resoluteness in the face of yet another Communist challenge. No one, to be sure, is educated about Communism by the film; but recruits who view it absorb the notion that Communism is evil, aggressive, and treacherous. They see the hammer and sickle spreading like a cancer over the map, and know it is the enemy, and that America must stop it.

Night of the Dragon, produced for the Defense Department by Guggenheim Productions of St. Louis, has a little more class. This film is designed to "explain" the Vietnam War. It is in color, has Charlton Heston as narrator, and lots of combat action. Heston starts off by talking about North Vietnamese infiltration and aggression, though he omits any mention of Diem's dictatorship. He refers to the Viet Cong as "terrorist agents" and "murder squads," though he says nothing of corruption in Saigon or the Geneva Accords' provision, defied by Diem, for all-Vietnam elections in 1956. The "Free World," declares Heston, has joined forces to put down these murderers: technicians from Japan and West Germany, fighting troops from Australia, New Zealand, and Korea, a medical team from the Philippines, and of course "the valiant South Vietnamese people," defending themselves against the aggressor from the north. South Vietnamese doctors are shown helping the people. Here is a South Vietnamese agricultural extension expert, sent by Saigon to provide insecticide and fertilizers to a village; here are South Vietnamese children paying close attention to their teacher in a government-built school; here are adults going to the polls to re-elect this democratic and benevolent government; here is the South Vietnamese army helping villagers to defend themselves against the Viet Cong terrorists. Amazingly, United States troops are almost nowhere to be seen. The final sequence shows what purports to be a real battle in which courageous South Vietnamese soldiers are dropped into a VC zone by helicopter and rout the enemy decisively.

Respect for authority, another basic motivational theme, is inculcated daily by the drill instructor and is also formally presented in four one-hour "character guidance" classes given by, of all people, the chaplain.

It is the chaplain's task to make trainees understand why they must be obedient. To this end he invokes, first of all, the Deity: "Wherever people live together, authority must exist. It is a need that arises out of the very nature of men. The man who believes in God would say that the source of authority, in the final analysis, is God. He would say it exists because God, the Creator, wants it to exist." [4] Thus does the foul-mouthed first sergeant, by the chaplain's grace, become an implementor of the Almighty's will.

Obedience, the chaplain further points out, is good for the soul: "The freest soldier is the soldier who willingly submits to authority. When you obey a lawful command you need not fear, nor worry. You can devote all your energies to getting the job done." Although Army regulations were modified after the Nuremberg trials to declare that a soldier is not duty-bound to obey an unlawful order and bears ultimate responsibility for his own actions, the chaplain does not mention this. If there are any questions or doubts, he says, obey first and complain later.

The chaplain also employs another tack—that obedience is a matter of honor because the trainee has taken an oath: "You solemnly swore that you would support and defend the Constitution of the United States against all enemies, foreign and domestic. You gave your oath that you would bear true faith, and you took this obligation freely, without mental reservation or purpose of evasion. In this you asked God to help you. This can only be done with respect for and loyalty to properly constituted authority." That they took their oath freely may come as news to draftees. But for them the chaplain has this further assurance: "The soldier who puts duty on the moral

4. This quotation and those that follow are taken from two Army Character Guidance Field Manuals. The citations here are, in order, as follows: Army Field Manual 16-5, *Character Guidance Discussion Topics,* p. 19; ibid., p. 20; ibid., p. 22; Army Field Manual 16-100, *Character Guidance Manual,* p. 7; ibid., p. 6.

basis of his Oath of Allegiance can 'look proud' even when he is scrubbing a GI can."

The chaplain does not limit his hymning of authority to the military setting. Significantly, he praises obedience as a virtue in its own right, regardless of where a man may find himself: "Only the conditions under which it is imposed distinguishes [sic] military from civilian authority. The soldier who promises himself that after discharge he will never again get a GI haircut or wear a uniform or clean a latrine is merely griping about a set of present conditions that he will eventually exchange for a new set—punching a time clock, catching a midnight plane at the command of his boss, or paying the taxes on his new house."

Also running steadily through the chaplain's lectures is the third major motivational theme of basic training; namely, that it is always wisest to go along with the system because, after all, it's much bigger than you. This message is reinforced during the brief classes given to recruits on the Uniform Code of Military Justice. These classes do not enhance the soldier's understanding of why he *should* fight, but they let him know what will happen to him if he *doesn't*: stiff punishments under Article 85 of the UCMJ for desertion, under Article 86 for going AWOL, under Article 87 for missing a troop movement, under Article 92 for failing to obey an order or regulation. If he talks back to his drill instructor, the recruit is taught, he can be court-martialed under Article 91 for insubordination; and if he misbehaves in any other way that is not specifically prohibited by the Code, he can be punished under the general article, Article 134.

The Army also places heavy emphasis upon the damaging effects of a less than honorable discharge. Trainees are shown a thirty-minute color film entitled *The Smart Way Out*, which begins with comedian Bob Hope warning recruits not to "cop out." Soon it is clear what Hope has in mind: a handsome young man appears on the screen, accompanied by a beautiful bikini-clad woman. As they frolic on the beach, the narrator promises "years of happiness" for trainees who go along with the system. Then the scene shifts to a dimly lit street corner, where four seedy-looking youths, unaccompanied by any women, are guzzling from a bottle of cheap wine. "Or," intones the narrator, "your life can be one of bitterness, loneliness, and poverty." It all depends, he explains, on whether you get an honorable discharge from the Army. The film goes on to trace the careers of two young draftees, one a super-straight guy who does his duty and receives an honorable discharge, the other a restless type who plays a guitar, goes AWOL to see his wife, and winds up with an undesirable discharge. Interspersed throughout this melodrama are swipes at draft dodgers, beatniks, and fellows who write letters to Congressmen.

Finally, the climax: the guitar player with the undesirable discharge can't get a job and is arrested by the police for vagrancy; Good Old Honorably Discharged Joe comes down to bail him out. It's a deception, of course—the number of undesirably discharged men who are arrested for vagrancy must be statistically insignificant—but the message is unmistakable: play it straight and you'll get all kinds of community approbation and veterans' benefits; deviate from Army norms and you're a loser for the rest of your life.

More effective than films or classroom lectures in indoctrinating recruits, however, are the informal methods of drill instructors. The drill instructor is in a much different position from the chaplain or other classroom lecturer. In the first place, his voice *must* be listened to. Beyond that, the trainee's growing personal identification with the DI causes him to take the latter's words seriously and may influence him to emulate his attitudes.

Since 1966 it has been Army policy to select drill instructors from among men who have seen combat in Indochina: the average new Army DI is 23 years old, was a small-unit infantry commander in Vietnam, and has re-enlisted once. His thoughts and attitudes are likely to be as rigidly in the military mold as his freshly starched fatigues, crew-cut hair, and mirror-shined boots. He tends to share the feeling of many older career men that civilian institutions—the family, the schools, even the church—have failed, and that only the Army can salvage the present generation of young Americans.

It is this state of mind that the DI gradually imparts to his trainees. When Army recruits march, DI's teach them to chant such cadences as "I wanna go to Vietnam/ I wanna kill some Charlie Cong," or "I wanna be an Airborne Ranger/ Living on blood and guts and danger." Explanations of military subjects are spiced with exciting stories of the DI's own experiences fighting "Communists" in Southeast Asia. Barracks bull sessions abound with references to "gooks," "dinks," draft card burners, and hippies—all subhuman creatures for whom the DI possesses nothing but contempt and whom he would kill in an instant. "Gooks" in particular are despicable little bastards who hate Americans and are almost unbelievably cruel and sneaky.

By the time trainees are finished with basic, they have heard so much talk about Vietnam that, unless they have previously formed a strong aversion to the war, many are actually anxious to get over there. Some are mainly curious, others are lured by the DI's tales of cheap cameras, stereo hi-fis, and whores—and some really want to kill "gooks."

IV

PREPARING MEN for war must inevitably involve a certain amount of nastiness. No one questions the notion that if soldiers are to be sent into combat they must be hardened to blood and pain. The questions that arise about basic training in America stem from doubts about the ends toward which this powerful conditioning process is directed, and from the fact that basic training does more than just prepare young men for war—it leaves a mark on their personalities that can be lasting and profound.

Given the present nature of American foreign policy, it is not surprising that the making of soldiers focuses on discipline rather than on rational justifications for fighting. Just as recruiting publicity avoids mention of the war in Southeast Asia and advances a variety of extraneous reasons why young men should join the army, so too does training concentrate on psychological conditioning that is related only by the tenuous thread of gut-level anti-Communism to the war which the soldiers are being primed to fight.

The military explains this by saying that its job is merely to get men to the battlefront, that it must do this in the best way it knows how, and that the way it trains men now is pretty much the way it trained men in 1942. In a narrow sense, the army has a point. But techniques used to motivate and discipline young men for participation in the Indochina War are not, merely because they were used or developed during previous wars, therefore justified by historical sanction or by the simple need to "get a job done." What was done to train Americans for World War II was tolerated largely because the war itself was morally and politically supportable. The same or similar practices applied in a moral vacuum are not automatically acceptable. Stripped of their moral underpinnings, they must be judged both by the end they serve, and by what they do to people.

In addition to its immediate impact upon the personalities of young recruits, basic training produces some longer-term effects that are more difficult to describe or to measure. Often, it is true, these effects are all to the good: many a juvenile delinquent has been "straightened out" by basic training, as officers like to boast. Often, however, these effects are not nearly so salubrious. "Much depends on the stability of the trainee," says Dr. Darrell C. Jewett, a former career psychiatrist in the Army who headed the Mental Hygiene Unit at Fort Ord. "Most young men are stable enough to recognize the artificiality of the training situation, and go along with it as a matter of expediency. Insecure young men, however, tend to personalize the process in their own thinking and emotions; it tends to shatter their sense of personal identity. And yet, because of their unresolved emotional conflicts with parental authority figures, they're unable to accept the identity the army asks them to assume—that of the highly aggressive man capable of killing without feeling."

Many such insecure youths go AWOL during or shortly after basic, and their army careers become little more than a series of frustrating and pointless wanderings from one stockade to another. When they finally get out of the army, they are embittered, confused, and uprooted.

Whatever its effects on the personalities of recruits, basic training very likely has an impact upon many young Americans' political views as well. This is not so much because the army engages in outright political indoctrination—it does so only to a limited degree—but rather because the attitudes instilled during basic training necessarily have political overtones. Thus, the automatic respect for authority drilled into the recruit by everyone from the DI to the chaplain carries with it an implicitly authoritarian view of society. Freedom lies in obedience; dissent is unpatriotic. Manliness means being the unthinking brute; good citizenship means despising Oriental Communists and not pondering too strenuously the subtleties of why America goes to war. To the extent that these attitudes are absorbed and carried on into adult life, basic training becomes a force for political docility in America, especially on matters of foreign policy. It serves as a kind of government-run incubator for what has come to be known as the Silent Majority.

The military in a democracy is always confronted, of course, with the dilemma that its own immediate demand for obedience is at variance with a basic tenet of democracy: that citizens should participate in the decision-making process. The American military, however, compounds the problem by insisting that what is appropriate in the army is also proper in civilian life, that discipline and uncritical acceptance of a leader's decisions are not merely unavoidable requirements of military organization, but universal virtues.

It would seem far more fitting for the army to differentiate between civilian and military value systems. Trainers could explain to recruits that for a short period of time they will be living in an abnormal environment, that in this abnormal environment obedience will temporarily be demanded in order to protect the normal environment, and that back in the normal environment, to which most trainees will eventually return, freedom is truly meant to flourish. Unfortunately, the day has not yet come when the military will admit it is abnormal. If anything, it increasingly sees itself as a bastion of the old virtues in a nation that is coming apart, and views basic training as a last chance to salvage a generation that is going astray.

Side by side with the question of the effects of basic training is the matter of the means employed. Just how essential are the brutality and harassment that go into the making of soldiers in America, most notably in the Marine Corps?

Older officers and drill instructors frequently grumble that basic training in the 1970's is too soft and that the Army is producing "fair weather soldiers." In *their* time, they declaim, training was really tough and DI's were really mean; nowadays the kids are coddled. The assumption behind these complaints is that there is a direct correlation between brutality in training and effectiveness in combat, that the more the drill instructor "thumps" the helpless recruit, the more he is really striking a blow against the enemy.

Whatever comfort this thesis may give short-tempered drill instructors, it doesn't bear much relation to reality. In World War II, when training methods were harsher than now, *less than twenty-five percent of the men in combat fired their weapons at all.* Brigadier General S. L. A. Marshall, the military historian, studied this phenomenon to determine why it happened. The reason so many trigger fingers froze, he found, was not that soldiers were badly disciplined or poorly motivated or lacking in the obedient attitudes that drill instructors seek to instill, but rather that the men had been inadequately trained in the importance of firepower and insufficiently encouraged to take the initiative in firing. In modern combat, Marshall wrote in *Men Against Fire* (1947), the soldier becomes isolated almost as soon as the firing starts; the most effective soldier is not the one who is trained to obey orders but the self-starter who is trained to act on his own initiative and without a general order.

In the years since World War II, military training has continued to emphasize obedience ahead of initiative, but it has pretty much solved the problem of firepower. Recruits, armed with much-improved automatic rifles, are now taught to quick-fire at pop-up targets as well as to hit the traditional fixed targets on the known-distance range. Judging from the body counts in Vietnam, this fire training is, if anything, too good, and it has little to do with hazing and thumping at boot camp. It certainly has nothing whatsoever to do with throwing young Marine recruits, without even the shadow of due process, into medieval institutions of torment.

Marines often contend that, man for man, they are better fighters than Army soldiers—a claim they base on their tougher and more brutal training. But while it may very well be true that Marine Corps training produces men who individually are meaner than the Army's, this *machismo* does not automatically translate into greater combat effectiveness. In point of fact, the Marines have not been notably more effective in Vietnam than the Army, while their casualty rate has been three times as high.

A more serious argument made for maintaining high stress, short of brutality, during boot camp, is that such stress helps steel a soldier for combat. This argument has considerable merit; but a distinction must be made among types of stress, as has been pointed out by Lieutenant Colonel William E. Datel, chief of the Mental Hygiene Unit at Fort Ord, who has studied the stress levels of basic trainees for nearly a decade. Recruits, he has observed, arrive at boot camp moderately anxious and without malice. By the middle of basic training, their anxiety has reached a peak of intensity and they are seething with anger. Their stress level, in fact, is actually considerably higher than that found in helicopter medics flying dangerous rescue missions or in soldiers anticipating an attack from the enemy. For even though the combat soldier's life is being threatened, his personal identity—unlike the recruit's—is not.

Datel believes that only *certain kinds* of stress are of any use in basic training. "Stress based on the rigors of training is one thing; stress based on loss of self is quite another. Training given to astronauts is no doubt highly stressful as well as effective toward accomplishing later mission performance, but it is extremely unlikely that such training results in stripped identity."

Datel and another Army doctor at Fort Ord, Lieutenant Colonel Llewellyn J. Letgers, have devised a new, experimental approach to basic training called the merit-reward system. It attempts to condition the behavior of recruits by using carefully controlled rewards rather than harshly imposed punishments. Each recruit, upon his arrival in boot camp, is given a small plastic-laminated card which he thereafter carries in the left pocket of his fatigue shirt. Three times a day the DI rates the recruit on such things as readiness for morning formation, neatness of bunk and gear, and over-all daily performance. Once a week the recruit is rated on physical training, rifle fire, written-test scores, and performance of assigned details.

To rate a recruit, the DI punches a hole in the appropriate place on the merit card. The merits thus accumulated, up to a maximum of fifty per week, may be cashed in by the recruit for privileges at different points in the training cycle. For example, a movie at the end of the first week of training "costs" thirty merits. A recruit might spend his earnings on the movie, or else might save them toward the seventy-merit privilege of going off post at the end of the fourth week of training. At the end of training, the top thirty-five percent of total merit earners are considered for promotion to Private First Class.

One purpose of the plastic merit cards is to give DI's a more positive means than physical and psychological harassment for controlling recruits. A second purpose is to minimize the attack on the recruit's personal identity, to reduce what Datel and other psychologists call the "stripping of self." Under the merit-reward system, Datel believes, it is possible to produce a soldier without breaking down the civilian first, to exploit the recruit's desire to be recognized for achievement rather than his fear of being punished for mistakes.

The new system has been tried on several basic training companies at Fort Ord and has been recommended by the Continental Army Command for consideration by all Army basic-training centers. There is no way of predicting, however, how widely it will spread: resistance from old-school DI's and officers is quite intense.

But whatever the fate of the merit card system, there remains something repugnant about *any* psychological conditioning process which treats human beings like dumb animals. Datel and Letgers compare their approach to the "token economies" adopted in recent years in mental hospitals and reformatories to control the behavior of schizophrenic and other disturbed persons. Using token rewards to reinforce desired patterns of behavior, many psychologists believe, is an even more effective way to condition people than is punishing them for infractions of rules. If this is so, then the use of token economies by the military may, in a sense, be more insidious than plain brutality, which, though painful, at least has the potential of exposing to recruits the coercive nature of their government's attempt to use them in a non-defensive war.

Perhaps the most basic question that must be asked is whether it is possible to train soldiers without any such animal-like conditioning at all. Unfortunately, the answer to that question is no, probably not. New habits of group living and cooperation must be instilled in a relatively short period of time, even if it is initiative rather than blind obedience that is sought. The particular degree of rote conditioning that is necessary, however, does very much depend upon the nature of the war being fought. The more spontaneous motivation there is for fighting, the less externally imposed discipline must be force-fed to recruits. As S. L. A. Marshall has observed:

> Men who have been in battle know from first-hand experience that when the chips are down, a man fights to help the man next to him, just as a company fights to keep pace with its flanks. Things have to be that simple. An ideal does not become tangible at the moment of firing a volley or charging a hill. . . . Yet above and beyond any symbol—whether it be the individual life or a pillbox commanding a wadi in the Sahara—are all of the ideas and ideals which press upon men, causing them to accept a discipline and to hold the line even though death may be at hand.

An army must have faith in its cause. For faith to be genuine and lasting, the cause must be legitimate. When a valid cause is lacking, no amount of brutal training, no amount of subtle brainwashing, can replace it for very long.

I WANT TO COME HOME ALIVE. IF I MUST KILL
OLD MEN, WOMEN, OR CHILDREN TO MAKE MYSELF
A LITTLE SAFER, I'LL DO IT WITHOUT HESITATION.

—Sergeant Raymond Hicks,
25th Infantry Division, U.S. Army, Vietnam

4. PAWNS IN INDOCHINA

AFTER basic training, the recruit, now a full-fledged soldier, settles down for an extended residency in America's
largest total institution. He undergoes a month or more of
advanced training in some given specialty—infantry, armor,
artillery, truck driving, cooking, clerking, or whatever—and
then receives a set of orders. Today these will impose on him
one of two alternatives: to pass his time in a garrison, or to
participate in a non-defensive war.

It is at this point that the ultimate purpose of basic training
becomes fully evident—it is to squeeze the soldier's personality
into a new, Janus-headed mold. On the one hand, he must be
meek, obedient, and agreeable towards his superiors; on the
other, he must be aggressive, cruel, and bloodthirsty towards
the designated enemy. He must, in other words, play the roles
of both nigger and killer. As one GI rather graphically put it,
"We're supposed to have no balls or four balls, but never just
two."

In his well-known book *Slavery*, Stanley Elkins describes how the slave's personality was to a great extent imposed upon him by the institution of slavery. The "Sambo" stereotype of the lazy, self-effacing slave who always managed to look happy was a result, not of the Negro's racial characteristics—the "Sambo" personality was not evident among Negroes elsewhere in the world—but of the paternalistic closed system of the Southern plantation. Toward the plantation owner, the all-powerful master who controlled every aspect of his existence, the slave came to act the way a child behaves toward an authoritarian father. He would try to please his owner by being servile and ever-smiling. His apparent laziness was due to a lack of opportunity to exercise initiative. Like a child, he would try mischievously to get away with things when his master was not looking, but he would always assume his best behavior in his master's presence.

Between this "Sambo" stereotype and the behavior and attitudes expected of enlisted men in noncombat situations, the similarities are quite striking. Though the army claims during basic training to be "building a man," it requires the soldier to behave toward his superiors like a child. The company commander assumes a fatherly role in many ways analogous to that of the slaveowner; he is, in fact, frequently referred to as "the old man." Also like the slaveowner, the commander exercises almost complete authority over the enlisted man's life; he may use or abuse the latter (within certain limits) as he sees fit. If the soldier should tire of his subservience and absent himself from duty, there are fugitive slave laws to bring him back.

The enlisted man must not only be obedient to specific rules and commands; like the American slave, he must display a fawning attitude in the presence of his superiors. He must salute and say "Yes, sir!," much as slaves were expected to smile and mutter perpetual agreement with their masters. When not in combat, he must shuffle impassively through his menial chores, without in any way challenging the system or the ultimate ends toward which his labor is put. As the slave was allowed to sit by the riverbank and sing, so he is allowed to drink beer at the enlisted men's club.

Quite unlike the slave, however, the soldier must also be able—upon a signal from his superiors—to shift into another, almost diametrically opposite role: that of killer. And he is expected to assume it with the same unthinking enthusiasm he must display in his role as nigger.

Ironically, the killer role is often easier to assume than the servile role, especially after the soldier gets used to it. It affords, at long last, an opportunity to release pent-up aggression and to establish a claim to a type of manhood. The pressures on the soldier's personal identity are removed, as are the restraints of civil society. Those dark and violent urges that seem to run through all men are uncorked and even glorified. The childlike soldier shoots and kills and bombs with the hearty approval of his "old man."

II

NON-DEFENSIVE wars are not necessarily all alike; but the Indochina War will serve, if not as an archetype, at least as a timely specimen. American soldiers have been caught up in it now for the better part of a decade, and it is vastly different from the major defensive wars that the country has fought. For the Americans, instead of fighting, as in the past, to expel aggressors from occupied lands, are now themselves in the role of foreign invaders. It is now American soldiers—tall, well-fed Occidentals from halfway around the globe, accompanied by the full panoply of their destructive technology—who enter a poor and simple Asian village to tell its inhabitants that they must abandon their thatched huts and farms, that if they don't they will be killed, and that in any event their possessions and livestock and crops will be destroyed.

Because the Vietnam conflict is different militarily, it is also different psychologically. It is a maddening, treadmill kind of war, filled with contradictions and absurdities. There are no great battles, no decisive turning points, just a lot of patrols and sweeps and bombing raids with no apparent progress and no apparent end, like a surreal baseball season in which deadly games are played out every day, without ever a pennant, ever a World Series. Soldiers advance into the jungle, then return to hot showers and cold beer at the base camp, almost as if they were coming home from the office. Pilots drop their napalm, and later relax over cocktails at an air-conditioned officer's club where they joke about their unseen victims like suburban commuters who have just driven through the ghetto on a six-lane freeway.

GI's habitually refer to the United States as "the world," as if Vietnam were somewhere off in space, so unreal as to stand morality on its head and permit almost any kind of behavior. For most of them, the one firm anchor of sanity is the knowledge that after a fixed period of time they will be leaving Vietnam.

How should a GI behave in such a bizarre setting? He does as his leaders say, and he does as his leaders do. He sees commissioned officers take potshots at Vietnamese villagers from jeeps and airplanes. He sees a battalion commander dub his helicopter a "Gookmobile" and record his kills on the fuselage in neatly painted rows of conical hats. He sees another battalion commander issue special olive-green badges bearing the words SAT CONG (Vietnamese for "kill Communists") to soldiers who prove they have killed a Viet Cong. He sees a brigade commander run a contest, offering a week of luxury in his own quarters to the soldier who racks up the unit's ten-thousandth kill. He sees his officers murder prisoners because taking them alive merely lowers the body count. He is told to cut off the ears of enemy corpses to verify claims of enemy killed. He sees and hears all these things—and he joins in.

Lance Corporal Gavino Tinaza volunteered for the Marine Corps in July 1967, with the express hope that "if I joined the Marines I'd get to Vietnam sooner or later." After boot camp, Tinaza remembers, he was so revved up that when he went home on leave he felt awkward because there was no drill instructor around, telling him what to do. "All my life I tried to be one of the best," he says, "and everybody said the Marine Corps was the best. I really did want to see combat. I didn't realize that Vietnam was something different from any other combat I've ever heard of."

Tinaza did see plenty of action. He was at Khe Sanh, Con Thien, the "Rockpile," and all around the DMZ. Along with other members of his company, he cut the ears off the VC he killed and with his bayonet carved on their chests the digits "L 3/4," to let the Vietnamese know that Lima Company, 3rd Battalion, 4th Marines, had struck again. But something began to impress Tinaza as odd: the reason he was supposed to be over there, to help the Vietnamese people, didn't seem to jibe with reality. "A lot of times I tried to communicate with the villagers, but they just turned around and walked away. I heard things like 'Yankee Go Home,' and other remarks that showed they didn't really want us around. My platoon got wiped out three times, and each time they filled it with replacements. The only reason we kept fighting was to stay alive. We never had any thought that we were fighting for freedom or anything like that."

Like so many other foot soldiers the government has sent to Vietnam, Tinaza found himself doing what the army wanted him to do—killing—but not for any worthwhile reason he could think of. He killed out of hatred, anger, the desire for revenge and the instinct to survive, and he kept from going crazy only by smoking marijuana. His hatred was directed toward the very people he was ostensibly defending—not so much the Viet Cong, whom he at least respected, but the *other* Vietnamese, who were supposed to be friendly and grateful but were neither. His anger was an inchoate resentment against his officers for giving him a hard time, against the Marine Corps for luring him into this mess, against the hippies back home for living it up and dodging the draft while he was slugging it out in the jungle. His desire for vengeance was directed not only at the Viet Cong and North Vietnamese, but also at any other Vietnamese who might in any way have been responsible for killing buddies in his platoon. His instinct to survive told him to shoot anything that might conceivably shoot at him, now or in the future. All these thoughts and

emotions welled up inside him, demanding an outlet. So Tinaza
became what he was programmed to become: a killer.

Most soldiers, most of the time, are able to restrain themselves from shooting Vietnamese civilians; but the emotions
which drive them to kill are often released in less lethal acts.
An Army memorandum on U.S.-Vietnamese relations, signed
by Lieutenant General Walter T. Kerwin Jr. and distributed
to all commanders in the II Field Force, Vietnam, in December
1968, provides a graphic description of the behavior of many
American soldiers. The memorandum urges commanders to
take immediate action to deter GI's from engaging in the following types of conduct:

a. Crop damage and/or pilferage. Armored carriers and other
   heavy vehicles have been indiscriminately driven through
   cultivated areas causing unnecessary crop damage and financial losses for Vietnamese civilians. . . .
b. Operation of motor vehicles on RVN highways. Difficulties
   arise from arrogance, lack of plain courtesy and failure to
   realize that many of the rural Vietnamese have little or no
   experience with larger motor vehicles. . . .
c. Destruction of real property. Effort is still being made to
   overcome the animosity of people in one village occupied
   by US troops for one week. During the week that the village was within a battalion defensive perimeter, civilians
   were barred from their homes, houses were damaged, furniture removed and damaged or destroyed, and foodstuffs
   were destroyed. . . .

Sometimes, in spite of the many frustrations that drive GI's
in Vietnam to anger, a soldier becomes so overwhelmed by the
senselessness of the war that he is unable to channel his aggres-
sions into the killing pattern sanctioned by the army. In that
case, Vietnam becomes another kind of hell. The soldier must
somehow pass the time until his Vietnam duty is up, staying
alive and trying to keep sane.

Private First Class Richard C. Cavendish Jr., of Richmond,
Virginia, enlisted in the Army for three years in 1968. In 1969

he went to Vietnam with the 1st Battalion, 28th Infantry, of the 1st Infantry Division—the famous "Big Red One" that left its permanent mark on the Vietnamese landscape by bulldozing in the jungle twenty-five miles northwest of Saigon a mile-and-a-half-wide swath in the shape of its divisional insignia. After five months in the front lines, Cavendish was wounded near Lai Khe and received a Purple Heart. While recovering, he began to realize that the war was pointless, and that he could not go back to combat. When he received orders to return to the field, he went AWOL to Saigon. After several months, he turned himself in, was court-martialed, served time in the stockade, and then returned to duty behind the lines as a truck driver. What follow are some of the brief notes and reflections he started jotting down about this time in a kind of diary:

MAY 15: This place does nothing but get me down. Can't get up.

MAY 17: Have gone on like this long enough. Will have to do something soon. Can't stand being involved in this war. Genocide! If I were black—wouldn't fight.

MAY 28: 3rd Brigade chaplain agrees this war is wrong morally but can give me no help.

JUNE 8: Went to sick call for nerves today. Rap, rap. Doc tells me to get my personal problems straightened out before expecting headaches and irritability to stop. Prescribed Florinal and Librium.

JUNE 20: Don't think I'll be able to live in the U.S. for much past my ETS [separation date], if until then.

JUNE 24: Frank is quite a help—really lifted my morale. Gave me ⅓ tab. Emergency only! Hope to see him and Boatman in Frisco in April. He says they will both be there. Can call Frank to pick me up at Oakland.

JULY 14: 62 days till DEROS [date of rotation out of Vietnam].

JULY 18: Many B-52 strikes around Lai Khe lately.

JULY 20: Went swimming today, just down the road past the water point. There was a papa-san and his baby-san washing when Ken and I arrived. They looked so peaceful and content. We made them nervous, I think, until they realized that we just wanted to groove on the water also. This war is so confusing. If it isn't taken one day at a time, if it's attempted to be comprehended as a whole, it will *blow the mind.*

JULY 21: Smoking much. The prices here are pretty good. The kids will trade anything for a carton of cigs.

JULY 22: Started a letter to Mom and Betty. Slept through a mortar attack last night. They woke me up during the return fire and then wanted us to get into a bunker.

JULY 23: 53 days to DEROS.

JULY 25: Spend much of the time sitting in shade drinking ice water, smoking, thinking. Want to go on R & R [rest and recreation] very much. Never a break. My nerves are worse than ever—I jump down throats at the slightest provocation. Can't write letters. Words are so useless. Started a letter to Mom and Betty yesterday. Nothing to say. Wish something would happen.

JULY 26: 50 days.

AUGUST 1: Someone is going to, soon, rent a full page ad in *The Washington Post* denouncing the war, go to the Pentagon and pour five gallons of the gas over himself and light a match. Can't think of a more effective way to protest the war for a Viet vet. [*At this point Cavendish was granted thirty days R & R. He flew to Sidney, Australia.*]

AUGUST 13: There is an entirely different mood in Australia. So alive and happy. Everyone does what they want. Think at this time I will go home and try to get Paul to help me get a discharge. I should qualify for a medical. Don't want to desert but can see little alternative.

SEPTEMBER 18: [*back in Vietnam*] Guard duty again at the ammo dump. No time off until DEROS unless I change things myself. Shot opium for the first time the other night. Nice rush-on, spectacular high. Have retrieved my acid. Don't know. Fork-lift trucks running around the dump like prehistoric monsters. Trying to groove again on the home scene. Can't—the States are a downer. Can't be identified with what the U.S.A. represents any more. Am going to get out of the Army one way or another. I want out! Now!

SEPTEMBER 20: B-52 bombing strikes every day shake the ground—are bound to scare the hell out of Charles Victorians [Viet Cong].

SEPTEMBER 21: Just finished writing to Deb asking for a divorce. Hope she takes it like a woman. Can't really be involved with anyone in that way until I become settled.

SEPTEMBER 22: Had better get on the ball. Am running out of friends to bum from. Don't feel single!

SEPTEMBER 26: Twenty days to go. If anything happens to me they will pay. Top [his first sergeant] is starting to fuck with me. Am going to ask to go into Lai Khe today. Take care of business and take a steam bath. Hope we make it.

SEPTEMBER 28: Into Lai Khe. Much hassle, no results. Everyone that I need to talk to is in the field. Would have liked to go to the steam bath but didn't have time. Just made it to the beer garden before catching chopper back.

OCTOBER 2: Closed my allotment out. Should be home by the end of the month!

III

RICHARD CAVENDISH made it home.[1] So do the majority of GI's who go to Vietnam. The date of rotation comes at last; the soldier packs his gear, clambers aboard a jet, crosses five time zones at the speed of sound, and is plunked down again in "the world." Another soldier, fresh out of training, crosses the time zones the other way and takes his place in the jungle.

The soldier who makes it home is not, however, home free. He still has months, sometimes more than a year, remaining in

1. When I met Cavendish in March 1970 at Fort Hood, Texas, he was reunited with his wife Deb, very happy about his marriage, and very unhappy about the nine months remaining in his three-year enlistment. I was saddened, though not surprised, to learn several months later that he had been court-martialed for his role in organizing a peaceful antiwar demonstration in Killeen, the town outside Fort Hood.

his term of enlistment. He is assigned to a base in the United States, usually, for some perverse reason, as far away from his home as geography permits. Then come the slow, miserable days as he waits for his time to run out, when he suffers through what one soldier calls the "post-Vietnam blahs."

Those final months in a soldier's career can be almost as miserable as his days in Vietnam. This may be difficult to imagine, considering the horrors of the Indochina War. But the soldier who survives that hell is in no mood to sit around and get hassled. He has killed and bled for Uncle Sam; he now expects to be treated like a hero, or at the very least like a man. Instead, however, the army demands that he revert to his pre-combat role of nigger.

Along with all the frustrations and hazards of Vietnam duty is a measure of freedom that the soldier out of combat is not allowed. The GI in Vietnam can smoke dope, let his hair grow, look grubby, wear a peace symbol—in short, be something of an individual. As long as he kills, or goes through the motions, he isn't hassled.

Back in the States, these liberties are gone. The soldier must conform, display obeisance, pass inspections—annoyances that he might once have tolerated as necessary preparations for combat, but which now, with combat behind him, seem totally without purpose. He must deal with officers and NCO's whose concept of a man's worth is determined by how he wears his uniform. And always, he must be prepared for punishment if he steps out of line. "My first sergeant took away my weekend pass because he didn't like the way I talked to him," says a Vietnam returnee at Fort Lewis. "It's disgusting. Never in my entire life have I been so much at the mercy of someone else."

The army keeps these short-timers in uniform in order to maintain its high force-in-readiness level. But there really isn't much for the soldiers to do. They play war games in which the enemy is always known as the aggressor, they stand guard duty, clean buildings and grounds—and every spring they train for urban riot control. Most soldiers kill time by thinking about the car they'll buy, the hair they'll grow, and the girls they'll screw when they get out. Sometimes the tedium and harassment get so bad that men actually volunteer to go back to Vietnam: anything to get away from where they are.

Finally—it's now two or three or four years since he started basic, more if he's had time in the stockade—the soldier approaches his ETS, his day of separation. A "career counselor" urges him to re-enlist, pointing to cash bonuses of up to $10,000 that the army pays to those who "re-up." If the soldier is not badly in debt, if he has even the slightest confidence in his ability to make it on the outside, he smiles at the re-enlistment counselor, grabs his discharge, and runs. He is still young, still with his life in front of him; but he is no longer the pimple-faced kid off the block. He has seen death, and maybe caused it. He has passed through an enormous total institution whose goal was to make him, not a man, but a sometime killer and a sometime eunuch—and the robotlike instrument of national policies seriously questioned or condemned by millions of his fellow citizens. What has it all done to him?

It is difficult to make sweeping statements in this regard; obviously, different men are affected in different ways. Thousands who survive are physically wounded: shrapnel is embedded in their bodies; limbs are missing; muscles are paralyzed. But hundreds of thousands more return to civilian life wounded in their souls and in their minds. Though there have been no formal studies on the psychological effects of Vietnam on returning soldiers, vast numbers have been hardened, disoriented, and embittered by their experience; and it is certain that the full impact of this war has yet to be felt by America.

Many of these men, like Richard Cavendish, say that they were "radicalized" by their experience in Indochina. But what does radicalization mean? On the surface it generally means a new political awareness, often accompanied by political involvement and activity. More fundamentally, however, it means a loss of faith, a sense of betrayal. Despite what their detractors say, most young Americans grow up with a basic trust in their country. They may laugh at the traditional symbols of Mom, apple pie, and the flag, but within most of them resides a quiet patriotism, a belief that theirs is the best country in the world, and that their government usually does what is right. In Vietnam, they cannot reconcile this faith in America's goodness with what they themselves, in the name of America, are doing. In their eyes, America now stands exposed as a lie, yet every day they risk their lives for it, and many of them even kill for it—an offense against their own consciences that can only be expunged by turning their enmity against the lie itself.

Among black GI's, many of whom came into the army hoping to "make it," this radicalization is particularly acute. Wallace Terry II, a former *Time* magazine correspondent, interviewed several hundred black soldiers during his two years of reporting in Vietnam. He found black GI's fed up with fighting and dying in a "white man's war." Sixty-four percent of those he interviewed felt that black men should not be fighting in Vietnam, that their true struggle was against racism in the United States. "A frightening number," reports Terry, "schooled in the violent art of guerrilla warfare, say they would join riots and take up arms if necessary to get the rights and opportunities they have been deprived of at home."

For many American soldiers in Vietnam, perhaps the majority, the effect of the war is not so much radicalization as alienation. Their loss of faith is apolitical, inchoate, almost unadmitted. They had expected to feel some pride in soldiering for democracy; instead they felt only anger and moral uncertainty. They are greatly dissatisfied with the army, with the quality of their leadership, with the pointlessness or halfheartedness of the war. They do not actively protest or dissent, or even talk much about their thoughts with friends; many of them, in fact, believe that the war ought to be decisively escalated. But they are afflicted by a strong and lingering malaise.

Vietnam affects soldiers in other ways that are difficult to calculate. Many decent, sensitive young men become calloused and indifferent. They used to care about hurting other people, now they don't give a damn. They become pugnacious, intolerant, irritable, prone to violence. Their prejudices are reinforced and they don't worry about overcoming them. They adopt a kind of Manichaean outlook on life, viewing the world in terms of good guys and bad guys. This works well (or seems to) when one has an enemy to fix on; at best, however, it distorts reality, both in war and in peace.

Many veterans find that they have difficulty relating to others, particularly women, with tenderness. And they must prepare themselves as well to cope with people, civilians, who question their participation in the war. "When I got back," recalls a 19-year-old ex-sergeant who won five Bronze Stars in Vietnam, "I felt mixed up. Everywhere I looked people were relaxed, talking and laughing. It dawned on me I didn't know how to act with peaceful people. I was afraid of what stuff they might ask me. And it was especially hard when I found out some people thought everything I'd done in Vietnam was all wrong. I shouldn't even have been there, they said."

When soldiers leave the army, most of them try as best they can to repress memories of their Vietnam experience. Many recognize that the war has done something to them, inflicted a permanent mark that goes beyond mere loss of innocence. They tend not to join the American Legion or the Veterans of Foreign Wars, feeling no common bond with survivors of earlier and better wars.

In part this is because America didn't win *their* war. Their fathers were heroes, honored by a grateful nation; *they* were merely unknown soldiers, slogging through the mud while their President spoke of peace. In part, though, their reticence is deep-felt and born of doubt. They have little to boast about and prefer to keep to themselves. It is easier, more comforting, to consign Vietnam to some deep recess of the mind, to think of it as a year spent on another planet or in a different incarnation. What would be accomplished by talking? Who would believe them? Who could possibly understand? Who would really care?

So they wander back to their homes, these non-defensive warriors, each harboring inside of him a dark and ugly secret, a psychic cyst that no surgeon can excise. Scattered throughout America are hundreds of thousands of these psychic cysts. Most may never burst open; but most, also, will never go away.

PART **III**

THE ARMY KEEPS A LOT OF
STRANGE DUDES OFF THE STREET.

—*Private Paul Solo*

5. MISFITS

EVERY WEEK at Fort Dix, New Jersey, the Army's major Northeastern training base, there are an average of four suicide attempts, or "gestures," as the Army calls them. Nine actual suicides occurred at Fort Dix in 1968, six of them among trainees. Among the deaths by suicide in 1969 was that of Private David L. Swanson, 21, of New Britain, Connecticut.

Swanson graduated from Pulaski High School and attended two local community colleges before being drafted. His father, a tool and die maker, describes him as "the most nonviolent kid on earth. He was interested in music and the arts. He was a good sculptor." According to his mother, David did not participate much in sports. He didn't smoke and he didn't drink.

Army records show that Swanson began basic training on August 4, 1969, and reported to sick call on August 5 and 6 complaining of chest pains. He was returned to duty both times. On August 8 he slashed his left wrist in a suicide "gesture," was bandaged up at the hospital, and ordered back to duty again. The following week he was briefly seen by two

Army psychiatrists at the Brigade Mental Hygiene Consultation clinic; both recommended his return to duty.

On August 29, Swanson slashed his wrist a second time, and for this was given an "Article 15"—nonjudicial punishment—by his company commander. He was again bandaged up at the hospital, seen by yet another psychiatrist, and returned once more to his unit. The new psychiatrist's report paralleled the earlier ones: Swanson had an immature and dependent personality, but there was no sign of mental disease warranting treatment or separation from the Army through medical channels.

Swanson wrote his parents about his difficulties and his suicide attempts: "I can't sleep and I can't stand all this harassment. . . . I hate it here and will do anything to get out. I can't run and my heart keeps skipping beats and I fall and they keep yelling at me to get up and stop bluffing. . . . I have seen two psychiatrists but only for about five minutes each. How two different people and for such a short time can help anyone is beyond me. . . . We were allowed to go on pass this weekend and when I returned, a sergeant asked me why I came back and said they didn't want me around because I was a dud. . . . I can't stand it any more. . . . Please help me."

His parents did try to help. They got in touch with their Republican Congressman, Thomas Meskill (now Governor of Connecticut), an Air Force veteran. One of Meskill's assistants, Mrs. Barbara Norris, called Fort Dix and got through to Swanson's company commander. She mentioned that Swanson was suicidal and wanted to know what was being done. "He thought it was some kind of joke," Mrs. Norris says. " 'Oh, yeah,' he said, 'We gave him some pills and we shrunk his head.' "

On August 28, Congressman Meskill received a letter from Swanson himself in which the young recruit said he could not stand Army life and that he had been the butt of abusive treatment by his superiors. Swanson added that he knew he would try to kill himself again and that this time he would not fail. Mrs. Norris immediately called Fort Dix again to advise Swanson's superiors of the seriousness of his suicidal inclinations and to request continuing psychiatric attention for him.

The Army says appointments were made for Swanson at the Mental Hygiene Clinic for September 24 and October 1. But on Saturday, September 20, after having been denied a pass, the young recruit went AWOL to his home in New Britain, where his parents found him the next morning, dead from an overdose of sedatives.

Meskill charged the Army with being "grossly negligent and responsible for this man's death." Major General William A. Becker, chief of Army legislative liaison, replied that "proper care and caution were exercised in regard to his treatment." In subsequent correspondence, the Army admitted that Swanson suffered from "a long-standing personality problem," but cited a statement in one of its psychiatrists' reports that "with time and leadership, he [would] be able to adjust to military life and perform satisfactorily." The private's suicide, in the Army's view, was thus in no way attributable to its own actions; rather, it was the fault of Swanson's defective personality.

Swanson's case is indicative of several widely prevailing assumptions that underlie the army's policy toward military misfits. First is the idea that military service is good for everyone—that discipline and authority are what all youths need these days. Second is the notion that, with the application of time-tested principles of training and leadership, every young civilian can be converted into a soldier if the army sticks at it long enough. A third assumption is that concern for the psychological well-being of enlisted men is not in the military's province—that if a soldier is in a state of emotional distress, well, that's just too bad for him.

This last-mentioned attitude is reflected in the role assigned to military psychiatrists. This role is not one of providing therapy for enlisted men in distress (except superficially through the administration of tranquilizers and other drugs), nor, as often in civilian life, of aiding patients in manipulating their environment. It is, rather, to demonstrate to misfits that there is no alternative to accepting their fate as soldiers. This usually involves telling possibly disturbed enlisted men that there is nothing seriously wrong with them and that they should concentrate on soldiering. Implicit in this approach to "treatment" are an acceptance of the military's right to manipulate young people, and the assumption that the root of a distressed soldier's trouble is not the army and what it is doing to him, but rather his own deficiencies, his inability to "cope."

Sometimes the insistence of the psychiatrist upon the legitimacy of the army and the responsibility of the soldier to adjust to it can reach quite bizarre extremes. Military stockades are full of prisoners who simply cannot or will not adjust to the military's demands. Because conditions inside these stockades are so oppressive both physically and psychologically, some prisoners become suicidal; they slit their wrists, swallow poison, or otherwise harm themselves out of despair and a desperate urge to attract help. The army's treatment of such prisoners is to bandage them up or pump them out, and then throw them back in the stockade—this time into segregation cells.

Just this sort of thing happened to several prisoners at the Presidio stockade in San Francisco who later took part in the now-famous "mutiny." A reporter asked Major Terry Chamberlin, then director of the psychiatric unit at the Presidio, how he justified such treatment of suicidal prisoners. "We've found from vast experience in the Army and lots of other places," he explained, "that you help people best by trying to help them in the situation in which their suicide attempt occurs." In other words, it is in the prisoner's own interest to be returned to a stockade segregation cell; this teaches him the vital lesson that one must always adjust to one's environment, no matter how intolerable or abnormal it is.[1]

1. Most psychiatrists in the military view themselves, nonetheless, as bootleggers of mercy into an otherwise unmerciful environment. But in the course of assisting the army to control its soldiers, they often devise some interesting justifications of their role. Many contend that by insisting that young men adjust to the military, they are helping to prepare them for later adaptation as civilians. As one career psychiatrist expressed it, "On the outside people who break rules are punished. If they steal, they are sent to prison. In the military it is the same. Men who go AWOL are punished. The rules may be different, but the basic problem isn't." When it was pointed out that there is a significant difference between going AWOL and stealing, just as there is a difference between refusing to kill—another military crime—and killing, and that one *has* to

Of course, most misfits in the army do not wind up by committing or attempting suicide—the far more common response is, and always has been, to flee. In 1823, the Army adjutant general reported that desertions totaled about one-fourth of the enlistments for the year; in 1826, they came to more than half. In 1871, some 8,800 men—one-third of the Army—went over the hill. All of those who ran had originally been volunteers.

Today, despite the draft, the Vietnam War, and the onset of what has been called "permissiveness," the AWOL rate is not nearly as high as it was a hundred years ago; it *is* high enough, however, to indicate that a substantial number of young people have great difficulty adjusting to the behavioral demands of the military.

During 1969, one out of every five Army recruits went AWOL during his first few months of training, and one out of seven soldiers was illegally absent at one time or another. All told, there were 206,303 absentees during the year in the Army alone, and tens of thousands more in the other services. Some of these men were intentionally seeking to avoid service in Vietnam; but the vast majority, perhaps ninety percent by army estimates, were apolitical youngsters, square pegs who were simply tired of being forced into round holes.

What kind of kid becomes a military misfit? The answer obviously varies, and psychologists who have studied the problem have found that there is no systematic way to predict who the misfits will be, and thus no really effective way to keep them out of the army by screening. Misfits do, however, tend to share a number of common characteristics. A large majority are high school dropouts, and a substantial percentage come from broken homes. Often, according to counselors who have dealt with them, they are slow-witted loner types who are not particularly attractive or likable. In civilian life, most of them have been losers many times over. In the military, this pattern is repeated.

One irony is that the youths who become misfits share many

consider the environment to which people are asked to adjust, the psychiatrist answered with a knowing smile, "Ah, yes, that is true. But these are social issues, not psychological issues."

of the characteristics of those who become "lifers," soldiers who fit so well into the army that they don't want to return to civilian life. Among lifers as among misfits there is a disproportionately high number of high school dropouts and youths who have had unhappy, often chaotic childhoods. Many lifers, like many misfits, are emotionally unsettled before going into the army. In each group are a substantial number who easily fall for the military's sales pitch—young men who want to get away from home, who want to find a masculine identity, who are desperately searching for a "second chance." The dividing point comes after they have been exposed to military life: for the lifer, the authoritarian environment of the army turns out to offer a viable solution to his conflicts, while the misfit discovers that his conflicts are aggravated by the military, not resolved.

It is not hard to locate the sources of the misfit's troubles. For one thing, he finds it difficult to maintain his emotional stability in an institution where he is buffeted around like a worthless being, for such treatment confirms his worst fears about himself. He expects the army to *care* about his problems; instead he encounters an impersonal organization that doesn't care, that only wants him to play the nigger and the killer. If he is a poor learner or a slow adjuster, he suffers humiliation at the hands of his peers as well as his superiors.

Often it is a family problem that heightens his distress in the military. Stationed far from home, unable to take many leaves, and unaccustomed to extended separation from his family, he grows anxious about what might be happening in his absence. If, on top of this, the responsibilities that he thought he was running away from keep coming back to haunt him, he grows even more distraught at his helpless captivity in the military.

Unquestionably, the military has neither the time nor the facilities to deal in an individualized way with young people's emotional problems, much less with their family problems; nor can it provide a proper environment for psychological care when the military setting itself is in fact a principal source of the misfits' misery. The most sensible thing the army could do with soldiers who are patently in psychological distress would be to return them to the civilian environment. There, even if they can't be cured of all their problems, at least the strains on their personality would be diminished. But the army prefers to punish misfits rather than let them go. When, as is almost always the case, the emotionally burdened soldier eventually violates one of the myriad rules established to control his behavior —usually the rule against absence—the army brands him a criminal, hauls him before a court-martial, and subjects him to the whims and dictates of military law. Thus are the stockades filled.

II

JIM ALLGOOD has lived almost all of his life around Earlimart, California, in the heart of the San Joaquin Valley. Allgood's parents were born in Oklahoma and migrated to the valley shortly after World War II. They have always lived on the brink of poverty. His father worked as a farm laborer and truck driver until pulmonary emphysema forced him to retire; he still works part-time as a night watchman, against doctor's orders. Allgood's mother is unable to work because of high blood pressure. Were it not for state disability payments, the family would be unable to make ends meet.

Allgood was the second oldest of seven brothers and sisters. His older brother, an epileptic, was unable to hold down a steady job, and it was on Jim's shoulders that the burden fell of being the family's chief breadwinner. He dropped out of high school in the tenth grade to work on potato farms. Later he got a job in a chemical factory in Los Angeles, and for a time he drove a diesel trailer truck. He also married.

It is hard to know exactly why Jim Allgood is unable to cope with non-parental authority. He never adjusted well to school, and despite an above-average IQ consistently received near-failing grades and got into quarrels with school authorities. Always an outsider, he rarely spent time with other teenagers. His aloofness may have had something to do with the fact that he was very self-conscious of his family's poverty; he preferred menial labor on behalf of his family to association with other youths in school. An Army psychiatrist would later report that he was "deeply, excessively and quite dependently attached to his parents."

In January 1966, Allgood received orders from his draft board to report to the induction center in Fresno. He was so frightened he didn't even go. Another notice came, and in February, scared to the bone, he went. "I tried to tell them that I knew I couldn't take Army life. I asked if I could speak to a doctor, but all I got to see were sergeants. They said they all heard the story before and I should move along. Just before I took the oath I talked to one sergeant who told me, 'We can't do anything about it here, but when you get to Fort Ord they can do something about it there.' "

With that advice under his belt, Allgood's military career began. It was, to say the least, an inauspicious start. As the bus carrying new recruits from Fresno approached Los Banos, about fifty miles away, Allgood told the driver he had to use a bathroom. The driver pulled into a gas station and let the recruits out for a rest stop. Shaking with fear, Allgood sneaked away and hitchhiked home. He arrived in the middle of the night, woke up his family, and burst into tears.

The next morning Allgood's father, a veteran of World War II, called up the reception station at Fort Ord and asked to speak to a chaplain. He told the chaplain that his son's induction had been a mistake, that his son couldn't make it in the Army. The chaplain said to send Jim on to Fort Ord, where he would refer him to a psychiatrist.

Mr. Allgood drove his son to Fort Ord the following day and left him in the care of the chaplain he had spoken with. The chaplain, however, turned out to be an airborne trooper and Vietnam veteran who was awaiting a second combat tour. When he told Allgood he would not refer him to a psychiatrist, Allgood escaped and hitchhiked home again.

This time he stayed a month before turning himself in. At one point he told his father that perhaps if he committed suicide, the insurance money would be worth more to the family than he would. When he returned to Fort Ord, he was charged

with AWOL and placed in the stockade to await trial. The social worker at the stockade mentioned the possibility of a hardship discharge, and Allgood expressed a strong desire for one.
Meanwhile, his father telephoned the base and told an officer in
the adjutant general's office that his son had talked about suicide. As a result of his father's call, Allgood was at last referred
to a military psychiatrist.

The psychiatrist was the head of the Mental Hygiene Clinic,
Major Darrell C. Jewett, a career medical officer with six years
in the Army behind him. Jewett remembers the interview
well: "Throughout the interview, Allgood continued to cry,
wring his hands, and blubber like a small child caught in a
frightening and unpleasant situation. He was an extremely pas-
sive-dependent personality who related to most people as if
they were his mother or father and he was a frightened child
who had to cling to them for safety. He responded from the
very beginning of his contact with the Army by shaking all
over, by being sick in his stomach, by bursting into tears or
screaming in frustration. He talked a great deal about killing
himself. He was so afraid of the aggressiveness in basic training—the guns, the bayonets, the hand-to-hand combat—that he
would rather have been dead than accept the aggressiveness demanded by the Army."

Unlike the psychiatrists who interviewed David Swanson,
Jewett strongly recommended that Allgood be discharged.
"The subject is basically unsuitable for military service," he
wrote, "and has little capacity to respond to rehabilitative efforts and measures. It thus would appear prudent for both the
military and the subject to consider separation from the service
for reasons of unsuitability." In the tactful world of military
psychiatry, this was hard-hitting language.

Allgood's incompatibility with the Army was so strikingly
visible that the court-martial which tried him for AWOL was
lenient. It convicted him but suspended his sentence, permitting
him to return to the reception barracks to await the outcome
of administrative discharge proceedings. Unfortunately, Allgood could not control his fearful impulses. One night, just
after he had fallen asleep, a training corporal came by his bunk

and started screaming. Actually, the corporal was screaming at somebody else, but Allgood awoke in a panic and struck him in the face. The corporal hauled him down to see the officer in charge, and the officer, who didn't like Allgood anyway, told him that he needed to learn military discipline and that he was therefore dropping the discharge procedures and ordering him to report to basic training.

Allgood went through the first week of basic in a state of extreme anxiety. He could do nothing properly and felt totally inadequate. He consulted a chaplain and attempted to calm himself by reading the Bible. This worked for a few days; but finally he could take no more. Once again he ran away—this time for two and a half years.

Life was hard for Allgood during this period, but it was better than being in the Army. He realized he could not stay at home, for he would surely be caught if he did. With his wife and a friend, he moved around the San Joaquin Valley, driving a potato truck and doing other agricultural work. This time, he told himself, he would be smart: he'd get a lawyer. He saved what money he could, and after several months found an attorney in Bakersfield who said he would take the case for $5,000. At that rate, Allgood thought, he'd have to be AWOL for ten years, so he gave up on lawyers.

In 1968 he got a job at a filling station in Santa Cruz. It was there, in October, as he was coming out of an evening movie with his wife, that an FBI agent suddenly approached with his revolver drawn. "Hold it right there, Allgood," he shouted, and Allgood obeyed. He was searched, handcuffed, driven to Fort Ord, thrown in the stockade, and charged with desertion.

While in the stockade, Allgood was seen by another Army psychiatrist, Captain Robert Elias. As Jewett had done two and a half years earlier, Elias recommended that Allgood be discharged: "Patient demonstrated a disorder of character and behavior which is not amenable to treatment in the military setting. . . . It is clear at this time that he will never be an asset to the military service and should be considered for separation under AR 635-212 [unsuitability]."

Another officer, Captain James T. Jones, was assigned as the

Article 32 investigator for Allgood's desertion charge. (An Article 32 investigation is the military equivalent of a grand jury hearing.) Allgood cried during his entire interview with Jones. In his report to the Staff Judge Advocate, Jones, too, recommended that Allgood be discharged and that the desertion charge be dropped: "I think that this man should be thoroughly checked by a psychiatrist and boarded from the Army without trial by court-martial. In my opinion, this man is not capable of functioning effectively in any military environment. I do not think it would serve any purpose to bring him before a court-martial board."

By this time, Allgood's case had become something of a conversation piece among senior officers at Fort Ord. The youth was obviously a classic misfit: a good husband, a loyal son, and a hard worker in civilian life, yet a total washout in military surroundings. But besides being a misfit, Allgood was also a runaway, and thus, in the opinion of the Staff Judge Advocate, Colonel Orrin Stribley, a criminal who deserved to be punished. Setting aside the judgment of the Article 32 investigator, Stribley recommended court-martial. Major General Thomas A. Kenan, commanding general at Fort Ord, concurred.

Fellow prisoners in the stockade urged Allgood to get a civilian lawyer as quickly as possible. They suggested Richard Silver, a young local attorney, who agreed to take the case for considerably less than $5,000. Silver promptly petitioned for a writ of habeas corpus in the U.S. District Court in San Francisco, alleging that General Kenan had "no basis in fact" for denying Allgood's discharge. Judge Alfonso J. Zirpoli agreed, and issued a writ releasing Allgood from military custody.

Judge Advocate Stribley was incensed. "There is nothing in the regulations requiring that there be a basis in fact for the General's decision," he insisted. "It is strictly up to the commander's discretion." What Judge Zirpoli had suggested was the radical notion that a soldier has a *right* to a discharge if he is clearly unsuitable for military duty according to the Army's own psychiatrists.

Horrified at the thought of doctors and civilian judges telling commanders what to do, the Army has appealed to the Ninth

Circuit Court of Appeals. Meanwhile, Allgood waits in Earlimart, happily reunited with his wife and driving a truck once
again, wondering why the Army is so determined to get him
back.

III

EVERY RULE has its exceptions, even the military's "no-exit"
rule. A very small number of soldiers—about two or three percent—are discharged each year for incompatibility with the
army. For such acts of mercy, however, the army extracts its
pound of flesh: most unfitness discharges are punitive in nature,
carrying with them a loss of veteran's benefits and a stigma that
adversely affects future chances for employment.

Military regulations provide that a man may be discharged
prior to the end of his enlistment on one of the following principal grounds: (1) medical reasons; (2) hardship; (3) unsuitability; (4) unfitness; (5) bad conduct; or (6) becoming a conscientious objector after induction. Some of the regulations
sound compassionate on paper; in practice, however, they are
not.

Most of those who are discharged on medical grounds are
soldiers who are wounded in action or have prior medical difficulties that were not detected at the induction center. Ironically, the standards for staying in the army are lower than the
standards for getting in. This is partially due to the fact that
once a man puts on the uniform, the army becomes responsible
for his service-connected medical problems; if it admits to the
existence of a permanent disability, the federal government
must provide compensation for the rest of the man's life.[2]

2. Unless the soldier happens to be General Earle G. Wheeler, chairman of the Joint Chiefs of Staff, the government is not eager to bear this
expense. General Wheeler, who suffered a mild heart attack in 1967,
retired as chairman of the Joint Chiefs in 1970. The Army then graciously
found him to be "permanently unfit for duty by reason of physical disability of 70 percent," a determination which entitles him to an annual
tax-free pension of $27,000.

Mental illness is included among the possible grounds for medical discharge, but the number of psychiatric discharges is unduly small. Army Regulation 40-501 provides that soldiers may be psychiatrically discharged only when there is evident neurological damage, recurrent psychotic episodes, or neuroses severe enough to require frequent hospitalization. Repeated AWOL's, drug abuse, or suicide "gestures" are not symptoms of mental illness, but "transient personality disruptions of a non-psychotic nature and situational maladjustments due to acute or special stress." As such, they do not "render an individual unfit because of physical disability."

Hardship discharges, like psychiatric separations, are almost never given. Recruiters may talk about the wonderful benefits of military service, but when it comes to discharges, the army's tune suddenly changes. Military service is now a hardship for everyone; everybody has a family he would like to support. Unless the hardship is extreme, of recent origin, and supported by a plethora of notarized statements and forms, the army's attitude is simply "Tough luck."

It is equally difficult to establish oneself as a conscientious objector, as the army is not readily amenable to the notion that soldiers can be pacifists. Most misfits, in any case, are emotionally rather than philosophically at odds with the military, though the two categories cannot always be so neatly disjoined.

Army policy is murkiest in the nebulous zone of unsuitability/ unfitness/ bad conduct. Regulations distinguish among the three approximately as follows: "Unsuitable" soldiers are those who "try but can't"—soldiers who are inept, apathetic, or suffer from alcoholism, homosexual tendencies (without having committed overt homosexual acts), bed-wetting, or other character or behavior disorders which interfere with military service. "Unfit" soldiers are those who "can but won't"— soldiers who become involved in "frequent incidents of a discreditable nature," who fail to pay just debts, engage in perverse or homosexual acts, or use drugs. Discharges for bad conduct come about most frequently as the result of courts-martial for specific offenses. Bad-conduct and unfitness discharges are invariably dishonorable to one degree or another. Unsuitability discharges are usually "general"—neither honorable nor dishonorable.

One major problem with these discharges is that their issuance depends solely on the will of a soldier's commander, or, in the case of bad conduct discharges, a court-martial. Commanders are notoriously arbitrary in granting discharges. Much of the time they feel compelled to make examples of misfits; they intentionally punish them and make them as miserable as possible before even considering a discharge. Often a chain reaction develops. A maladjusted soldier is thrown into the stockade for his first or second offense of AWOL. His bitterness and anguish are thereby increased, and he commits another offense. This time the punishment is more severe, and the vicious circle continues.

Most of the character and behavior disorders that might cause a commander to consider a soldier unsuitable do not become evident until he has committed enough discreditable acts to make him also classified as unfit. In like manner, most of the acts which are grounds for calling a soldier unfit are also punishable by court-martial. This blurring of the lines gives the commander that much more power to punish. Most commanders will not take a psychiatrist's word that a man is unsuitable; they want to see overt acts to prove it. As a result, the misfit who acts out his troubles is more likely to be discharged than the misfit who suffers in silence—but also much more likely to be court-martialed and imprisoned.

The army, of course, does not punish misbehaving soldiers merely to satisfy the sadistic urges of its officers. At the root of the army's predilection for punishing rather than discharging distressed soldiers is its fear that if misfits are simply returned to civilian society, discipline will collapse.

As with most military arguments, there is some validity to this one. It *is* easier to run an army on the assumption that everyone must be a good soldier or suffer the consequences, and in some ancient armies, misfits and misbehavers were simply taken out and killed. But presumably in the post-Freudian age we have become a little more sophisticated and a little more humane. We appreciate the fact that not all persons have the emotional stability to cope with certain types of stresses, and that inability to adjust is not a criminal offense.

We also know that it is *not* true, as many commanders like to think, that the army can make a soldier out of anyone. For this reason, we establish standards to weed out civilians who should not be taken into the army because in all likelihood they will not become good soldiers. We recognize that these standards are at best inexact, and that many young men who are rejected for military service might in fact have made adequate soldiers, while many others are accepted who later turn out to be very bad army material. Why, then, do we insist on punishing those young men who we *know* can't adjust to military life, while letting free those young men who we only *suspect* will not be able to adjust?

The reason, says the military, is that there is a difference between rejecting civilians who will probably be unfit, and discharging soldiers who obviously are unfit. Keeping out undesirable civilians does not interfere with military discipline; letting out undesirable soldiers does. Thus, while it may not be equitable to punish emotionally troubled kids simply because they happen to be in the army, it is demanded by military necessity.

One must always subject arguments of *raisons d'état* to the closest scrutiny, for it is usually the greatest injustices that are perpetrated behind such reasonings. In the present instance, discipline is unquestionably weakened to some extent if soldiers see a member of their unit getting discharged while they have to serve till the end of their enlistments. But most GI's are intelligent enough to understand that if the soldier getting discharged is emotionally disturbed and unsuitable for duty, it doesn't do much good to keep him in.

Moreover, discipline is never perfect anyway. Some is lost by *retaining* men who are nothing but headaches to the command and possible sources of danger to their fellow soldiers. More is lost when men who could legally be boarded out of the army are constantly running AWOL. The real issue is whether keeping and punishing misfits results in a net gain or loss of efficiency, and if it results in a net gain, whether the suffering inflicted upon misfits is a fair price to pay for this gain. It would seem that the gain, if any, is small, and not worth the human price that is paid for it.

What, then, is to be done about military misfits? In the first place, the army ought to make it easier for people to adjust. A lot of the soldiers who go AWOL would stick around if the army weren't quite so hard to take—if their sergeants didn't razz them for being "duds," if someone truly cared about their problems, if they could have more time off and be stationed closer to home.

Secondly, when it becomes evident that a young man really is incapable of coping with the military, the army should not be so reluctant to let him go. The all-or-nothing dilemma that officers like to paint—let one out and you'll be letting everybody out—is in fact a false one. Army discharge regulations themselves are premised on the assumption that there *is* a meaningful distinction between "letting everybody out" and providing responsible, humane treatment for troubled young Americans who are placed under military custody. The difficulty is that, in practice, the military so narrowly interprets its own rules on hardship and unsuitability that soldiers who clearly ought to be separated are instead arbitrarily retained and often punished.

Thirdly, military psychiatrists ought to be given the power to determine when a distressed soldier should be discharged. At present, this power is in the hands of the commander; psychiatrists can only recommend.

Most important is the need to change the army's attitude toward punishment. Except in the unusual circumstances of an all-out defensive war, there can be no justification for sentencing chronic AWOL's and misfits to the stockade. Wherever possible, misfits should be discharged through psychiatric channels *before* they violate rules that would subject them to court-martial. Some form of punishment is unquestionably necessary to deter misbehavior and faked maladjustment, but it should be punishment that fits the crime. In the case of misfits who go AWOL, confinement in stockades during peacetime or a non-defensive war is much too severe a punishment. Far more appropriate and beneficial to all concerned would be the transfer of such men back to their draft boards for assignment to two or three years of service in a less stress-causing civilian environment.

6. OBJECTORS

FOR AS long as there has been an army in America there have been citizens who rebelled against what they considered to be its illegitimate powers. The roots of their objections were not psychological but political—they felt the military had interfered with their liberties beyond its proper authority to do so. Such attitudes account at least in part for the fact that the British had almost no success in converting colonial militiamen into aggressive campaigners against the French.

The Revolution itself was marked by a number of mutinies. On New Year's Day, 1781, six regiments of the Pennsylvania Line rebelled; many had signed up in 1777 for three years and were angry that their enlistments had been extended. Washington wanted to crack down on the Pennsylvanians, but Brigadier General Anthony Wayne prevailed upon him to negotiate. A representative of Wayne met with a committee of sergeants representing the mutineers. Wayne agreed to discharge all soldiers who had served three years, and about half the Pennsylvanians went home.

Three weeks later the New Jersey Line mutinied. This time Washington did not bargain. He surrounded the New Jersey camps with loyal New England troops and trained cannons on them. Then he placed the three most prominent mutineers on the parade ground in front of the troops, formed a firing squad of the twelve next-most-prominent activists, and forced them to execute their comrades.

The ending of the war provoked another series of riots among troops anxious to go home. Congress did not want to release the army until terms of the treaty with Britain became final; the men wanted their discharges and their mustering-out pay at once. On June 18, 1783, a group of eighty mutinous soldiers marched from Lancaster to Philadelphia, where they barricaded Congress in the Pennsylvania State House and demanded immediate redress of their grievances. The mutiny fizzled, however, when the members of Congress boldly walked out of the building and the troops failed to fire.

During the War of 1812, many New England militiamen refused to cross the border into Canada on the grounds that no invasion of the United States had taken place. Thirty-five years later, General Winfield Scott started off for Mexico City with some ten thousand volunteers, about a third of whom were twelve-month enlistees. By the time Scott arrived at Puebla, these short-termers' enlistments had expired, and nearly all of them went home.

Lincoln's army during the Civil War was plagued by desertion and draft evasion. Although improved machinery for enforcing the laws did much to reduce these problems in the twentieth century, the War Department listed 337,649 draft evaders during World War I.

A generation later, Americans again demonstrated their dislike for extended military service in far-off places, especially for non-defensive purposes. After Japan's surrender in September 1945, GI's demanded to be brought home—they had fought to defeat an aggressive enemy, but they were not interested in being global policemen. On Christmas Day in Manila, four thousand soldiers marched on the Twenty-first Replacement Depot Headquarters carrying banners that read WE WANT SHIPS.

Two weeks later, some twelve thousand GI's assembled in the bombed-out Philippine Hall of Congress to renew their demand. Tens of thousands of other soldiers demonstrated that week in Hawaii, Korea, Guam, Saipan, France, and Germany. In London, 1,800 officers and enlisted men signed a telegram to Washington: "We want an explanation of delayed return. . . . We are tired, homesick, disgusted men . . . eligible for discharge December 1, 1945. In European theatre over 30 months." Letters to Congressmen of similar import arrived at the rate of several thousand per day. If some recent actions of dissenting GI's seem angry and intemperate, it is worth remembering that, by contrast to some of their free-spirited predecessors, citizen-soldiers today are relatively docile and obedient.

Resentment of the military's powers, of course, has not always taken the form of outright disobedience or vociferous demands to be brought home. Commonly, it has been privately expressed by low-ranking soldiers with a kind of stoical sense of resignation. The resistance among citizen-soldiers to the military's powers today is a blending of these grumblings with more overt forms of action, some traditional, some uniquely *au courant:* protest marches, underground newspapers, unionization, avoidance of contact with the enemy, and application for discharge on grounds of conscientious objection.

It is hard to establish an accurate accounting of the number of political objectors in the ranks. Major General J. F. Freund, Deputy Chief of Staff of the Army for Intelligence, says that "at one time the total strength of dissident personnel in the Army was 285. This number increased by November, 1969, to a high of 547. In December, 1969, the number dropped to about 525, and it has now stabilized at about that level."

To count only "hard-core dissidents" who have been identified by military intelligence, however, is to grossly underestimate the extent of disaffection within the armed forces. The dissidents counted and constantly watched by the army are those who might accurately be described as full-time activists; they help publish underground newspapers, they regularly work at GI coffeehouses, they organize demonstrations, petitions, and local union chapters. But these activists, while relatively few in number, are merely the visible tip of a large iceberg. To them must be added the thousands who occasionally take part in marches, who sign petitions (1,365 active-duty GI's signed a single antiwar petition that ran in *The New York Times* on November 9, 1969), and who help distribute the underground papers. Besides these are the tens of thousands who *read* the underground papers, wear peace symbols, flash the V-sign or throw the clenched fist, smoke grass, or mutter "Fuck the Army" and mean it. All told, those disillusioned with far more than just working conditions and chow come to a quite sizable number.

Political disaffection is manifested mostly in myriad small and inconspicuous ways. It occurs in the anonymity of the darkened movie theater when GI's holler and cheer as Arlo Guthrie, in *Alice's Restaurant*, shouts "Kill, kill, kill" for the benefit of an induction center psychiatrist. It emerges in letters to parents and friends, or in the idle chatter of barracks bull sessions.

Sometimes it comes out on the job. A member of the band will intentionally play off key, a mechanic will take five days to perform a simple repair, a clerk will forge another man's orders to get him out of overseas duty, an armed forces newscaster will denounce military censorship.

Surface forms of resistance occur in Vietnam as well as at home. Peace medallions and hippie beads are commonplace on the front lines, and nearly everyone smokes the cheap and potent Vietnamese marijuana.

More significant is the growing number of GI's who intentionally avoid contact with the enemy. One articulate infantry platoon sergeant wrote in a letter that

Almost to a man, the members of my platoon oppose the war. While quite a few oppose the war on moral or political grounds (several were members of anti-war groups while they were in college) the majority are simply fed up with the drudgery of life in the field. This feeling is compounded by the easy life of men in the rear. . . . The result is a general malaise which pervades the entire company. There is a great deal of pressure on leaders at the small unit level, such as myself, to conduct what are popularly referred to as "search and avoid" missions, and to do so as safely and cautiously as is humanly possible.

Another front-line soldier, who aligns himself politically with Barry Goldwater and Ronald Reagan, says: "Our battalion commander will tell you that we'll have ambushes set out tonight, and maybe he'll even believe it. But there won't be any ambushes. The grunts [infantrymen] will just go out and call in by radio and say they've set up at the ambush point. But they'll really check into some ARVN compound and smoke pot and drink beer and make out with the boom-boom girls. Then in the morning they'll come back in."

It is around such acts of protest and semipassive resistance that there has emerged in the past few years what has come to be known as the GI movement. Like other recent political and cultural groundswells, it is a broad and amorphous affair. There is no central headquarters issuing directives to scores of disciplined operatives; the movement is too anti-militaristic to be organized in such a fashion. Nor are there any outstanding leaders who are widely respected as spokesmen or spiritual guides. The GI movement is a lot of little people doing a lot of little things, sometimes individually, sometimes in concert. The common political bonds are two: opposition to the Indochina War, and support for the citizen-soldier's right to dissent.

Those who identify with the GI movement represent a wide cross-section of America's men-in-arms. Among them are disillusioned junior officers, angry blacks, college graduates (twenty-six percent of the enlisted men separating from the armed forces in 1969 had attended college), late-blooming rebels who find their identity in opposition rather than in submission to the army, and a few ideological revolutionaries who enter the army specifically for the purpose of political organizing.

The motives of the participants are equally varied. Some have been radicalized by their service in Vietnam and seek to express their new political consciousness; some desire to strike back at the lifers and the military machine that harass them;

some are merely struggling to assert their individuality or protect their sanity.

Even among the more ideologically-minded GI's there is a broad spectrum of motives. Some see resistance within the military as a means of ultimately stopping the Vietnam War, or at least preventing future wars of a similar nature. Others view GI organizing as an effort to build radical political consciousness among working-class youth. A few dream of neutralizing the military as a repressive force, or even converting it into a revolutionary force that might, as in Russia in 1917, join in a general uprising.

For most GI's, however, the prime consideration is not some distant political objective but the immediate, existential need to *do something*. As soldiers, the war in Vietnam for them is a living reality, not the abstraction that it is for most civilians. The sense of being manipulated is also a daily experience. The soldier who detests working for a cause he finds abhorrent feels happier, freer, more self-respecting when he is stuffing envelopes with copies of an antiwar newspaper. He fears reprisal, he even expects it, but he joins the movement anyway.

Almost every major base in the United States and Europe has had its rumblings of anti-army activity. One of the early groups to form was at Fort Jackson, South Carolina. In January 1969, Private Joe Miles, an articulate black socialist, got a tape recorder and some tapes of Malcolm X's speeches, and began playing them in the barracks at night. Black and Puerto Rican soldiers started attending these sessions, and they created a group called GIs United Against the War in Vietnam. Soon the group expanded to include a number of white soldiers as well.

GIs United decided to organize around the issues of constitutional rights for soldiers and an end to the Vietnam War. It circulated a petition asking the commanding general to make available on-post facilities after normal duty hours for an open meeting to discuss the war. Several hundred soldiers signed the petition, but Fort Jackson officials refused to accept it on the grounds that it represented a form of "collective bargaining."

With the help of civil liberties lawyers, GIs United sued for a declaratory judgment that soldiers have a right to petition military authorities and to hold peaceful meetings on base. The suit was recently rejected by a federal appeals court.

At Fort Bliss, Texas, near El Paso, another group of antiwar GIs got together in the summer of 1969. These were predominantly white, well-educated draftees (their first chairman, Private Paul Nevins, had been drafted out of graduate school while working on his doctorate in political science), and they called themselves GIs for Peace. "What we're asking for is our rights," said Nevins. "We still believe that American society can be radically transformed for the better through non-violent action. As every soldier knows, America has witnessed too much violence. We desperately need a peaceful alternative."

GIs for Peace launched an extremely literate newspaper, *Gigline*, to serve as a forum for news and ideas. It opened a movement center, provided legal help for soldiers, filed complaints with the Inspector General's office, wrote to Congressmen and Senators, forged links with the local press, and got involved in community projects in El Paso.

One after another, leading activists in the organization were transferred to Vietnam, Korea, Germany, or other stateside bases; yet no sooner would one "troublemaker" be removed than another would pop up to fill his place. GIs for Peace scored one of its greatest successes on January 15, 1970, when General William C. Westmoreland, Army Chief of Staff, was greeted in El Paso by a picket line of eighty active-duty soldiers carrying signs proclaiming PEACE IS PATRIOTIC and WE PROTEST STOCKADE BRUTALITY.

Another antiwar organization, the Movement for a Democratic Military, traces its origins back to the summer of 1969. Seamen Tom Csekey, André Carlson, Robert Mahoney, and Jack Noel, all then stationed at the North Island Naval Station, San Diego, were growing restless. They'd been hassled several times for possessing antiwar literature and posters; finally, they decided to get together and start a newspaper. Working with a civilian commune that published the San Diego *Free Press* (now the *Street Journal*), they created a lively, irreverent paper for sailors which they called *Duck Power*.

Meanwhile, at the sprawling Camp Pendleton Marine Corps base thirty miles to the north, an angry group of black, Chicano, and white Marines was also developing plans for a newspaper and some antiwar actions. "A lot of guys got together and we discussed exactly what was going on in the military," recounts Sergeant Jack Anderson, one of the black Marine organizers. "We realized that we were being oppressed and that we shouldn't just sit passively and take it. We couldn't be silent because we know that the lifers interpret silence as complacency."

In November 1969, the Marines and the sailors joined forces, initially to co-sponsor Vietnam Moratorium activities, then more lastingly to form MDM. They agreed upon a twelve-point program—an eclectic mix of Black Panther, white radical, and other GI movement demands—around which they set forth to rally new members. These points were: (1) the right to refuse politically objectionable duty such as Vietnam or riot control; (2) the right to collective bargaining for soldiers; (3) an end to cruelty in basic training and military stockades; (4) removal of military courts-martial from the chain of command and provision for trial by a jury of one's peers by rank; (5) a minimum wage for soldiers equal to the minimum federal wage for civilians; (6) an end to "sir"-ing and saluting and other privileges of rank; (7) an end to racism; (8) freedom for all political prisoners; (9) an end to the glorification of war by the military; (10) abolition of the draft; (11) immediate U.S. withdrawal from Vietnam; (12) full constitutional rights for soldiers.

Much less radical than MDM is another group of disenchanted soldiers—in this case, officers—who have banded together into a loosely knit association they call the Concerned Officer's Movement. Most of its members are Washington-based junior officers, including two who, until they joined COM, prepared daily intelligence briefings for the Chief of Naval Operations.

COM's members view themselves as loyal, responsible officers with an obligation to express themselves on vital issues. Paramount in their program, states their May 1970 newsletter,

. . . is a fervent opposition to the continuing effort in Vietnam. COM decries the military policies that turned an internal political struggle into a nation-destroying bloodbath. . . . COM further abhors the military mentality that promotes absurd measures like the body count; that leads to the indiscriminate slaughter of innocent civilians; that destroys land and villages and calls it victory. COM is opposed to the preponderant share of national resources devoted to the military. . . . Within the military structure itself, COM supports free expression of dissenting opinion. GI movements with legitimate grievances have too long been suppressed by a military hierarchy that considers honest questioning a threat to its power.

Probably the largest, or at least most far-flung, organization within the GI movement is the American Servicemen's Union, which claims (doubtless with some exaggeration) several thousand card-carrying members stationed everywhere from Long Binh to Fort Dix. In theory, the ASU is patterned after civilian labor unions. It has a national office in New York headed by ex-Private Andy Stapp, and about a dozen locals that tend to be fairly autonomous. Membership costs $1, and each member carries a wallet-size card with the union's ten-point program, similar in its essentials to MDM's.

Becoming an established trade union like the Teamsters, however, is the last thing the ASU has in mind. It *is* interested in GI power, but not for the purpose of obtaining better fringe benefits or fatter paychecks. In the short run, union members hope that, by sticking together, enlisted men will be able to fight back against "lifer harassment." In the long run, they envision a powerful union enabling soldiers to refuse objectionable duty, although that day admittedly is quite far away.

The union, at least on its leadership level, has unabashedly Marxist overtones. *The Bond*, the union's newspaper, is not only anti-lifer and anti-war but frequently anti-capitalist. One of its popular themes is that GI's are fighting a rich man's war that benefits only David Rockefeller and his cohorts.

Andy Stapp, the affable ASU chairman who now sports a Lenin-like beard, is an outspoken revolutionary socialist. A product of upper-crust Philadelphia society, he won three letters in high school athletics and made dean's list at Penn State. When he volunteered for the draft in 1966, it was with the conscious intention of radicalizing American enlisted men. At Fort Sill, Oklahoma, he was court-martialed for refusing to surrender socialist literature he kept in his footlocker. To his aid came a delegation from Youth Against War and Fascism, a New York–based Trotskyite splinter group with which he has been aligned ever since.

II

THAT THE military is worried about the growing disaffection of its soldiers is evident from its twofold approach to youthful dissent: on the one hand, a greater degree of tolerance for such nonpolitical forms of rebelliousness as longer hair, rock music, mod clothing styles, and even marijuana; on the other hand, a consistent policy of suppressing, to the greatest extent possible, the expression of political views that run counter to official dogma.

The Navy, traditionally the most hidebound of the services, has taken the lead in liberalizing its regulations on appearance and dress. Under recent orders promulgated by Admiral Elmo Zumwalt, Chief of Naval Operations, sailors may now sport beards, sideburns, and mustaches, as long as they are neatly trimmed, and have greater freedom in their choice of off-duty attire. The Army and Marine Corps have revised their regulations to permit slightly lower sideburns, as well as modified Afro haircuts for black soldiers. In like manner, penalties for smoking marijuana have been greatly relaxed, especially in Vietnam, and many army units have shifted from an emphasis on punishment to a concern for rehabilitation of hard-drug users.

These recent concessions to the Aquarian generation have been accompanied, however, by a concerted effort to deter political expression. The army can tolerate soldiers who smoke marijuana, just as it has tolerated soldiers who drink; what it cannot tolerate are too many GI's who think—and speak—for themselves.

The most potent deterrent to those who might entertain the thought of protesting or somehow resisting the army's powers is simply the omnipresence of fear. For a valid psychological comparison, one must visualize an almost wholly totalitarian society, where no one can be trusted, where everyone is watched, where rules mean whatever the rule-enforcers say they mean, and where punishment is swift and arbitrary. Courage rapidly fades in such an environment; one's first concern becomes survival.

Fear is constantly reinforced by low-level harassment. Denial of weekend passes, restriction to base, and assignment to unpleasant or unnecessary details are typical measures employed against "troublemakers." A confidential memorandum prepared for the command at Fort Carson, Colorado, for example, describes how the Army planned to keep five antiwar GI's from attending a Moratorium rally in Colorado Springs. One of the activists, the memorandum said, could be kept on base by an inspection; another could be assigned to guard duty; and a third would be kept busy "cutting new unit orders" for arriving troops. The other two men, Specialists Fifth Class Tom Roberts and Curtis Stocker, both editors of the underground newspaper *Aboveground*, presented more ticklish problems:

1. Roberts: 46th Arty. Cannot come up with any sound, above criticism type reason to keep Roberts on post. The best they have to offer so far is that Roberts may accompany LTC Munson (XO) on an evening Army aircraft flight and be forced into an RON [remaining overnight]. This is pretty flimsy at best.
2. Stocker: 47th Hosp. Cannot devise any logical, reasonable action to be taken which would *not* be highly suspicious (comment: I believe there is good reason to expect Stocker's appearance in Acacia Park during the evening of 15 October, since this area is his old "stomping ground").

Roberts and Stocker ultimately did attend the rally in Acacia Park, along with about seventy-five other GI's from the base;

but Stocker might not have made it if he hadn't been cleverer than his superiors. On October 14, his commanding officer, Major Alonzo C. Perry, asked him what he planned to do the following day. Stocker replied that he was due to speak in Colorado Springs at 6:30 in the evening. On the day of the rally he was scheduled to get off duty at 4:30. At three o'clock, however, he was told to report to his unit's orderly room at the end of his normal duty hours. There Major Perry ordered him to remain until shortly after six o'clock. This crude and rather obvious stratagem might have succeeded were it not for the fact that the Moratorium rally actually began at 8:30, not 6:30. Stocker jumped into his car and covered the sixty-five miles to Colorado Springs with minutes to spare.

Punitive transfers are another favorite technique. Soldiers active in an antiwar group at a given base will be reassigned to another installation, usually one that is small and out of the way. Private Joe Miles, who launched GIs United at Fort Jackson, was quickly transferred to Fort Bragg and then reassigned again to a desolate outpost near the Arctic Circle. Seaman Robert Mahoney, one of the antiwar sailors in San Diego who helped found *Duck Power*, was rewarded with a transfer to Midway island. Sergeant Michael C. Sanders, an honor guard at the Tomb of the Unknown Soldier, did nothing more than tell a reporter from his hometown paper, the Louisville *Courier-Journal*, that he was opposed to the Indochina War; he was promptly reassigned to combat duty in Vietnam.

Another widespread practice is surveillance of GI's suspected of engaging in antiwar activities. Recent headlines have revealed the extent of such surveillance beyond the bounds of the military itself. Thus, according to former Captain Christopher H. Pyle, who served at the headquarters of the Army Intelligence Command at Fort Holabird, Maryland, the Army uses nearly one thousand plainclothes agents to keep track of the lawful activities of such civilian organizations as the NAACP, the Southern Christian Leadership Conference, and the American Civil Liberties Union. The 116th Military Intelligence Group, for example, maintains a staff of twenty agents whose job is to infiltrate political groups and observe politically active persons in the Washington, D.C., area. Some agents of the 116th have grown beards and long hair to pass as college students; others have posed as news photographers to get pictures for their files, and at one time even maintained a videotape truck marked "Midwest News."

That this kind of intelligence effort should be mounted against *civilians* who protest government policy gives some indication of the lengths the army goes to in "taking care of its own." It is generally assumed that within every group of dissenting GI's there are at least one or two MI (Military Intelligence) or CID (Criminal Investigation Division) informants. Also taken for granted is that every meeting of any import is attended by an adequate number of agents, and that every outdoor protest rally is photographed by a virtual platoon of intelligence shutterbugs.

One of the most astonishing examples of such surveillance involved Seaman Roger Priest, a husky sailor assigned to the Pentagon who singlehandedly wrote and published an antiwar newsletter called OM. He was eventually court-martialed on a variety of charges. As the Navy was subsequently to admit at a pre-trial hearing, Priest was followed for several months by no less than twenty-five agents of the Office of Naval Intelligence—a state of affairs exceeding the young sailor's most grandiose suspicions. At one point, ONI obtained a District of Columbia sanitation truck to make a special pickup of Priest's trash. Another time, when Priest spoke at an antiwar meeting in Cleveland, six of the fifteen people in the audience were Navy agents.

The mentality of overzealous military intelligence officers is fairly well represented by the following memorandum which fell into the hands of antiwar GI's at Fort Rucker, Alabama:

Commanders should be alert for the following indicators: a. Display of Pacifist Peace Symbols; b. Subscription to and/or possession of dissident newspapers; c. Membership in, and/or support of New Left, pacifist, anti-Vietnam, communist and racial groups.

These may indicate that the individual supports causes which are not in the best interests of national security.

During the past year, my office has undertaken investigations of some 15 soldiers who chose to display the Pacifist Peace Symbol on their private automobiles. This action was taken with full realization that the Pacifist Peace Symbol has been adopted by the New Left, the dissident elements of our colleges, and the communist front organizations whose declared mission is to use the military youths as pawns, to organize and direct dissident elements of the military services. . . .

Display of the Pacifist Peace Symbol is, in almost every case, used to show overt contempt for law and order and indicates that the person displaying such symbols is anti-military, anti-Vietnam and anti-establishment. Invariably, it is the person with character defects, the pot-smoker, the amoral, the immature and/or the irresponsible who displays this symbol: the PINKS, PUNKS, and PIMPS, if you will.

While the display of this symbol is not a basis for a limited investigation or a flagging action under AR 600-31, it is sufficient basis for close and continuous monitoring of a subject's conduct while he is at Ft. Rucker. In each case, where a dissident is identified, we have asked the commanding officer and immediate superiors to report any information of an adverse nature which may come to their attention concerning the subject.

Our efforts have been rewarded with four dissidents discharged as undesirables, two placed in confinement and the remainder much wiser for our association.

Besides monitoring the activities of soldiers, the various military intelligence agencies stay in touch with businessmen, police, and politicians in the towns surrounding military bases. They have ways of encouraging such civilians to cooperate in controlling undesired forms of GI expression.

A case in point: The December 1969 issue of the Fort Carson paper *Aboveground* was set to be printed by a Colorado Springs firm, Peerless Graphics, on the 12th of that month. On the afternoon of December 11, agents of Military Intelligence, the FBI, and the local police paid a visit to the firm's offices—the upshot of which was Peerless's last-minute refusal to do the job. What kind of pressure had the visitors applied? "Well," said a spokesman for the firm, "we try to do business in a town where we are, you might say, respected. See? And we weren't going to irritate them. They didn't say we couldn't print it. But they wanted copies of the paper. They wanted this and they wanted that, and I just wasn't going into a thing like that."

Foremost among the targets of military intelligence are the antiwar coffeehouses that have sprung up around a dozen bases throughout the United States since 1967. The coffeehouses were conceived as a means of bringing GI's and civilian radicals closer together. They also provide a hangout, a congenial ambiance, where soldiers who are turned off by the military can meet and talk and listen to music and maybe decide to do things. The civilian staffers do not get directly involved in organizing GI's, but they can provide soldiers with access to legal help and publicity, and generally stimulate their interest in opposing the war.

From the start, the military intelligence apparatus kept a very close watch over the coffeehouses. Civilians involved in the project were investigated. The New York-based United States Servicemen's Fund, a kind of left-wing USO that helped finance many of the coffeehouses, was deprived of its tax-exempt status. At every base where a coffeehouse was opened, officers warned their men that it would be inadvisable to be seen visiting it.

The tactic found most effective was to bring pressure against the coffeehouses through the civilian communities in which they are located. In town after town, the pattern repeated itself: Military and FBI agents would make the rounds of realtors and local politicians. Leases and licenses to operate coffeehouses would mysteriously disappear or be challenged. Civilian arrests on trumped-up charges would be made.

At the Shelter Half coffeehouse near Fort Lewis, Washington, which the Army tried unsuccessfully to put off limits, two civilian staff members were arrested by Tacoma police and charged with corrupting the morals of a minor: a GI under 21, it seems, had used the Shelter Half's table soccer game—the kind of "crime" that occurs hundreds of times a day at USO's everywhere.

In Muldraugh, Kentucky, just outside Fort Knox, the opening of a GI coffeehouse in 1969 prompted the city council to order a "thorough investigation" by the police chief of any person applying to open a business. The chief determined that, under the terms of a new ordinance, the coffeehouse managers were not of good character and repute. Their license application was turned down.

Not to be outdone by local officials, the Meade County grand jury launched its own investigation. Many of the coffeehouse staff members, said the county attorney, "participated in civil rights demonstrations in Louisville" or have "come from New York." That was enough for the grand jury, which indicted six of the staffers for conducting a public nuisance. The whole matter is now in the federal courts.

In Columbia, South Carolina, a much larger and more sophisticated city than Muldraugh, the community response was even harsher. Circuit Judge E. Harry Agnew sentenced three operators of UFO, oldest of the GI coffeehouses, to six years in prison for maintaining a public nuisance, while police put padlocks on the coffeehouse itself. The court-ordered closing of UFO followed by several months the tossing of an incendiary bomb through the door of the Fort Dix Coffeehouse Project in Wrightstown, New Jersey—an attack reminiscent of earlier bombings at the Shelter Half in Tacoma and the Green Machine coffeehouse outside Camp Pendleton.

III

THERE ARE four things a state can do to citizens who are strongly opposed to participating in a war: coerce them to fight in it, imprison them, allow them to serve the country in some other way, or leave them totally alone. Until the Enrollment Act of 1863, America followed the last-mentioned course; since then, whenever conscription has been imposed, America has preferred coercion or imprisonment. Only in an extremely niggardly fashion has the government provided alternative means of service for citizens conscientiously opposed to war.

The first federal conscription law during the Civil War allowed persons who declared their religious opposition to bearing arms to be employed in hospitals or to be excused from all obligation upon the payment of $300, which was put into a fund for the sick and wounded. During World War I and again since 1940, draft boards were authorized to assign religious objectors to noncombatant military duty or to civilian work of public importance. Today most conscientious objectors fulfill their two-year obligations by working in civilian hospitals or social welfare agencies. Those assigned to noncombatant military duty usually serve as medics.[1]

Two basic assumptions have underlain American laws regarding conscientious objection: first, that it ill behooves a democracy to force citizens to bear arms when it is against their consciences, and second, that persons sincerely opposed to war and killing do not make good soldiers.

These sensible assumptions have been largely offset, however, by two other tenets of national policy: first, that only *religious* objection to military service should be recognized by the state, and second, that objection cannot be to a particular war but must be against the entire concept of killing under any circumstances. For a long time, the only citizens whose consciences were deemed to be worth respecting were those who belonged to established pacifist churches—Quakers, Mennonites, Seventh Day Adventists, and the like.

In the past few years, the Supreme Court has widened the definition of conscientious objection to what are probably the broadest limits possible under present law. The Military Selective Service Act of 1967 exempts from combatant military duty any person

who, by reason of religious training and belief, is conscientiously opposed to participation in war in any form. As used in this subsection, the term "religious training and belief" does not include essentially political, sociological or philosophical views, or a merely personal moral code.

1. A few conscientious objectors in the Army are sent to Fort Detrick, Maryland, where they are used as human guinea pigs in nonlethal chemical and biological warfare experiments.

According to the Supreme Court's interpretation, the phrase "religious training and belief" does not require a belief in God or membership in an organized church, and religious belief *can* encompass philosophical, political, and social views, so long as it does not consist *exclusively* of such views. The determining factors, the Court ruled in *U.S.* v. *Seeger* and *U.S.* v. *Welsh*, are whether the objector's opposition to all killing is sincere, and whether it derives from a belief "which occupies in the life of its possessor a place parallel to that held by . . . God" in the lives of formally religious persons. Under this liberal definition of "religious training and belief," a handful of humanists and agnostics have been classified as conscientious objectors in the past few years, usually after lengthy court battles.

The initial power to determine which civilians should be designated as conscientious objectors does not lie, however, with judicial bodies but, as prescribed by Congress, with the Selective Service System. Under the best of circumstances, it is difficult and basically improper for an executive agency of the government to pass judgment upon the beliefs of citizens; by assigning this distasteful task to the same federal agency that is charged with conscripting the bodies to fight wars, Congress has added to this fundamental impropriety a very serious conflict of interest.

It is, obviously, the desire of the Selective Service System to minimize the number of conscientious objectors; it has a built-in bias against the individual and in favor of the manpower needs of the state— a bias that extends from the most unsophisticated of the four thousand local draft boards to the very pinnacle of the Selective Service System in Washington. Thus, when the Supreme Court ruled in the Welsh case that conscientious objection could be based on deeply held moral and ethical views, as well as traditional religious beliefs, Selective Service Director Curtis W. Tarr promptly issued instructions to local draft boards to be particularly stringent in assessing ethical or moral convictions. Any citizen claiming conscientious objection on ethical or moral grounds, he advised, should be made to prove that his views were "gained through training, study, contemplation or other activity, comparable in rigor and dedication to the processes by which traditional religious convictions are formulated." Since the Supreme Court had said nothing about "rigorous training," Tarr's directive represented a quite gratuitous and unwarranted restriction on the scope of the Court's decision.

Because the granting of conscientious objector status was for so long limited to members of specific religious sects, it was never considered possible for men to become conscientious objectors after they had donned a military uniform. Congressional legislation applied only to the classification of civilians; the army itself would not admit that soldiers might also become pacifists.

In 1945, an Army private named Henry Weber refused to train with his rifle when ordered to do so. He was sentenced to six months confinement at hard labor, then ordered again to train with the rifle. Again he refused and again he was court-martialed. At his trial he explained, "I do not mind being in the medics or any other place, just as long as I don't have to hate and kill other people." This time he was sentenced to death.

Weber's sentence, after a series of public protests, was reduced to life imprisonment, then to twenty years, then to five years and a dishonorable discharge. But it was not until 1962 that the military finally adopted regulations for recognizing conscientious objectors *within* its ranks.

The army's guidelines for classifying conscientious objectors are similar to those of the Selective Service System, except that they are even stricter. A soldier must be sincerely opposed to killing by reason of religious training and belief. His opposition must be to participation in all wars and not merely to a particular war. In addition—and this is the trickiest part—he must be able to prove that his conscientious beliefs grew out of his experience *prior* to entering the army, but did not become crystallized until *after* his entry into the service. If his views were well formed before he entered the army, he loses; if, on the other hand, his beliefs were prompted solely by his experience in the army, he also loses. His views, in other words, must not only conform to the finely drawn official definition of conscientious objection, they must also have developed at just the right time and at just the right speed.

Applying for conscientious objector status within the military is as laborious a process as its favorable outcome is unlikely. Three out of four applications for such discharges are rejected, and the soldier who then sticks by his beliefs must be ready to spend time in the stockade. He must also be wealthy or prepared to go into debt, since court fights are expensive.

The first thing an objector in the military must do is learn of his right to apply, as well as the procedure to follow. This itself is likely to prove difficult, since accurate information on conscientious objection is notoriously hard to come by within the military. Were it not for the existence of civilian antiwar counselors, most GI's would remain quite unaware of their rights in this regard.

Second, a soldier must notify his commanding officer in writing of his intention to seek objector status. The commanding officer may react with anger and a string of epithets—"coward," "peace creep," and the like. Whatever the commander says, the applicant must brace himself for the harassment that is sure to follow in the days ahead.

Third, the soldier must prepare and submit his written application, which, to be effective, must be a lengthy, self-analytical document backed up by supporting letters from clergymen, teachers, and other respectable persons. The heart of the application is a series of essays in which, as prescribed by Defense Department Directive 1300.6, the soldier is required to explain the nature of his "religious training and belief." He must state "how, when, and from whom or what source [he] received the training and acquired the belief which is the basis of his claim." He must expound upon the "circumstances, if any, under which [he] believes in the use of force." And he must describe "the actions and behavior in [his] life which . . . most conspicuously demonstrates [sic] the consistency and depth of his religious convictions."

Next, the applicant is interviewed by a military psychiatrist and by a chaplain. The purpose of the psychiatric consultation is to determine whether the soldier is free from mental disorders. (The apparent implication is that a man strongly opposed to killing may well have something the matter with his mind.)

It is the chaplain's function, as a Pentagon personnel officer puts it, to "smoke out those claims that are not based on religious training criteria." Although some chaplains are genuinely fair-minded towards conscientious objectors, a great number are "gung-ho" types who find it extremely difficult to conceive how a man can have valid religious objections to defending God-fearing America against the menace of atheistic Communism.[2]

Finally, the soldier seeking recognition as a conscientious objector has the right (which it is wise to exercise) to a hearing and interview by a middle-ranking officer who is "knowledgeable in policies and procedures relating to conscientious objector matters." Usually this officer is a lawyer in the Judge Advocate General's Corps or a captain in personnel. After discussing with the soldier all aspects of his beliefs, the officer makes a report and recommends approval or disapproval of the application. His judgment is given considerable weight.

The ultimate decision on the application is made at the departmental level in Washington by an advisory board consisting of representatives from the offices of the Chief of Chaplains, the Judge Advocate General, the Surgeon General, and the Chief of Personnel. The evaluation takes anywhere from a few days to six weeks. If the decision is negative, there is no practicable method of appeal within the military. The soldier

---

2. The role of an army chaplain is in general an anomalous one, and quite arguably unconstitutional. He is not merely a clergyman providing religious succor to soldiers, but is a commissioned military officer, paid by the state, promoted in rank like any other officer, and sworn to uphold the policies of a secular President. His role in judging conscientious objector applicants derives from his specific military status as a staff officer of the commander: "The chaplain is a member of the staff of the commanding officer, and is the consultant of the commander and his staff in matters involving the spiritual welfare of the command, public religious observances, morality, morale and character building" (Army Field Manual 16-5).

can refuse to cooperate with the army while he seeks a writ of habeas corpus from the federal courts, but in so doing, he invites punishment by court-martial, or even shanghaiing to Vietnam, and there is no guarantee that he will ultimately succeed. His only certainties at this point are that he will be imprisoned by the military and billed by his lawyer.

A case can be made—and army spokesmen occasionally make it—that the military's procedure for classifying conscientious objectors is fairer than that of Selective Service. Military applicants, it is pointed out, may have a lawyer present during their interview with the hearing officer, whereas civilian objectors may not be accompanied by counsel during their draft board hearing. In addition, the fact that decisions in the military are made at a national level, rather than by a local body, ensures uniformity and a stricter adherence to official guidelines.

While these points are in themselves valid, and while it is true that the military has taken several steps since 1968 to improve its classification procedures, it is nonetheless also true that the army can *never* be a genuinely fair judge of conscientious objectors. For, if empowering the Selective Service System to pass on the beliefs of civilians creates a substantial conflict of interest, the degree of such conflict inherent in having the military rule on its own conscientious objector claimants is staggering.

Soldiers' conscientious objector applications are, and by their nature must be, filled with derogatory references to the army and its mission. Objectors write and talk about the senseless killing by the army in Indochina, the repulsive dehumanization of basic training, or—as one applicant wrote—"the overwhelming evil of the entire system." How can men who have made their careers out of the business of war be expected to rule dispassionately on the fate of young people who proclaim that everything they stand for is immoral? One might as well ask the directors of General Motors to pass upon the sincerity of Ralph Nader.

Moreover, the military does not like to discharge soldiers for *any* reason. Thus, many conscientious objector applications are rejected without any evidence that the claimant is insincere or that his beliefs are totally nonreligious. During the first three years of the massive build-up in Vietnam, the Army approved almost no conscientious objector discharge applications—not because the objectors were wanting in conviction, but because it simply was not Army policy then to recognize them. In 1968, after federal courts asserted their right to review military conscientious objector cases, that policy was changed. In 1969, the Army acted favorably on 194 out of 943 applications for conscientious objector discharge, a rate of twenty-one percent; in 1970 the approval rate was only slightly higher. By contrast, nearly eighty percent of the conscientious objector claims of soldiers in the West German Bundeswehr are approved—at least partly because in West Germany the classification of conscientious objectors in the military is made by a *civilian* board of examiners.

Clearly, the power to judge the conscientious beliefs of young Americans should be taken out of the hands of the military and the Selective Service System and delegated to some new and impartial judicial entity. Far more necessary, however, than a change in the manner of administering conscientious objector classification is a change in the way in which conscientious objection is defined. It is absurd in this day and age to insist that conscientious opposition to war be grounded in some form, however broad, of religious belief—the more so since the Constitution forbids any establishment of religion. It is similarly illogical to require that an objector be equally opposed in conscience to all wars, when it is obvious that the only really relevant war is a current war.

So long as the President retains the power to commit the army to undeclared, non-defensive wars, it should be enough to be a conscientious objector that a citizen be deeply and sincerely opposed to killing in the war he is being asked to fight. Anything more stringent than that is a gross deprivation of liberty.

IV

THE ISSUES of conscription in general and conscientious objection in particular are not unique to our own society. It may be instructive, therefore, to see how another country—one closely related to our own politically and culturally—has handled the problem.

Of all the imperial nations of modern times, the most lastingly successful was Great Britain. Yet Britain managed to build its empire without eroding liberty at home; there was no conscription imposed in any of its non-defensive wars. A draft was adopted only when the country's security was directly threatened—during World War I, and from 1939 to 1955.

During the first of these two brief periods, British policy toward conscientious objectors was not a model of enlightenment; hundreds of sincere objectors were trapped in a "cat and mouse" game in which they were court-martialed and imprisoned two, three, or more times for refusing to accept combat duty. But unlike the United States, Britain learned something from its experiences in the first great war. By the time Hitler marched into Poland, England was prepared to protect the freedom of conscience it was about to begin fighting for.

When the bill reinstating conscription was introduced in the House of Commons in 1939, the government made it clear that there would be no persecution of those who held honest scruples against killing; the government's primary concern would be to see that provisions for conscientious objection were not abused. When Parliament approved conscription, therefore, it also approved a procedure for recognizing conscientious objectors which stands as a monument to Britain's centuries-old tradition of political tolerance.

Under this law, which remained in effect until the end of conscription in 1955, the sole criterion for judging conscientious objectors was sincerity. The nature of the objector's beliefs was of no concern to the state; he could be motivated by religious, moral, economic, political, sociological, or astrological ideas; he could be opposed to all war, or he could merely be opposed to fighting Hitler. What mattered was not *what* he thought, but how honestly and deeply he held his convictions.

Men between the ages of 18 and 41 were given a choice of entering themselves either on the military register or on a provisional register for conscientious objectors. Those who inscribed themselves on the military register were drafted; those who claimed to be conscientious objectors had to state their views in a written application and then appear before a local tribunal for classification.

These tribunals were created for the exclusive purpose of classifying conscientious objectors; thus they avoided the conflict of interest that characterizes American draft boards. There were sixteen local tribunals throughout the United Kingdom, each consisting of five members, and six appellate tribunals consisting of three members each. Great care was taken by the government in selecting persons to sit on these bodies. The chairman of each local tribunal was always a county judge; other members were men of high caliber who could be relied on to be impartial in matters of conscientious objection. Those appointed to the appellate tribunals were citizens of outstanding reputation and considerable legal experience, such as retired judges and civil servants.

A young man seeking conscientious objector status first filled out a form on which there were no trick questions about theological intricacies but simply a space for "any statement you wish to submit in support of your application." He then appeared for a hearing before his local tribunal.

Unlike the hearings conducted by American draft boards, those in England were public; the applicant could be represented by counsel or by a friend; he could call witnesses to testify under oath, and have the expense of transporting himself and his witnesses paid for by the Ministry of Labour.

More importantly, the applicant could express his convictions to the best of his ability without worrying whether or not they would fit into a wafer-thin definition of acceptable beliefs. Many of those who were granted exemption were Socialists who insisted that they could not participate in what they viewed as a war for capitalist gain. Others were Indians and

Pakistanis who refused to fight in the British army so long as their own nations remained subjugated colonies. A few were avowed Nazi sympathizers who said they could not in good conscience fight against the German Reich.

After hearing the applicant's case, the local tribunal could assign him to one of four classifications: unconditional exemption from all national service (reserved only for the most tenacious objectors); permanent registration as a conscientious objector with the obligation to perform civilian service; transference to the military register for noncombatant duty; and, in complete rejection of the applicant's claim, transference to the military register for combat duty.

Objectors assigned to civilian service were often employed in civil defense and fire-watching. They were also engaged in farming, relief or hospital work, or in private business which was deemed to be of benefit to the country. Military noncombatants were usually assigned to the Labour Corps, similar to the American Seabees.

An applicant could appeal an unfavorable classification within twenty-one days to the appropriate appellate tribunal. In making his appeal, he would have the benefit of a written decision from the local tribunal. His appellate hearing would be public, and he could again have the assistance of counsel. The Ministry of Labour would again reimburse him for transportation costs.

Statistics for the years 1939–48 show that the British tribunals, even during this period of dire national emergency, were eminently impartial in their judgment of conscientious objectors[3] Out of a total of 61,227 men who inscribed themselves on the provisional conscientious objector register, 2,868, or five percent, were granted unconditional exemptions. Nearly 23,000, or thirty-eight percent, were permanently registered as conscientious objectors and assigned to civilian service. Some 17,000, or twenty-eight percent, were assigned to noncombatant

3. For complete statistical data, as well as an excellent account of British policy toward conscientious objectors, the reader is referred to Denis Hayes's *Challenge of Conscience* (London: Allen and Unwin; 1949).

military duty, and approximately the same number were denied conscientious objector status and ordered to combat duty.

The British were equally fair to conscientious objectors whose beliefs were formed subsequent to entering the armed services. Under the British law, a soldier could petition an appellate tribunal, which, after evaluating his application, could advise the War Office to discharge him as a conscientious objector. Appellate tribunals considered 808 such applications from servicemen over the years 1939–48, of which 587 were acted on favorably.

Even a soldier who had been court-martialed could apply to an appellate tribunal for release from the military after having served three months of his sentence. If the tribunal found his conscientious objection claim to be valid, it could order him freed from prison, discharged from the army, and assigned to appropriate civilian work, just as though there had been no military service or court-martial.

Because most British citizens believed the survival of their nation to be at stake, the overwhelming majority of young men chose to enroll on the military register.[4] The provisions for conscientious objection were not abused, and the over-all war effort was probably aided by the government's enlightened policy. Manpower was allocated in such a way that people were assigned to the tasks for which they were best motivated. At the same time, the armed services were not weakened by the presence of resentful conscripts. As a 1944 Ministry of Information booklet explained:

> We hold that a man whose deepest feelings are outraged by combatant military service should not be pressed into such service. Not only will he suffer, but also—a point frequently overlooked—the Service will suffer. Nobody wants to attack an enemy strongpoint in the company of fellow soldiers who are rootedly opposed to fighting.

Nobody, apparently, except the Americans in 1971.

---

4. In 1939, 2.2 percent enrolled as conscientious objectors; by the time of the Battle of Britain, the rate had dropped to 0.5 percent.

PART IV

WHEN YOU GO INTO THE ARMED FORCES, YOU GIVE UP
A HELL OF A LOT OF THINGS. BUT I'VE NEVER
THOUGHT YOU GIVE UP YOUR RIGHT TO SAY WHAT YOU THINK
IS RIGHT AND WHAT YOU THINK IS WRONG.

—General David M. Shoup,
Former Commandant, U.S. Marine Corps

7. THE LOSS OF RIGHTS

DANIEL AMICK and Kenneth Stolte are two of the most unlikely criminals a jailer could expect to meet. Amick is a gentle, soft-spoken young man who enjoys reading, thinking, and playing music. Stolte has a leaner, tougher face, but soon reveals a calm, detached, almost mystical personality and a deep commitment to nonviolence.

Amick grew up in the suburban fringes of Los Angeles. His father, a Church of Christ minister for twenty years who now sells World Book encyclopedias, passed on to him a religious approach to life, though Amick's outlook is more contemplative, of a more Oriental cast, than his father's. He was drafted in 1967.

Stolte attended Catholic schools in Maryland, then in southern California when his parents moved west. (His father, an ex-Marine, sells life insurance.) By the time he was 18, he had left home and switched to a public high school. He studied at a local college for about a year before being drafted and sent to Fort Ord for basic training. There he ran into Amick.

"I first flashed on Amick after a long day of training," Stolte recalls. "There was this dude, sitting up in his barracks meditating and burning incense." The two recruits found they had a good deal in common—a mutual interest in spiritual matters and a shared distaste for organized killing.

After basic training, Amick got a job as trumpeter in the Fort Ord band, while Stolte was given orders to report to Fort Polk, Louisiana, a jumping-off point for Vietnam-bound infantrymen. He refused, however, to board the plane. He told his commanding officer that he was prepared to serve in Vietnam as a medic, but that he would never carry a gun. For some reason the Army neither brought charges against him nor sent him to Fort Sam Houston for training as a medic. Instead, he remained at Fort Ord as a clerk in the hospital.

Amick and Stolte spent a lot of time together as the months dragged on. Stolte would go over to Amick's barracks and they would listen to music or discuss things that they had read. Occasionally they talked about the nature of the Army and Stolte's conscientious objector application, which had been denied. Most often they talked about Zen Buddhism, Gandhi, the Bible, and Kahlil Gibran's *The Prophet*.

Increasingly, too, they discussed the Vietnam War. Amick, who was more of a reader, got hold of books about Asia such as William Lederer's *The Ugly American* and *A Nation of Sheep*. He followed Vietnam developments in the San Francisco *Chronicle* and *U.S. News and World Report*. He was impressed by the antiwar statements of retired Lieutenant General James Gavin, which he read in several magazines and newspapers.

One night in February 1968, shortly after the Tet offensive, Amick and Stolte went down to the post library to visit a friend who worked there. He told them to go into a back room and wait until he got off duty. In the back room were a typewriter and a mimeograph machine. To kill time, Stolte sat down at the typewriter and began knocking out a statement of personal belief. When he was finished, he showed it to Amick and asked him what he thought of it.

Amick mentioned a few things he probably would have

phrased a little differently, but said he pretty much agreed with it.

The statement was innocuous enough by normal civilian standards. It did not encourage victory for the Vietcong or defeat for the United States. It did not urge the violation of any law or the disobeying of any order. It expressed much the same sentiments that Senator Eugene McCarthy was then voicing in his electoral challenge to President Johnson.

"We protest the war in Vietnam," the statement began. It continued:

> We know that war will never bring about peace. Peace can only be obtained through peaceful means. War cannot be rationalized, justified, or condoned . . .
>
> The greatest contribution America can make toward world peace is to become a peaceful nation. The communist paranoia that we possess does not justify what we are doing to the country of Vietnam and its people . . .
>
> Do the American people want this war? Do we, who *must* actively participate, have any desire for this war? Then why do we have it? Why do we allow it to continue day after day? . . .
>
> We are uniting and organizing to voice our opposition to this war. If you want to be constructive towards building a better world, then stop being destructive. If you really want to work for peace and freedom, then join us in our opposition. We are organizing a union in order to express our dissension and grievances. If interested and wish further information, then contact:

PVT KEN STOLTE JR.	PFC DANIEL AMICK
US 56 707 892	US 56 707 839
USAH, FT ORD, CALIF.	52ND ARMY BAND, FT ORD, CALIF.

Stolte was a little uncertain about the last paragraph—the word "union" was quite strong, and he wasn't sure if he should use it. He had heard about the American Servicemen's Union and even written once to Andy Stapp, but he realized that he was too much of a loner to be a real union organizer. Amick also had doubts about this paragraph, but finally they agreed to let it stand.

Their friend in the library was still on duty, so Stolte decided to make a stencil and run off some copies of his statement on the mimeograph machine. "The machine was right there—it was like destiny," Amick said later. "Just for the fun of it—I think he wanted to see something he'd written being published—he ran off about two hundred copies. The first fifty were pretty bad. We took the others down to my room at the band barracks and put them in my locker. They just sat there for a couple of days, and then Stolte came by one night and said, 'Why don't we pass some of them out?' "

Around eight o'clock on the evening of February 21, 1968, Amick and Stolte, in civilian clothes, walked to the enlisted men's club and left a few copies of their statement on some tables. They tacked a few more onto telephone poles and stuck one on the side of an old armored car. As they walked by the Third Brigade chapel, they handed some out to passing GI's. Soon they had gotten rid of all their copies and returned to Amick's barracks.

"Before we did any of this, I read books on the Constitution and civil liberties," Stolte remembers. "The right of the people to petition, what free speech meant, and so on. We felt pretty sure they couldn't do anything to us, even though we were saying something we knew a lot of people weren't going to like. We felt it was our right to say this. Our idea was that the Constitution is the supreme law of the land and all other laws are subservient to it."

The MP's picked up Amick that night; Stolte, the following morning. They were thrown into cells and interrogated separately by military intelligence agents: Who was behind the leaflet? The Communists? Students for a Democratic Society? Joan Baez? (Fort Ord authorities entertained a particular dread of Joan Baez, whose Institute for the Study of Non-violence was then located in nearby Carmel. Once, an Army information specialist played one of her songs on the Fort Ord morning radio show over Station KIDD in Monterey; he was roundly chewed out, and warned never to so much as mention "that draft-dodger's wife" again.)

Amick and Stolte tried to explain the spontaneous nature of their act, but the intelligence men were skeptical. In Amick's wallet they found a telegram from a friend in the form of a haiku poem. What did it mean? the agents wanted to know. What was the code?

The Army charged Amick and Stolte with two offenses under the Uniform Code of Military Justice: first, that, in violation of Article 81, they had conspired to "publicly [utter] disloyal statements"; second, that, in violation of Article 134, they had issued their statement "with design to promote disloyalty and disaffection among the troops and the civilian populace," and that the "statement was disloyal to the United States."

Their three-day court-martial was conducted with the efficiency and seclusion that the Army prefers in potentially controversial trials. The motion by the defendants' civilian attorney, Francis Heisler, to dismiss the charges, on the grounds that the accused had done nothing more than exercise their constitutionally protected right of freedom of speech, was summarily denied by the military judge. For the prosecution, it was enough to establish that the defendants had printed and distributed the leaflet, and this was hardly difficult to do: Amick and Stolte, who had signed their names and serial numbers to the statement and had never wished or tried to be stealthy, readily admitted responsibility for their act.

There was no proof offered by the prosecution that Amick and Stolte had shared a "design" to promote disloyalty and disaffection among the troops and the civilian populace, no evidence introduced that they had actually promoted any such disloyalty or disaffection, no effort to explain how the leaflet or any phrase in it was "disloyal to the United States." Indeed, during cross-examination, all of the prosecution witnesses who had read the leaflet admitted that their encounters with the defendants' mimeographed prose did not cause in them the slightest twinge of disloyal or disaffected feelings.

Amick, testifying in his own defense, said he grew up in America believing he had certain rights and was never told when he entered the Army that he had lost those rights. "In this country, the government is—well, the government is by the people, for the people, and of the people; and the people are the ruling voice through their representatives, and any individual has the right to speak out for or against government policy. And the minority is protected by the rights of the First Amendment."

He said he did not feel at all disloyal to the United States and had no desire to bring about disloyalty in others. He had read the statements of senators and retired generals against the war in Vietnam, and it never occurred to him that their statements might be disloyal. He said that he had never ceased to perform his military duties, and that neither he nor Stolte advocated that anyone else not perform assigned duties.

Stolte, in his testimony, said he had always been taught that Americans could express their opinions, and he believed that if there is anybody who should express his views on the Vietnam War, it is the soldier who has to fight it.

The court-martial found the two soldiers guilty on both charges and sentenced each of them to four years of confinement in Fort Leavenworth, forfeiture of all pay and allowances, and dishonorable discharge from the Army. The commanding general at Fort Ord, Major General Thomas A. Kenan, reduced the confinement to three years instead of four. On appeal to an Army court of review, both the verdict and the sentences were upheld.

II

THE CASE of Amick and Stolte, along with many similar cases in the last few years, raises a serious question: to what extent do citizens lose their constitutional rights when they don a military uniform? Or, putting it another way, are there any legal limits to the powers that the military acquires over citizen-soldiers?

It is important, in considering the complexities posed by this question, to recognize how recently the problem of soldiers' rights acquired urgency. Two hundred years ago, the question of whether a soldier lost his constitutional rights could not have been asked. America was ardently committed to the notion that all citizens were endowed with certain fundamental rights—

rights considered to be inalienable, not merely granted to the people by a benevolent government. Government itself was a creation of the people and possessed only those limited powers that the people deemed necessary for the performance of its functions.

This concept of limited government and inalienable rights was carefully spelled out in the original Constitution and the first ten Amendments. The only place in the Constitution where the Framers distinguished between the rights possessed by all citizens and those possessed by soldiers was in the Fifth Amendment, which guaranteed the right to indictment by grand jury, "except in cases arising in the land or naval forces, or in the militia when in actual service in time of war or public danger."

In point of fact, the distinction between citizen and soldier was, in the minds of the Founding Fathers, almost entirely an academic one. The "land and naval forces" of the federal government comprised an extremely small number of voluntary professionals—at the time of the Philadelphia convention, these forces numbered exactly 718 men *in toto*—and it was only these few full-time professionals who would not be entitled to indictment by grand jury, and would be subject to the Articles of War, a code of military justice modeled after that of the British army. Every other soldier in America was a citizen-soldier, a part-time militiaman, entitled to all the inalienable rights and privileges of other citizens except "when in actual service in time of war or public danger."

Three developments, all relatively recent, have clouded the Framers' original conception of the citizen-soldier and brought to the fore the previously meaningless question of soldiers' rights. First, the number of full-time soldiers subject to the Articles of War (now the Uniform Code of Military Justice) has risen from 718 to three million. Second, a good many of the three million are not volunteers. Third, considerable doubt has spread of late as to whether all the wars that America fights are truly necessary. If America is involved in a non-defensive war that is not essential to the survival of the nation, there is a serious question as to whether a "time of war or public danger" exists that is serious enough to justify the abridgment of inalienable rights.

Those who maintain that the American soldier today has no claim to the citizen's normal constitutional protections invariably contend that it makes no difference whether a time of legitimate war or public danger exists. It does not matter, they say, whether a war is defensive or non-defensive, declared or undeclared, right or wrong. It is enough that a man is in the army. Once he takes the oath of service, he automatically surrenders many of the rights that belong to him as a civilian.

Several arguments are commonly advanced to support this position. Army officers frequently argue, for example, that "you can't have democracy on the battlefield." Soldiers cannot debate whether to obey an order from their superior. Instant obedience is essential for an effective military force; without it, an army becomes little more than an armed rabble.

Another frequently heard assertion is that soldiers must relinquish their own rights so that the rights of others may be protected. According to this view of things, society is divided into two classes: the defenders and the defended. Soldiers are the defenders; their lot is one of sacrifice. Unless they are willing to give up their rights, the rights of everybody will be lost.

Sometimes, the "war power" of the federal government is invoked as both the reason and the legal justification for restricting soldiers' rights. A long list of historical examples is cited to buttress the argument that, when war is being waged, the right of the government to defend itself must supersede the rights of the individual. During the Civil War, President Lincoln suspended the privilege of habeas corpus; civilians who spoke against the war policies of the Republican administration were rounded up and tried by military commissions. During World War I, civilians advocating draft resistance were prosecuted by the federal government, and during World War II, thousands of Japanese-American citizens were herded into concentration camps in total disregard of the Fifth Amendment. If, in the name of waging war, the federal government can so brazenly deprive civilians of their constitutional rights, it can certainly do the same to soldiers.

Another, more sophisticated argument is that the function of the army is to respond effectively and reliably to the will of the nation's civilian leaders. To achieve this reliable response, cohesion and solidarity within the army are essential. Cohesion can only be obtained through unquestioning obedience to orders as transmitted through the chain of command. Anything less than unquestioning obedience would create the possibility that the will of the nation's political leaders might be thwarted.

Perhaps the ultimate argument against allowing free speech in the military is that to do so would open the doors to a politicized officer corps. Officers would go around the country proselytizing for military interests or for themselves. Civilian control of the military would no longer be assured. American politics might begin to resemble Argentina's.

All of these arguments have some validity as well as some flaws. But even when their valid points are taken together, they do not add up to a sufficiently compelling case to justify depriving three million citizens of what are, after all, inalienable rights.

The flaws in the arguments for restricting soldiers' rights are, moreover, quite substantial. Many of the arguments are based on oversimplifications of reality or on distortions of what those who advocate soldiers' rights are saying.

Few would contend, for example, that there should be democracy on the battlefield. It is almost universally agreed that soldiers in combat must obey lawful orders without group debate or majority rule or any of the other processes of civilian democracy. It does not necessarily follow, however, that soldiers must lose all their rights at all times, simply because they are soldiers. Workable distinctions can be made between battlefield conditions and homeside duty, between wartime and peacetime, between on-duty responsibilities and off-duty rights. The Fifth Amendment makes just such a distinction when it suspends the right of militiamen to grand jury indictment only "during time of war or public danger" and when the militiamen are "in actual service." Surely the nation's security is not endangered if an off-duty soldier in North Carolina is permitted the same rights as, say, a civilian clerk in the Pentagon or a New York City policeman.

Similarly, the assertion that soldiers must give up their rights so that the rights of others may be preserved has merit only up to a point. It is true that soldiers, by the very nature of their occupation, must give up a great deal. They have no power to choose assignments (although they could have) and lack even the right not to risk their own lives. But this does not mean that they must also lose the right to speak, to listen, to think, to complain, and to be entitled to due process of law—at least when they are not in battle.

Moreover, the notion that in order to defend freedom it is necessary to suspend it is based upon a somewhat primitive understanding of the way in which freedom is likely to die. It is certainly true that if a foreign invader were to occupy America, the rights of citizens would be obliterated; but it is also true that such foreign conquest is a very improbable eventuality. A much more ominous danger is that freedom will die of disuse—that out of fear of foreign occupation or military defeat, Americans will do away with their freedom themselves. If the Constitution is truly to be kept alive, the exercise of constitutional rights is just as essential as is the slaying of distant enemies.

As for the government's "war power," it is not unlimited even in time of war, and in time of peace or undeclared war, when civilians enjoy the full spectrum of rights guaranteed by the Constitution, it is unfair and unnecessary to penalize soldiers simply because they were either highly motivated or unlucky enough to have been accepted into the army.

The argument that unquestioning obedience is needed to ensure compliance with the will of the nation's political leadership is also open to some dispute. Few Americans would contend that soldiers have a right to disregard or, worse yet, to override, legitimate political authority. But what is wrong, when the times call for it, with *questioning* obedience? When political authority is of doubtful legitimacy—when soldiers are ordered to take part in a war that is undeclared and non-defensive—it is going too far to insist that they must not only follow orders, they must also surrender their right to criticize the policy behind those orders.

The last argument cited against soldiers' rights—the danger of politicizing the military, raising the spectre of an ultimate military take-over—has considerable merit in the abstract. The question of soldiers' rights must be viewed, however, in the context of an imperfect civilian-military relationship in which the army has already been substantially politicized.

It is certainly not unusual nowadays to find high-ranking officers speaking out on public issues—occasionally even in outright opposition to prevailing policies, as when General John P. McConnell, then Air Force Chief of Staff, criticized Vietnam bombing restrictions before the Senate Preparedness Subcommittee in 1967. But even when, as is more common, officers speak in support of official policy, the political import of their pronouncements is hardly any less. General William C. Westmoreland, for example, while on active duty as commander of American forces in Vietnam, appeared on *Meet the Press* and before a joint session of Congress to urge support for highly controversial policies. Since taking over as Army Chief of Staff, Westmoreland has averaged more than one speech a week before Rotary Clubs and other gatherings.

Lieutenant General Lewis W. Walt, assistant commandant of the Marine Corps, is another frequent public speaker. One of his favorite themes is that those who oppose the Vietnam War must bear part of the responsibility for the deaths of American soldiers.

Major James N. Rowe, a personable and articulate Green Beret officer who spent five years as a captive of the Viet Cong, appeared on at least twenty television shows in 1969 with congressional supporters of the Vietnam War. On several shows, he questioned the patriotism of Senator George McGovern and said his former captors were making political capital out of the statements of Senators J. William Fulbright, Mike Mansfield, and Wayne Morse. When a reporter asked Rowe if he was concerned about breaching the separation of the military from politics, he professed no misgivings. "We are entering an age of ideological conflict where the political and the military are married into one. If somebody says you can't speak and stay in the military, I would resign."

Perhaps most significantly, this sort of political involvement is no longer only a matter of individual military men speaking out; it is now carried on in a highly systematic and organized fashion. Throughout the country the army operates a network of speakers bureaus, using active-duty officers, usually Vietnam veterans, to boost the war effort. Thus, at Sixth Army headquarters alone there are thirty speakers on tap, ready to carry the word—in uniform—to every available rostrum in California.

None of this speechmaking can be said to create a real threat to civilian control of the military—at least not yet—but it certainly belies the notion that the military in America is divorced from politics. It also makes it difficult to muster sympathy for those who argue that enlisted men, even out of uniform, should not be allowed to speak their minds as citizens. The danger of military take-over, such as it is, lies not in any words that might be uttered by rank-and-file soldiers, but in the potential acts of high-ranking officers. An army of enlisted men unafraid to exercise their rights might well, in fact, be a bulwark against coups, rather than a contributing cause.

There are additional, positive reasons why soldiers should be entitled to constitutional rights. One is simply that soldiers *are* different from civilians, in that—unlike policemen and firemen, for example, from whom courage and obedience to civilian authority are also demanded—they can't quit their jobs. To trap them *and* to deprive them of their rights is a double injustice not inflicted on any other segment of society. Moreover, precisely because soldiers must make the greatest sacrifices in the defense of freedom, it is all the more improper and incongruous to deny them the rights once deemed inalienable by the Founding Fathers.

Another significant difference between servicemen and civilians is the isolation to which the former are, most of the time, subjected. They are stationed at out-of-the-way bases and on ships at sea, cut off by geography from the give-and-take of civilian politics and removed by law from the protection of civilian courts. With this isolation, furthermore, goes a constant exposure to the whims and preachings of the state. "By handing boys over to the arbitrary and complete domination of the government," the late Senator Robert A. Taft once observed, "we put it in the power of the government to indoctrinate them with political doctrines then popular with the government. In wartime it is bad enough; in peacetime it is intolerable."

The military, it may be argued, *should* have a chance to discipline and—to use its own term—indoctrinate its men. But in a democracy, it should not also have the power to prevent them from hearing and expressing other viewpoints. This is particularly important now that the individual soldier, as was established at Nuremberg, bears ultimate responsibility for his actions.

But perhaps the most compelling reason why soldiers' rights should be carefully safeguarded is that, of all citizens, it is soldiers who are most directly subjected to the sufferings brought about by unwarranted presidential wars. Citizens need protection against the illegitimate exercise of military power. They cannot be protected if they lack even the right to make their grievances known.

To be sure, the exercise by soldiers of constitutional rights would create certain risks. It is possible that if GI's were allowed to discuss and criticize the policies of their government without fear of punishment, a number of them might conclude that those policies were wrong or misguided, a number that would vary, in large measure, with the nature of those policies. But it is the very purpose of the Bill of Rights to create risks for the government—to ensure that its policies are always subject to scrutiny by the people, and that the people can change those policies if they see fit to do so.

Often it seems that underlying the arguments against rights for soldiers is the fear or assumption that American servicemen are either stupid, unpatriotic, or unusually susceptible to enemy propaganda. If GI's are allowed to talk, read, and question, many officers appear to believe, they will inevitably wind up acting against the best interests of their country.

This view ignores two very important realities. First is the fact that American soldiers, though they obviously vary in intelligence and gullibility, are not about to turn their country over to an enemy. If a large number of them should question the wisdom of a policy, then there is probably something wrong with the policy, not with the soldiers. The second reality is that the army always retains the power to punish illegal *acts*. If a soldier runs from the enemy or refuses a lawful order or engages in an actual mutiny, the military has full power to court-martial and convict him.

Short of a national emergency, and certainly short of a congressional declaration of war, there is neither need nor justification for denying to soldiers the freedoms over which they stand guard. As Supreme Court Justice Hugo Black wrote not long ago: "The Framers balanced the freedoms of religion, speech, press, assembly and petition against the needs of a powerful central government, and decided that in these freedoms lies this nation's only true security. They were not afraid for men to be free. We should not be."

III

IT IS over the course of the past few years, and particularly since the escalation of America's intervention in Indochina, that the battle to define the scope of soldiers' rights has raged most fiercely. The battle has involved GI's, commanders, Congress, and the courts. It is likely to go on for quite some time.

One notable issue in the conflict has been whether the federal courts have the power to interpose themselves in strictly military affairs. For nearly two centuries, a unique situation has existed within the army: military commanders have been able, in effect, to order men to cease exercising their constitutional rights and to punish them if they disobey. At the same time, the military has enjoyed an exemption from the scrutiny of federal courts.

In civilian society, by contrast, it has been since 1865 an

express federal offense for any civilian law officer to interfere
with the exercise of constitutional rights. In addition, the federal courts have long had the power to act on a citizen's claim
that his constitutional rights have been infringed.

The special immunity of the army from civilian law and
civilian courts has been up until recent times a matter of mutual
preference: commanders have always felt it necessary to exercise complete control over their troops without having to
worry about what a judge might say; the federal courts, in
turn, have not been inclined to open the Pandora's box of protecting soldiers' rights. For many decades they accepted military cases only when the question of proper military jurisdiction was raised. Their caseloads were heavy enough with
civilian disputes; it seemed more practical to let the army handle
its own problems.

Gradually and reluctantly, however, the Supreme Court came
to the conclusion that it could not take strides in protecting the
rights of civilians and at the same time ignore the millions of
citizens who happen to be soldiers. In 1953, in *Burns* v. *Wilson*,
the Supreme Court ruled for the first time that federal courts
can, on habeas corpus, consider denials of a soldier's constitutional rights during court-martial proceedings. Since then, federal courts have extended their habeas corpus powers to the
review of infringements of soldiers' rights in situations other
than military trials. In *Brown* v. *McNamara* (1967), the Third
Circuit Court of Appeals held that the federal judiciary has
the power to determine whether the military has followed
proper due process in administrative proceedings—in Brown's
case, it was an application for discharge as a conscientious objector. A South Carolina district court ruled in 1969 that the
propriety of a commander's imprisonment of soldiers prior to
trial could be examined by the federal courts. In San Francisco,
a federal district court judge issued a temporary restraining
order in 1970 forbidding guard brutality in the Treasure Island
brig. Similar rulings have emanated from other benches, and it
is now accepted doctrine that, just as the federal courts have
found it proper to protect the civil rights of blacks against
infringement by state and local authorities in the South, it is also

within the scope of the courts' powers to protect soldiers against denial of their rights by military authorities.

One of the greatest difficulties in protecting the rights of soldiers, however, is the often-enormous gap that persists—no matter what the courts may say, no matter what even the military's own regulations may say—between pronouncement and reality.

The right to communicate with members of Congress, for example, is one of the few soldiers' rights that is specifically guaranteed by statute. The law says:

> No person may restrict any member of an armed force from communication with a Member of Congress, unless the communication is unlawful or violates a regulation necessary to the security of the United States.

The practicalities of writing to a Congressman are something else again. Soldiers are warned against going outside the chain of command and taking their gripes to a civilian legislator. GI's who insist on exercising this right do so at their own risk. The chances are great that a soldier who "breaks faith" with the army in this fashion will be suitably remembered—and the army has many ways of remembering.

In early 1970, Captain Charles J. Sanner, an Army doctor who had served twelve months in Vietnam, wrote to then-Senator Charles Goodell about a problem that concerned him greatly. Captain Sanner was spending the remainder of his two-year military commitment as chief medical officer of the Armed Forces Examining and Entrance Station in Albany, New York, and every day he talked to dozens of men who were being drafted into the Army in ignorance of their right to hardship and other types of deferments. Why not introduce a bill, he suggested to Senator Goodell, requiring local draft boards to inform young men of the various categories of deferment and the methods of appeal? Sanner also noted that many youths were being high-pressured into enlisting by false or misleading inducements. He thought an investigation of unethical practices by military recruiters might be in order.

An aide to Goodell forwarded Sanner's suggestions to the

Selective Service System for its comments. She received no direct response from the Selective Service System, but got an immediate reaction from Captain Sanner. Selective Service, it seems, had passed on Sanner's name to the First Army District Recruiting Command, which oversees the Albany induction center. A few days later, Sanner was called by the personnel section of the First Recruiting District and ordered, over the telephone, to report to a new permanent duty station in Maryland within seventy-two hours.

Sanner inquired into the reasons for his transfer orders and was told that they came about because he had "caused trouble." He appealed the order to First District headquarters, pointing out that if he were removed from the Albany induction center, a civilian doctor would have to be retained on a fee basis to replace him, resulting in considerable expense to the Army. He also observed that transferring officers to two permanent duty stations within five months is contrary to long-standing Army policy. In his case, it would necessitate breaking the lease on a home and losing several months' rent as a result. And it would mean that his wife, who had completed half of a post-graduate term at the state university, would be unable to finish her studies and would forfeit her tuition.

The First Army District turned down Sanner's appeal. Senator Goodell asked Secretary of the Army Stanley Resor to cancel the transfer as an illegal infringement of a constituent's statutory right to communicate with him. Resor refused.

A right similarly "guaranteed" by Army regulations is the right to complain to the "IG"—the Inspector General of a post or unit. The IG is a kind of military Mr. Fix-it who is empowered to investigate allegations of injustice and to straighten out snarled red tape. If a soldier gets past the sergeant at the door, the IG can in fact be effective on certain types of problems. He is good at uncorking stalled paychecks, for example, or arranging for overdue leave. His zeal and effectiveness are limited, however, by his position as a staff officer of the commanding general—he is not about to tackle a complaint that requires changes in the system or creates discomfort at the officers club.

The chief problem with seeing the IG, however, is not that he won't be inclined to help, but that repercussions at the company level are likely to follow. "Once you go to the IG, you've had it," says a GI at Fort Hood who went. "They start giving you extra details, working you harder, making life a little more unbearable."

Another right that exists more pristinely on paper than in reality is one guaranteed by the Fourth Amendment: to be secure from illegal searches and seizures. In theory, the military recognizes the Fourth Amendment, and the *Manual for Courts-Martial* explicitly states that evidence obtained as a result of an unlawful search is inadmissible at a trial. The reality, however, is that a GI's possessions are constantly and routinely subject to inspection. MP's may stop and search automobiles at any time. In addition to regular barracks inspections, there are the unannounced "shakedowns" that usually take place at least once a month—typically, in the dark of night.

The surprised soldiers are awakened and ordered to stand on their footlockers so that nothing can be rearranged. While MP's guard the doors, an officer comes by and searches each wall locker and footlocker. If he desires, he can strip-search soldiers as well. The object of the shakedown is to uncover "contraband": liquor, dope, stolen property, unauthorized literature. Although material obtained in a shakedown would probably be excluded by a fair-minded court-martial, thousands of GI's have been fined, demoted, imprisoned, or otherwise punished—usually nonjudicially—as a result of these pre-dawn raids.

Of all the rights set forth in the Constitution, the most precious are those guaranteed by the First Amendment: freedom of speech, of the press, of peaceful assembly, and of petition for redress of grievances. But it is precisely these rights, held so dear by the Founding Fathers, that the military is most determined to restrain.

On the surface, military regulations appear to authorize a wide range of political and communicational activities. Under Army Regulation 381-135, GI's have the right to receive written matter through the mails and to keep one copy of any book, newspaper, or pamphlet. (Possession of more than one copy implies intent to distribute, which, depending on the material involved, can be illegal.) Army Regulation 600–20 allows soldiers stationed in the United States to participate in public demonstrations when they are off duty and out of uniform, although not when "violence is reasonably likely to result." Defense Department Directive 1344.10, applicable to all four services, permits soldiers to vote, express personal opinions on political candidates and issues, join a political club and attend its meetings when not in uniform, sign a petition for specific legislative action or to place a candidate's name on the ballot, and write letters to newspaper editors expressing nonpartisan personal views.

In like manner, a 1969 Army memorandum to commanders, entitled "Guidance on Dissent," sounds like a Jeffersonian paean to First Amendment freedoms:

In our system of Government, we do not ask that every citizen or every soldier agree with every policy of the Government. . . . The right to express opinions on matters of public and personal concern is secured to the soldier and civilian alike by the Constitution and laws of the United States. . . . It is the policy of the Department of the Army to safeguard the service member's right of expression to the maximum extent possible, and to impose only such minimum restraints as are necessary to enable the Army to perform its mission.

On the subject of freedom of the press, "Guidance on Dissent" is quite specific:

The publication of "underground newspapers" by soldiers off-post, on their own time, and with their own money and equipment is generally protected under the First Amendment. . . . A commander may not prevent distribution of a publication simply because he does not like its contents. . . . A commander must have cogent reasons, with supporting evidence, for any denial of distribution privileges. The fact that a publication is critical—even unfairly critical—of government policies or officials is not in itself a grounds for denial.

On top of this, military spokesmen frequently point out that soldiers always have the right to say what they want in private. Such assertions are supported by the *Manual for Courts-Martial*, which states that "expressions of opinion made in a purely private conversation should not ordinarily be made the basis for a court-martial charge."

It looks good, it sounds good, and to a certain extent it is good. Soldiers do vote, do receive literature of all kinds through the mail, do take part in peaceful demonstrations. But what the regulations and memoranda do not convey is the virtually unlimited power the military still retains to obstruct the free exercise of First Amendment rights whenever it chooses to do so. Nor do they convey the alacrity with which soldiers who persist in exercising their rights are punished—not necessarily for the specific act of expressing themselves, but punished nonetheless. It takes great courage to exercise one's rights as a citizen-soldier in the American army, and such courage should not be necessary in a democracy.

The means of obstruction are plentiful enough. Is there an antiwar demonstration scheduled near the base? Then simply cook up a reason to keep soldiers on duty. GI's at the Presidio had their leaves canceled on Easter Sunday 1969 because of a peace march in downtown San Francisco. They were confined to the post and, in memory of Christ's resurrection, given civil disturbance training. At Fort Lewis, Washington, on the occasion of a Saturday peace march in Seattle, the commanding general suddenly assigned all base personnel to "post beautification" chores.

Are GI's meeting to discuss political issues? Then simply arrest them and release them later. This happened in 1969 to thirty-five members of the American Servicemen's Union who held a meeting during off-duty hours at Fort Lewis.

Is a soldier expressing, in speech or writing, views of which the commanding general disapproves? Then assign him to guard the latrine—or, better yet, banish him to Vietnam.

So absolute is commanders' power within the army structure that they don't even have to obey the army's own regulations.

This was the discovery of soldiers on several bases who had taken the "Guidance on Dissent" memorandum at face value.

The GI's at Fort Bliss who publish *Gigline*, for example, sought official permission to distribute their newspaper in accordance with memorandum guidelines. They submitted a formal request for distribution rights, along with two sample copies of their publication. Three weeks later came the terse reply: "Attached request for permission to distribute Volume I, Number 5 of the *Gigline* on Fort Bliss is disapproved." No explanation, no "cogent reasons"—just "disapproved." Similar applications for distribution rights have been turned down at Fort Bragg, Fort Ord, and North Island Naval Station (San Diego), among other places.

At Fort Bragg, soldiers who had been denied permission to distribute their paper *Bragg Briefs* took their case to a federal district court. The government lawyer, in arguing against the soldiers' claim that the prior restraint imposed on distribution of their newspaper amounted to unconstitutional censorship, did not beat around the bush. "The First Amendment," he contended, "is not applicable to servicemen. The only question is whether the choice here, prior restraint as opposed to subsequent action, is reasonable and necessary to the protection of good order and discipline within the command. Under the circumstances, we believe that it is." The federal judge agreed.

In 1969, a civilian requested permission to hand out at Fort Bragg flyers containing the remarks of three U.S. Senators about Vietnam, excerpted from the *Congressional Record*. Three months after submitting his request, the civilian finally received a letter from the Fort Bragg provost marshal, disapproving it without explanation. Even Senator Sam Ervin of North Carolina—a high-ranking member of the Senate Armed Services Committee and a steadfast supporter of American policy in Vietnam—was incensed when he heard about this incident. Three things angered Ervin, a stern defender of the Constitution: the disapproval itself, the absence of explanation as called for by Army guidelines, and the three-month delay in acting. "The refusal appears to be not only an unconstitutional interference with the right of free expression, but also a dangerous infringement upon the role of a Senator as a representative of the people," Ervin complained to Army Secretary Stanley Resor. "While I find myself in substantial disagreement with the views quoted in the flyer, still I strongly contend every person has the right to bring his opinions to the attention of his fellow citizens. The right to free expression is . . . one of the most fundamental rights of all."

Freedom of expression is discouraged in other ways. Soldiers who attend demonstrations during off-duty hours and in civilian attire, as permitted by army regulations, are followed, photographed, interrogated. So are soldiers who display peace symbols or put antiwar bumper stickers on their cars or are seen with "too much" unapproved literature.

When all else fails, there is punishment. Private Wade Carson was sentenced to five months in the Fort Lewis stockade for distributing an underground newspaper; the charge was brought under UCMJ Article 134, a catch-all provision prohibiting "all conduct of a nature to bring discredit upon the armed forces." Private Richard Gentile, one of the Presidio 27, attended a peace march on Saturday, October 12, two days before the "mutiny," in civilian clothes and on what is normally an off-duty day; he returned to base after the march and was thrown in the stockade for having been eight hours AWOL.

Sergeant Don Sherman left Fort Lewis one evening to participate in a Moratorium discussion with students at Tacoma Community College. He returned twenty minutes late, was charged with being AWOL, given sixty days restriction to base, and demoted to Private First Class. Private Francis Lenski, an active member of GIs for Peace at Fort Bliss, was returning to his barracks from an afternoon at the firing range when a sergeant picked him up for the court-martial offense of "failing to render the proper courtesies during retreat ceremonies" —he had neglected to stand at attention during the sounding of retreat.

The multifarious forms of intimidation, obstruction, and punishment employed by the army to deter soldiers from exercising First Amendment rights guaranteed in many cases by its own regulations indisputably create what the Supreme Court has called a "chilling effect" on such exercises. Yet the Supreme Court has never condemned the army for infringing upon the First Amendment. In fact, the Court has never said *anything* about the applicability of First Amendment rights within the military, leaving the law in this area about as murky as the law can get. And the longer the law remains murky, the longer the army can do as it pleases.

The history of First Amendment cases, both civilian and military, casts at least some light upon the state of the law, but not much. During World War I, the Supreme Court upheld the conviction of a civilian named Schenck under the 1917 Espionage Act. Schenck's crime had been to distribute leaflets condemning conscription. The Court's decision, written by Justice Holmes, set forth for the first time a judicial reading of the First Amendment's application in wartime:

When a nation is at war many things that might be said in time of peace are such a hindrance to its effort that their utterance will not be endured so long as men fight, and that no court could regard them as protected by any constitutional right. . . . The question in every case is whether the words used are used in such circumstances and are of such a nature as to create a clear and present danger that they will bring about the substantive evils that Congress has the right to prevent.

In Schenck's case the "substantive evil" was interference with recruitment. The Court concluded that his leaflet created a clear and present danger that the evil would be brought about.

The army at the time did not worry much about "clear and present dangers." It sentenced one private to three years confinement (subsequently reduced to three months) for saying that the United States and Germany were both wrong in going to war and that "Woodrow Wilson is no more a Christian than you fellows, as no Christian would go to war." Another soldier was sentenced to two years for declaring that really everyone, including the President, was either an anarchist or a socialist, though they were afraid to admit it. One GI who criticized the war in a letter to his mother was imprisoned for six months.[1]

By the 1940's, the Supreme Court had become more forbearing toward wartime dissent, but the army decidedly had not. A private who called President Roosevelt "the biggest gangster in the world, next to Stalin," received a year in the stockade. A lieutenant was court-martialed for offhandedly remarking, when someone mentioned Roosevelt, "What has that sonofabitch done now?"

In recent years the Supreme Court has substantially liberalized its interpretation of the First Amendment, going so far as to declare, in *New York Times* v. *Sullivan* (1964), that verbal or printed attacks upon public figures must be made with actual malice or reckless disregard for the truth in order for the speaker or writer to be subject to civil or criminal penalties. The highest military court, the Court of Military Appeals (COMA), has advanced a bit too, picking up the language of the "clear and present danger" test and even asserting, in 1960, that "the protections in the Bill of Rights, except those which are expressly or by necessary implication inapplicable, are available to members of the armed forces" (*U.S.* v. *Jacoby*).

The trouble with these recent pronouncements, however, is that what the Supreme Court says in civilian First Amendment cases has no immediate effect upon the army, and what the Court of Military Appeals lends rhetorical sanction to bears almost no relation to what courts-martial hand out in the way of sentences. COMA's proclamation that constitutional rights are available *except* . . . , etc., is in fact something like the Red Queen announcing that there will be "jam every other day"; as the Queen explains to Alice, it is always jam tomorrow or jam yesterday, but never jam today.

The non-applicability of High Court dicta can be seen in a number of First Amendment cases of recent years. Lieutenant Henry H. Howe Jr., a young Army officer stationed at Fort Bliss, took part in a small and peaceful demonstration in down-

1. These and other cases, as well as the World War II cases mentioned below, are cited and discussed in an article by John G. Kester: "Soldiers Who Insult the President," *Harvard Law Review*, June 1968.

town El Paso in 1965. His participation in the half-hour protest march was in accordance with regulations; he was off duty and in civilian clothes, and there was little likelihood of violence.

At the demonstration Howe carried a handmade picket sign which read on one side, END JOHNSON'S FASCIST AGGRESSION IN VIETNAM and on the other side, LET'S HAVE MORE THAN A CHOICE BETWEEN PETTY IGNORANT FASCISTS IN 1968. Strong language, to be sure, but criminal language? The military professes to allow its members to discuss political issues and candidates, and though 1968 was then a long way off, it was fair to assume that President Johnson would be a candidate for re-election. More important, the Supreme Court had just pointed out, in its *New York Times* v. *Sullivan* decision, that protected speech under the First Amendment "may well include vehement, caustic and sometimes unpleasantly sharp attacks on government officials."

If Howe had been a civilian, he could never have been prosecuted. But Howe merely *looked* like a civilian; underneath his mufti, the Army maintained a twenty-four-hour-a-day lien on him. It was, in fact, an undercover military policeman observing the demonstration who suggested to El Paso police that Howe be arrested. The El Paso police obligingly trumped up a charge of suspected vagrancy, took Howe down to the police station, and then turned him over to military authorities. The Army promptly accused him of two offenses under the UCMJ: using contemptuous words against the President (Article 88), and conduct unbecoming an officer (Article 133).[2]

2. Article 88 makes it a crime for officers to use contemptuous words against governors, members of Congress, various Cabinet secretaries, as well as the President and Vice-President. Officers who pick the right public officials, however, need not fear punishment. Navy Captain Robert J. Hanks published an essay in 1970 in which he singled out for severe criticism Senator J. William Fulbright of Arkansas, and was almost as contemptuous towards him as Lieutenant Howe had been towards Lyndon Johnson. Hanks wrote that Fulbright's speeches "could prove as dangerous as the fulminations of those who advocate immediate and complete unilateral disarmament of the United States." He was not even reprimanded for his outspokenness. In fact, his essay, entitled

A Fort Bliss court-martial convicted Howe on both counts and sentenced him to two years in Leavenworth. His commanding general reduced the confinement to one year. On appeal, the Court of Military Appeals upheld his conviction by employing Holmes's "clear and present danger" test in a most remarkable fashion:

> The evil which Article 88 of the Uniform Code . . . seeks to avoid is the impairment of discipline and the promotion of insubordination by an officer of the military service. . . . That in the present times and circumstances such conduct by an officer constitutes a clear and present danger to discipline within our armed services, under the precedents established by the Supreme Court, seems to require no argument.

Why "no argument"? Very likely because if the Court of Military Appeals *had* entertained an argument, the Army would most assuredly have lost it. At no time was it ever asserted, much less proved, that Howe had sought to impair military discipline or promote insubordination among the troops. He had urged no disobedience of orders, incited no one to illegal acts; he had not, for that matter, even addressed himself to soldiers. His expression of political views was conducted miles away from the nearest Army base and without the slightest outward sign that he was associated with or concerned about the military. There was, in short, no clear and present danger to anything or anyone—except, in the event, to Howe himself.

Much of the same may be said of the case of Captain Howard Levy, the Army doctor sentenced to three years in prison for, among other things, promoting "disaffection and disloyalty" among the troops in violation of Article 134. Levy had not picketed or distributed leaflets; the evidence brought forward against him on this charge consisted of a letter Levy had written to a career sergeant who was a friend of his, and testimony concerning some of his private remarks to fellow soldiers at Fort Jackson—precisely the kind of personal, non-public communication that the Army insists is permissible.

"Against All Enemies," was published in the *U.S. Naval Institute Proceedings;* it won him a gold medal and $1,500 cash.

The letter and many of Levy's remarks were critical of American policy in Vietnam. At the court-martial, Levy's civilian defense attorney, Charles Morgan Jr., asked the military judge to clarify whether the Army had to prove Levy's words actually created some danger, or whether the words themselves constituted the crime:

JUDGE: It's not the words, it's the consequence of the words, the creation of disloyalty and disaffection.

MORGAN: Does he have to prove then—does the prosecution have to prove that somebody was actually disloyal or disaffected?

JUDGE: No, no. No, no. He must prove that—the prosecution has the burden of showing that the natural and reasonable tendency of these words is to create disloyalty or disaffection.

That is to say, it *was* Levy's words, and not the danger they may or may not have created, that constituted the offense.

Words also caused the conviction of Privates George W. Daniels and William L. Harvey Jr., black Marines stationed at Camp Pendleton in 1967. Daniels and Harvey, both from New York City, had been promised assignments in aviation; instead, they were placed in the infantry. Over a period of time they came to share the increasingly widespread belief that the war in Vietnam was a "white man's war" and that black men didn't belong there.

Daniels and Harvey expressed their views frequently in private discussions. What they advocated was the *idea* that black men don't belong in Vietnam. Sometimes they suggested that black Marines should *ask* not to be sent there. In fact, Daniels himself had gone to his captain to request just that, and his captain had told him he'd see what he could do.

One hot summer afternoon in July 1967, Daniels, Harvey, and about a dozen other Marines, mostly black, were sitting under a tree, eating, talking, and listening to a record player. It was a friendly bull session, wide-ranging and open. Many opposing points of view were heard. Participants drifted away; new ones ambled by.

Daniels and Harvey expressed their usual position that black men shouldn't fight in Vietnam. They also urged black Marines who felt this way to make their views known to their commander.

The next morning, some eighteen black Marines, including Daniels and Harvey, reported to company headquarters to request "mast," as was their right under Marine and Navy regulations.[3] The men were orderly and respectful. The company commander met with a few of them individually, although he did not hold a formal mast. Some of those he spoke with asked not to be sent to Vietnam; others asked for changes of assignment; two asked for hardship discharges. No "nonnegotiable demands" had been presented; no demands, in fact, of any type. When the talking was over, the Marines left quietly. None of them—either then or subsequently—committed illegal acts. Several of them later served in Vietnam.

A few weeks later, however, Harvey and Daniels were charged under Article 134 with causing and attempting to cause insubordination, disloyalty, and refusal of duty. Daniels was convicted and sentenced to ten years in prison. Harvey was convicted of a lesser offense—making disloyal statements with design to promote disloyalty—and given a six-year sentence.

On appeal, Daniels and Harvey contended that they were guilty of no crime. They had committed no illegal acts, urged no one else to commit illegal acts, and no illegal acts were known to have been committed as a result of anything they'd said. They had expressed a view, shared and also expressed by many other GI's, that the war in Vietnam was wrong. They had also expressed the desire, as had many other soldiers, not to fight there. But the only "clear and present danger" created

3. "Mast" is a meeting with one's commander to express grievances or complaints; perhaps in the old days it used to be held under a ship's mast. The *Marine Corps Manual* explicitly states that "personnel availing themselves of the right to request mast in good faith may do so without fear of prejudice to their interests."

by their words was the danger that a handful of Marines would lawfully request mast.

Nearly three years after their court-martial, the Court of Military Appeals ruled on their case. It reversed their convictions on a technical ground—the military judge had given deficient instructions to the jury—but rejected their free speech arguments. "The aggregate of the accused's activity was not a trivial hazard but a clear and present danger to impairment of the loyalty and obedience of . . . blacks in the company," the Court concluded.

What, then, *is* the law on free speech in the military? The law is ultimately uncertain because the Supreme Court has yet to speak. But the combined impact of recent military court decisions leads to at least one clear conclusion: if a soldier does not like a particular war, there's virtually no lawful channel through which he can safely express himself. Letters and private conversations are out (Levy). Leaflets are out (Amick and Stolte). Off-base demonstrations are out (Howe). And bull sessions and collective masts are out (Daniels and Harvey).

In order to convict a soldier using any of these forms of expression, all that a court-martial need determine is that the soldier's words are disloyal in and of themselves (Amick and Stolte), have a "tendency" to create disloyalty without necessarily having created it (Levy), or have created more than a "trivial hazard" of disloyalty (Daniels and Harvey). Since it is not really clear what disloyalty is (the military judge in the Levy case defined it as "import[ing] not being true to or being unfaithful to an authority to whom respect, obedience or allegiance is due and tending toward insubordination, refusal of orders or mutiny"), a court-martial need not be very rigorous in reaching a determination. Almost anything it deems disloyal or dangerous is, *ipso facto*, disloyal or dangerous.

The law as it stands now, in short, does not guarantee free speech. Quite to the contrary, it guarantees to the army almost unlimited power to repress free speech.

Of course, the army does not suppress all critical expression. To do so would not only be impossible, but would destroy morale more effectively than could the words of any dissident GI. The military is also constrained by another factor: public relations. Having the law on one's side is not everything; one must be able to *use* the law. And the army has been reluctant to prosecute free speech because courts-martial create bad publicity. Consequently, in the last year or so, there has been a noticeable trend away from prosecutions in First Amendment cases and a growing preference for quieter forms of punishment, such as reassignments and undesirable discharges.

Exactly how publicity-conscious the Army has become was revealed by its "Guidance on Dissent." The chief purpose of this 1969 memorandum was not to promote the cause of civil liberties but to warn commanders in the field against overreacting and thereby damaging the Army's image. "In the past few weeks there have been press reports suggesting a growth in dissent among military personnel," it began. "It is important to recognize that the question of 'soldier dissent' is linked with the Constitutional right of free speech and that the Army's reaction to such action will—quite properly—continue to receive much attention in the news media. Any action at any level may therefore reflect—either favorably or adversely—on the image and standing of the Army with the American public."

Specifically, the memorandum urged commanders to do two things before quashing an outburst of free speech: consult with their Staff Judge Advocate, and more important, get in touch with Army headquarters in Washington, where cooler heads would presumably discourage them from flying off with a half-cocked mutiny charge. The message apparently got through.

The message also got through, however, to the House Armed Services Committee, where it was, to say the least, frigidly received. When Secretary Resor came before the committee to present the Army's 1970 posture statement, he was greeted by a chorus of gnashing teeth.

Congressman Charles E. Bennett of Florida told Resor that "the dissent paper concerns me more than anything I have ever read from the Army. . . . It is just nauseating to me to think that such a publication would be possible from the

Army." Congressman John E. Hunt of New Jersey proclaimed: "I have never read anything which to me was more repugnant than this particular documentation." Committee Counsel John R. Blandford chimed in: "I think it is one of the most damaging documents ever put out by the Army." The late L. Mendel Rivers of South Carolina, then committee chairman, heartily agreed.

Resor tried to explain the intent of the memorandum: "I think it is very important to the Army that we adopt a position that appears to the public as a wholly reasonable position and not an arbitrary one, and that is all we are trying to do. The military is under attack from many elements, and if we are going to survive, we must show that we are acting in a reasonable way and show that we are standing up for the Constitution. That is all we are doing."

Talk of "reasonableness," however, could not placate Chairman Rivers. Turning to Chief of Staff General William C. Westmoreland, who was also in the hearing room, he fumed: "General Westmoreland, I will bet my hat that you don't agree with it. Now, if you have got one drop of South Carolina blood left in your veins, you don't agree with it. . . . It is very difficult for me to compose myself, and I am stopping myself right now."

Under pressure from Rivers and his cohorts, the Defense Department backtracked. In September 1969, it issued a new set of directives, applicable to all four services. Although the Army's "Guidance on Dissent" was not officially superseded, the new guidelines manifested a very different spirit. Gone was the original memorandum's assertion that "disagreement with policies of the government is the right of every citizen." Gone was the requirement that commanders must "have cogent reasons, with supporting evidence, for any denial of distribution privileges." Absent, too, was the policy commitment "to impose only such minimum restraints [on free expression] as are necessary to enable the Army to perform its mission."

The flap over the relatively restrained language of "Guidance on Dissent" is indicative of the obstacles in Congress to reform of the military. But there are no Mendel Riverses on the Supreme Court (at least not yet), and a number of First Amendment cases are currently winding their way up the federal court ladder. It may be that the Supreme Court, which has not entirely broken away from its old "hands-off-the-military" tradition, will refuse to hear these cases. But with a large standing army now seemingly a permanent part of the American landscape, it seems unlikely that the Court will abandon millions of present and future citizens to the unchecked whims of their commanders. Clear-cut judicial guidelines are necessary, and the Court cannot shirk its responsibilities much longer.

In the meantime, the struggle goes on between citizen-soldiers, their lawyers, and the army. It would not be wrong to say that some progress has been made. In 1969, at a House Appropriations Subcommittee hearing, Lieutenant General Albert O. Connor was asked why the Army was not more forcefully clamping down on dissident soldiers. Connor replied that "we don't have the same freedom we used to exercise in this area." The "freedom" Connor so nostalgically referred to is the "freedom" to suppress free expression.

8. THE COURT-MARTIAL SYSTEM

CIVILIAN LAW in America is designed to do two things: to punish wrongdoers and to protect citizens against state power. Law in the military, on the other hand, has only one primary function: to subjugate the individual to the will of the state.

Courts-martial are the ultimate capstone of the military system, the guardian of the commander's power and the final enforcer of discipline. The system is simple. The commander accuses and a court-martial punishes. There were 109,000 courts-martial in the armed forces in 1969; convictions were obtained in ninety four percent of them.

Courts-martial do not have the protective powers that civilian courts possess. They can only punish or acquit, they cannot grant other forms of relief. A soldier cannot appeal to a military judge for a writ of habeas corpus; he cannot obtain from a court-martial an order restraining illegal action by his superiors. He can never come out of a court-martial with a net gain; at best he can escape serious loss, and even that does not happen very often.

That military law should be a weapon of the commander is not surprising, considering its origin and the purpose for which it was designed. American military law derives from the British Articles of War, which in turn hark back to the Roman Articles of War. These were harsh, autocratic codes of discipline intended to keep in line mercenaries of the king or emperor, not to assure justice to citizen-soldiers of a democracy.

When the Continental Congress needed a military code in 1775, it hastily adopted the British Articles of War, including its provisions for branding, flogging, and other bizarre punishments. After the Revolution, the Articles were retained for the regular army, and for the militia when in actual service. Henry Knox, the first Secretary of War, thought some of its provisions to be grossly out of line with the Bill of Rights, and advised Washington that they should be "revised and adapted to the Constitution."

They never were. Minor changes were made during the nineteenth and early twentieth centuries; medieval punishments were abolished. But when the present Uniform Code of Military Justice was enacted by Congress in 1950, it retained, with only small modifications, the essential structure of courts-martial as established by the ancient Articles of War.

The fundamental principle of those Articles was that all punitive authority must rest with the commander—the power to accuse, the power to judge, and the power to sentence, powers that in civilian law are almost always divided. The same principle, though in less blatant form, underlies the UCMJ today.

The Uniform Code offers commanders four ways of punishing a soldier, depending on the gravity of the alleged offense (not counting, of course, the numerous informal ways a GI can be punished).

At the lowest level is what is called company punishment, generally known as an "Article 15," after the governing provision of the UCMJ. This is the most common form of military chastisement, accounting for four-fifths of all cases. There is nothing judicial about the procedure: the soldier's commanding officer accuses him of an offense, finds him guilty, and sentences him, all in the space of minutes. Sentences are, to be sure, of limited severity—for enlisted men, they may not exceed fourteen days restriction, seven days loss of pay, and reduction to the next inferior rank. Moreover, a soldier may refuse company punishment and demand a court-martial instead. In this case, however, he runs the risk of receiving a considerably stiffer sentence.

The second level of military punishment is the summary court-martial. This has been likened to a civilian magistrate's court, but that is an unduly flattering comparison. A more accurate one would be to a high school play in which everyone reads his lines badly and in which the outcome is known by all ahead of time. Trial is held before a single officer who need not be, and usually is not, a lawyer. The same officer also acts as prosecutor and then shifts hats again to play defense counsel. Returning to the role of judge, he can sentence the soldier to up to thirty days confinement and forfeiture of up to two-thirds of a month's salary.

The third type of punitive proceeding is called a special court-martial and is considerably more serious. There is a jury consisting of three or more members; the accused is entitled to defense counsel, and notes are kept by a clerk in case an appeal is made. Special courts-martial may impose sentences of up to six months confinement and a bad conduct discharge.

The highest form of criminal tribunal is the general court-martial. These panels contain five or more members; they may sentence to death, life imprisonment, or any lesser punishment. Because the possible penalties are so severe, one would expect the highest standards of justice to apply. Yet the command structure possesses almost the same undivided punitive power in general courts-martial as it does in the lower forms of trial and punishment.

Accusation initiates the proceedings in general courts-martial. Whereas in civilian courts indictment is presented by a grand jury, in the military, it is a high-ranking commanding officer— usually a general—who brings the charges and then convenes a court-martial to weigh them.

Article 32 of the UCMJ provides that, before charges are

formally filed against a soldier, there must be "a thorough and impartial investigation." This investigation is often described as the military equivalent of grand jury proceedings, and there are, it is true, certain similarities—the investigating officer holds a hearing at which the suspect may be represented by counsel, may cross-examine witnesses against him, and may present evidence in his own behalf. But there is a fundamental difference between this proceeding and that of a civilian grand jury: the investigator has no power either to indict or to throw a case out; his sole function is to report back to the commander. It is the latter who then decides, on the basis of the investigative report, the advice of his Staff Judge Advocate, and his own predilections and prejudices, whether to bring charges.

This system is biased against the prospective defendant in several ways. In the first place, there is built-in pressure upon the investigating officer to recommend prosecution under the heaviest possible charge, if that is what the general and his Staff Judge Advocate want (and it usually is). More important, the commanding general has the power to ignore the investigator's recommendation and to press ahead with charges purely upon his personal whim. This does not happen often (usually because the investigator recommends prosecution), but it happens frequently enough to cast doubt upon the system.

In the Presidio mutiny case, it was well known that Lieutenant General Stanley R. Larsen and his Staff Judge Advocate, Colonel James Garnett, strongly desired to bring mutiny charges against the prisoners who had sat down in the stockade. Two successive investigating officers, Captains Richard M. Millard and James Bradner Jr., could find no basis for such a charge and, at considerable risk to their own careers, said as much in their reports to General Larsen. But Larsen, not being bound to accept their findings, insisted on the mutiny trials anyway. Nearly two years later, a military appeals court ruled that the general had been wrong and the investigators had been right: the element of willful intent to override lawful authority was completely absent in the Presidio sitdown. But the "mutineers" had to wait for this verdict in prison.

The same thing happens in less publicized cases. Jim Allgood, the fear-struck private who kept running away from Fort Ord (see Chapter 5), was recommended for discharge by two military psychiatrists as well as by the Article 32 investigator in his case. The commanding general still insisted on pressing ahead with desertion charges.

After the power to accuse comes the power to judge and the power to sentence. These powers the commanding general does not exercise directly; rather, he does so through subordinates who are scattered throughout the courtroom.

Foremost among the general's proxies are the members of the court-martial itself. These men not only have the power to determine innocence or guilt, but also the responsibility of sentencing those whom they convict, a responsibility that in civilian courts is almost always assigned to the judge.[1] While nothing is more crucial to the quality of justice in any courtroom than the impartiality of the jury, this is especially so— given this added power—in military courts.

In civilian courts, care is taken to insure that juries are not obviously partial to either side; counsel for both defense and prosecution may challenge prospective jurors for cause, or may peremptorily challenge a substantial number of them, the exact number depending on the court. The goal of an unbiased jury is further promoted by the random selection of jurors from the entire community.

In the military, by contrast, court-martial members are handpicked by the commanding general. Typically, when a general court-martial is due to be convened, the Staff Judge Advocate asks the post's personnel section for the names of approximately twenty officers of varying rank who are available for courtroom duty—the names usually being selected from a roster maintained for such purposes. The Judge Advocate takes this list to the commanding general, who reads it over carefully. He knows many of the officers personally from either social or official functions at the base; the Judge Advocate may know some of the others. Article 25 of the UCMJ empowers the convening

1. The exception is when military defendants waive a jury trial, which they have been allowed to do since 1969. In such cases, the defendants are judged and sentenced by a single military judge.

authority to select for courts-martial "such members of the
armed forces as, in his opinion, are best qualified for the duty
by reason of age, education, training, experience, length of
service, and judicial temperament"—in other words, gung-ho,
career-minded officers. The general indicates his selection by
crossing off the names of those he doesn't want and putting his
initials next to each cross-off. The officers remaining on the list
are the court-martial members. Defense attorneys may challenge jurors for cause, but they can peremptorily challenge
only one of them.

When the defendant is an enlisted man, the defense has the
option of demanding that one-third of the jurors be enlisted
men. In practice, however, defense attorneys almost never make
such a request, since enlisted jurors are selected in much the
same manner as the officers—hand-picked by the commander
from among his tough-minded senior NCO's—and such men
tend to be even more unsympathetic toward fractious young
GI's than do commissioned officers.

Inevitably, the manner of selecting the jury taints the trial.
In the first place, jury members are not usually peers of the
defendant, who is most often a low-ranking enlisted man. In
the second place, as professionals, they are prone to a strong institutional bias against citizen-soldiers accused of a military offense. Toward those accused of general criminal offenses such
as robbery, rape, and murder, they may in fact be quite open-
minded; but they almost automatically take a dim view of anyone accused of bucking the system which they dutifully serve.

Beyond this, they cannot help but have in the back of their
minds the thought that "the old man" put them on the court-
martial personally. They are well aware that the general convened the court-martial after considering the Article 32 report;
evidently, he must think the defendant is guilty. And they also
realize that the general will personally be reviewing the judgment of the court. A finding of guilty, they know, cannot hurt
their careers; an acquittal just might. "If the case is a heavy
one," says defense attorney F. Lee Bailey, a former Marine
Corps jet pilot, "the officer in the jury sits there and reflects on

his career in the military. He says, 'If I do justice, my conscience will feel better for a couple of days, but that son-of-a-gun, the commanding officer, is going to remember me for years.' "

The Court of Military Appeals has made much the same observation, though a bit more tactfully: "Courts-martial are manned by officers whose opportunities for advancement and promotion are controlled largely by their commanding officers and it is no reflection on their honesty and integrity to conclude that they desire to make a fine record."

So much for the presumption that a man is innocent until proven guilty.

In contrast to the unanimous verdict of a twelve-man jury required in civilian courts, only a two-thirds vote of a court-martial jury is necessary to convict. Sentencing is similarly arrived at by a two-thirds vote, except that a three-fourths vote is needed to impose life imprisonment and unanimity is required for the death penalty.

Almost always, the commanding general is careful not to exert direct pressure on the members of the court-martial; this is expressly forbidden by the UCMJ.[2] But such intervention is hardly needed: all that is necessary is for the word to go out that the old man is "interested" in a particular case, and the court-martial can generally be counted on to come up with the appropriate judgment. If the jury members have any doubts as to exactly how harsh the commanding general wants to be, they need only impose an extremely severe sentence and let the general adjust it later as he sees fit.

As if his looming presence over the jury were not enough, the commanding general has other proxies in the courtroom:

2. In one extraordinary deviation from accepted procedure, the commanding general at Fort Leonard Wood, Major General Thomas H Lipscomb, embarked in 1966 upon an overtly calculated campaign to obtain tougher sentences at his base. He lectured officers about the dangers of lenient sentences and encouraged them to dole out stiff punishments so that defendants would be more inclined to negotiate guilty pleas. Lipscomb's strategy backfired when military appeals courts reversed or reduced sentences on ninety-three cases from his command.

both the prosecutor and the defense attorney are directly subordinate to his legal adviser, the Staff Judge Advocate. (Until 1968, the judge himself was a member of the general's command.) While it is no embarrassment for the prosecutor to be part of the same team as the general, it can be distinctly inhibiting for the defense counsel. His efficiency reports are written by the Staff Judge Advocate, and his future assignments, promotions, and leaves are in the hands of an officer who is rarely eager to see him perform well. If he is too zealous or too successful in defending GI's whom the commanding general wants convicted, he may henceforth be assigned only to prosecution. Or he may be taken off trial work altogether and given nothing but legal journeyman's work. Or, if the general and his Staff Judge Advocate get really mad, he may even be ordered to Vietnam.[3]

Though judges at general courts-martial are now assigned and rated by the Judge Advocate General's Corps rather than by the local commander, the commander does have the power to overrule a judge on certain important points of law. For

3. Examples of retaliation are legion. Ex-Captain Stanley R. Mazeroff, assigned to the Pentagon, got a lieutenant colonel acquitted in his first case. In the course of the trial he put a general on the stand and treated him rather roughly. His superior informed him that this was the last case he'd ever try for the Army; it was.

At Udorn Air Force Base in Thailand, Captain Terence G. Connor accompanied a client to his barracks while military investigators were searching it for drugs. Connor told the investigators that his client, an enlisted man, did not voluntarily consent to the search. The investigators searched anyway and found nothing, and Connor was promptly ordered off the base by Colonel David Mellish for "overzealous protection of a client."

In the Presidio mutiny case, one of the scrappiest defense lawyers was Captain Brendan Sullivan. While home on leave with exactly six months and one day remaining in his enlistment, Sullivan received telephone orders to ship to Vietnam. Since the Army does not send people to Vietnam for tours of less than six months, and rarely sends officers for less than twelve months, Sullivan was—to say the least—surprised and angered. He made a public protest, and after prodding from members of Congress, his orders were rescinded.

example, if the judge dismisses a charge that the commander would like to prosecute, the latter may reinstate the charge. This occurred in the case of Roger Priest, the Navy seaman who published an underground newspaper in Washington. Priest faced three charges: soliciting servicemen to desert, sedition, and making disloyal statements. Navy Captain B. Raymond Perkins, the trial judge, dismissed the first charge on the grounds that it failed to state the method of solicitation. Rear Admiral George P. Koch, who had initiated the charges against Priest, ordered Perkins to "reconsider" his decision because— though not a lawyer—he disagreed with the ruling "as a matter of law." The judge reinstated the charge, explicitly stating that he was acting on the admiral's orders.

Similar interventions have occurred in less controversial cases. At Fort Bliss, Texas, Private James H. Watson was charged by the Army with illegal possession of marijuana; he had been arrested at the Mexican border on New Year's Eve while off duty and off base. At his court-martial, Watson's lawyer contended that his crime was not service-connected; consequently, he argued, citing a 1969 Supreme Court decision, he could only be tried in a civilian court. The military judge, Major Daniel H. Benson, agreed and dismissed the case. But Lieutenant Colonel William E. Walker, the commander who had originally brought the charges, overruled Benson and directed him to proceed with the trial.

When a general court-martial is finished, the commanding general reviews its work. He may not increase the severity of the sentence; he may only approve it or reduce it. The important point here is that he is still involved—that the same man who initiated the criminal proceedings, selected the jury, and appointed the prosecutor and defense counsel, now gets a chance to pass judgment on their performance. If the court-martial members have been unduly lenient, the general finds out; if, in anticipation of his scrutiny, they have been overly ironhanded, he may temper their harshness with a minim of mercy. Then he orders the sentence he has decided upon to be executed.

II

THE DEFENDANT in a court-martial may not have much of a chance to win, especially if his alleged crime is anti-military in nature. But he will be accorded a number of procedural rights as his conviction draws near. Most of these look good on paper; in practice, they leave much to be desired.

The accused GI will, first of all, have the right not to testify against himself. Article 31 of the UCMJ, like the Fifth Amendment to the Constitution, allows a defendant to refuse to answer questions which might tend to incriminate him. The Article also requires, like the Supreme Court's *Miranda* decision, that a suspect be informed prior to trial of his right to remain silent; and it bars admission into the trial of coerced or illegally induced confessions.

There is no question that Article 31 is a bona fide safeguard. Nevertheless, its effectiveness is reduced by several uniquely military circumstances. In the first place, a soldier has very little privacy in the army; incriminating evidence may be obtained by a search of his locker in a shakedown or, if he is in the stockade, as accused soldiers often are, by the reading of his mail. Secondly, other GI's in his barracks can easily be pressured to talk by threats; when a high-ranking officer orders a nervous private to respond, alluding very credibly to the possibility of "consequences" if he doesn't, there is a strong incentive to obey. In addition, despite the assurance of Article 31, military interrogators have a bagful of tricks for persuading soldiers to answer questions.

Another safeguard contained in the Code is the right to counsel without cost. The military is quite proud of this right, claiming that it antedates by several years the Supreme Court's requirement in *Gideon* v. *Wainright* that all civilian defendants be provided with free counsel when they can't afford their own. But the right to counsel in the military does not extend to summary courts-martial, company punishments, or administrative proceedings in which undesirable discharges may be adjudged. (Until 1968, it applied only to general, not to special, courts-martial.) Moreover, the soldier's right to free defense counsel is limited to *military* lawyers—attorneys who, however skilled and devoted they may be, are inherently under a number of restraints. Not only does the Staff Judge Advocate keep a wary eye on them; they are also prohibited by law from seeking relief for their clients in civilian courts, even though such relief might be essential to the defense of the accused. The army's guarantee of free counsel, in other words, is something of a mixed blessing: it does assure defendants that they will have *someone* to represent them, but it discourages the use of unfettered civilian lawyers who might more effectively defend their interests.

Article 44 of the UCMJ extends to servicemen the right not to be prosecuted twice for the same offense. However, when the offense involves a violation of both military and state law, there is no prohibition against being tried and punished by both jurisdictions (though this rarely happens). More significantly, though a GI need not fear double jeopardy within the military for the *same* offense, if its nature is such as to incur the wrath of his superiors, he stands in perpetual jeopardy of being punished for almost any slight violation of the rules.

The right to discover evidence, cross-examine hostile witnesses, and obtain favorable witnesses is also protected in the UCMJ. Military defense counsel are provided liberal pre-trial access to the prosecution's evidence. Cross-examination is permitted at Article 32 hearings as well as during courts-martial. Defense counsel, however, do not have an inherent right to subpoena witnesses; they must receive permission from the prosecution to do so, and not infrequently such permission is denied.

Additional problems can arise over evidence that the military decides to classify in the interest of national security. At the trial of Captain Howard Levy, for example, it was revealed that the evidence which led to the charges against Levy was contained in a 180-page intelligence dossier; Levy's military defense counsel was permitted to read it, but he could not discuss it either with his civilian colleague, Charles Morgan Jr., or with

Levy himself. Ira Glasser of the New York Civil Liberties Union observed after Levy's conviction that "the obvious choice the army would seem to have is clear: either it must reveal the evidence to the defense or else it cannot introduce it. Yet in the weird world of military law, that choice need not be made. The evidence is both introduced and kept from defense scrutiny."

The right to reasonable bail is inherent in the concept of due process of law; if a citizen must remain incarcerated until his guilt or lack of guilt is established in court or upon review, he is effectively denied the presumption of innocence. In the military, however, there is no such thing as bail, and more than half of the prisoners currently in stockades have not yet been tried.

There are, to be sure, rules regarding pre-trial detention and imprisonment pending appeal. The pre-trial detention rule is, on the surface, both sensible and fair. The *Manual for Courts-Martial* states: "Confinement will not be imposed pending trial unless deemed necessary to insure the presence of the accused at the trial or because of the seriousness of the offense charged." But the rule's fairness falls down over the questions of who deems confinement necessary and what constitutes a "serious" offense.

Under the UCMJ, any commissioned officer can order an enlisted man arrested and confined. Confinement may be to barracks, to post, or in the stockade. At some installations, stockade confinement must be approved by a JAG Corps officer, as well as the officer who orders the arrest. Such approval, however, is issued quite routinely and informally; usually a company commander simply gets it over the telephone. There is no magistrate's hearing at which the accused can present his side of the story. And if one JAG officer should turn a commander down, he need only shop around until he finds one more receptive.

What, in the military's opinion, is a serious offense? Army Lieutenant William L. Calley Jr., charged with murdering more than a hundred unarmed Vietnamese, was deemed not to have been accused of a serious crime and was not even restricted to post. Private Richard L. Gentile, the Vietnam veteran stationed at the San Francisco Presidio who took part in a Saturday afternoon peace march, and was then arrested for having been several hours AWOL, was immediately confined in the stockade.

The rule on post-trial confinement is even more explicit than the pre-trial rule. Article 71 of the UCMJ states: "No sentence which includes, unsuspended, a dishonorable or bad conduct discharge, or confinement for one year or more shall be executed until affirmed by a board of review and, in cases reviewed by it, the Court of Military Appeals." Nothing could be more unequivocal: no soldier with a heavy sentence can be imprisoned until his appeal has been heard. Yet this rule—which is in fact, like every provision of the UCMJ, not simply a rule but a law, passed by Congress and signed by the President—is rarely, if ever, adhered to; GI's normally begin serving their sentences as soon as they have been convicted.

The right to appeal a court-martial verdict does exist in the military, but not in a very effective form. The first level of appeal is virtually useless: it is to the same commanding officer who brought the charges and appointed the court. The next level, to a court of review in Washington, offers more possibility for an impartial hearing. However, the backlog of cases awaiting review is so immense that convicted GI's—lacking the right to bail—often serve all or most of their sentences before their appeals can be heard. Bruce Petersen, a Fort Hood private convicted of possessing an almost invisible trace of marijuana, served thirteen months in Leavenworth before a court of review threw out his conviction. Similarly, most of the Presidio "mutineers" served more than a year in prison before their mutiny convictions were overturned.

Above the courts of review in the army's judicial hierarchy is the Court of Military Appeals (COMA). COMA was created by Congress in 1951 to serve as the supreme court of the armed forces; it was also expected to exert a "civilianizing" influence upon military justice. The court's three members are not JAG Corps colonels but civilians appointed by the President and confirmed by the Senate. They tend, however, not to be as civilian-minded as their non-military status implies; the latest appointee, for example, was William H. Darden, formerly chief counsel for the Senate Armed Services Committee and as favorably disposed toward military traditionalism as any four-star general.

COMA's value as an appeals court is further limited by its reluctance to hear many cases; all told, it reviews only about one percent of all courts-martial, and some of the appeals it has refused to hear have involved serious questions of constitutional rights—Captain Levy's case, for example, and the somewhat similar one of Privates Amick and Stolte. Any of the Judge Advocates General of the respective services can order COMA to hear an appeal if he wants to; but they invariably use this power only when it is in the army's interest to have an appeal decided, not in that of an individual soldier.

If soldiers are unsuccessful in their quest for appellate relief within the military, they have no statutory right to appeal to a civilian court; the military system is considered an entity unto itself, not (ordinarily) subject to review by the Supreme Court or any lower federal tribunal. A small number of military cases do manage to slip into the federal courts on petition for habeas corpus, but this is a difficult procedure, made even more formidable by the so-called doctrine of exhaustion of remedies: a federal court will not touch a soldier's case until he has unsuccessfully availed himself of every potential avenue of redress within the military, administrative as well as judicial. This can, and usually does, take years. Thus, by the time Captain Levy's petition for habeas corpus makes its way to the Supreme Court —if it ever does—nearly half a decade will have passed since his court-martial conviction.

Military men, naturally enough, tend to see the situation in much more positive terms. Captain Richard J. Selman of the Navy JAG Corps presents a view quite commonly expressed by high-ranking JAG lawyers and other service spokesmen when he claims that "For an accused in the military today, many of his rights exceed those of his civilian counterparts." However, it would be closer to the truth to say that, while many rights *have* been afforded military defendants in recent years, these rights create a semblance of fairness without altering the basic structure of military justice. That structure always has been and still is strongly weighted against defendants—particularly so against those of low rank and those accused of crimes against the military system.

III

AMERICANS HAVE been talking about changing the structure of military justice for the better part of a century. Draconian justice, it was felt, might be appropriate for Roman legionnaires, British redcoats, or even American professionals—but not for citizen-soldiers.

It was during World War I that masses of American citizens were exposed to military justice for the first time. There were half a million courts-martial during the war, most of them summary. In some cases the sentences were extraordinary: thirty years at hard labor for a GI who had insulted a sergeant; twenty years for a three-month AWOL; ten years for unlawful possession of a pass. One of the most shocking cases arose out of a fight in 1917 between white civilians and Negro soldiers at Fort Sam Houston, Texas, in which several persons were killed. Sixty-three Negro soldiers were charged with mutiny, fifty-five were convicted, and thirteen were sentenced to death. All thirteen were executed immediately after the court-martial, before their records could be forwarded to Washington or examined by anyone.

A movement for reform of military justice was begun after the war by—surprisingly enough—the acting Judge Advocate General of the Army, General Samuel T. Ansell. Ansell argued that the command-dominated structure of military justice was not only alien to the American spirit but harmful to the Army as well:

I contend—and I have gratifying evidence of support not only from the public generally but from the profession—that the existing system of Military Justice is un-American, having come to us by inheritance and rather witless adoption out of a system of government which we regard as fundamentally intolerable; that it is archaic, belonging as it does to an age when armies were but bodies of armed retainers and bands of mercenaries; that it is a system arising out of and regulated by the mere power of Military Command rather than Law; and that it has ever resulted, as it must ever result, in such injustice as to crush the spirit of the individual subjected to it, shock the public conscience and alienate public esteem and affection from the Army that insists on maintaining it.

Ansell drafted a bill that, had it been passed by Congress, would have radically altered the nature of American military justice. It provided, among other things, for a mandatory and binding pre-trial investigation, an independent military judge with the power to sentence, an eight-man jury selected by the judge, two peremptory challenges rather than one, a three-fourths rather than two-thirds majority for conviction, the right to civilian legal counsel, and a civilian court of review. The bill also provided that three of the eight jury members be of the same rank as the accused. With six votes needed for conviction, an enlisted-man defendant would thus be assured that men of his own rank—not officers or senior NCO's—would hold the balance of decision.

Ansell's bill was introduced in the Senate in 1920 by George E. Chamberlain of Oregon. Its reforms, however, were vigorously opposed by the War Department, which at this time was seeking to persuade Congress to enact universal military training. Congress was sensitive to the public's displeasure with both the excesses of army courts-martial and the prospect of compulsory training in peacetime. "I know that in my community," said Congressman John F. Miller of the House Armed Services Committee, "there is a growing opposition to compulsory military training, which grows evidently out of that reason, that they think if their boys get into military training they would then become subject to all this system of military courts-martial and that it is out of place, and is outclassed by the modern trend of progress."

Congress resolved its dilemma by rejecting both compulsory

military training and Ansell's proposals for reforming military justice; courts-martial would thus remain as bad as they were, but at least the mass of American youth would not be unwillingly subjected to them. Instead of the Chamberlain bill, Congress in 1920 adopted a very limited revision of the Articles of War. That was where matters rested up to and through World War II.

During that war there were over 1.7 million courts-martial, and though sentences were lighter on the average than in World War I, the aftertaste was bitter nonetheless. The subsequent outcry against military justice was if anything even more intense, and constituted, moreover, part of a general postwar outburst of anti-military criticism.

The response of the War Department was to appoint a board under Lieutenant General James H. Doolittle to study ways of making the Army more democratic, and another committee headed by Arthur Vanderbilt, a former president of the American Bar Association, to recommend changes in military justice. Vanderbilt's committee urged a lessening of command influence and a strengthening of military defense counsel. The net result of these recommendations, however, was that the Army and Navy quickly introduced legislation embodying mild reforms but actually making few alterations in the basic court-martial structure. War Department pressure led to passage of this legislation, the Elston Act, in 1948; but it was so unsatisfactory to advocates of reform that when Secretary of Defense James Forrestal appointed another committee to propose uniform rules for all four services, the reformists bombarded the new group with angry demands for change.

Letters poured in with suggestions. Governor James E. Folsom of Alabama wrote: "I have one recommendation to make, that enlisted men try enlisted men and that officers try officers. This is an old common law which has been handed down for hundreds of years, that every man is entitled to be tried by his peers." Governor Ernest W. Gibson of Vermont, a former Army lawyer, urged that the commander's power to appoint and rate court members and defense counsel be abolished:

We were advised, not once but many times on the Courts that I sat on, that if we adjudged a person guilty we should inflict the maximum sentences and leave it to the Commanding General to make any reduction. . . . I was dismissed as a Law Officer and Member of a General Court-Martial because our General Court acquitted a colored man on a morals charge when the Commanding General wanted him convicted—yet the evidence didn't warrant it. I was called down and told that if I didn't convict in a greater number of cases I would be marked down in my Efficiency Rating; and I squared right off and said that wasn't my conception of justice and that they had better remove me, which was done forthwith.

The military justice committees of the American Bar Association, the War Veterans' Bar Association and several other legal organizations called upon Forrestal's panel to recommend the complete removal of command control from courts-martial. They proposed instead a system which would empower a commander to bring charges against a soldier and to control the prosecution, but which would leave selection of the jury, handling of the defense, and post-conviction review to others.

The armed forces campaigned actively against the movement to limit command influence over courts-martial. Generals Omar Bradley and Dwight Eisenhower, the Army's two highest-ranking officers, publicly defended the rights of commanders to try their own men. In the end, the committee's proposals for a uniform code incorporated only moderate changes in the court-martial system. "In contrast with the Chamberlain bill of 1920," complained Professor Arthur Keeffe of Cornell Law School, "this proposed uniform code . . . is a sorry substitute." Congress enacted it anyway, along with a peacetime draft; it took effect as the Uniform Code of Military Justice in 1951.

The UCMJ's minor reforms included the provision permitting enlisted defendants to require that one-third of their court-martial members be enlisted men (though not necessarily of the same rank as the defendant). Directed at the problem of command influence was Article 37, which made it unlawful for a commander to "censure, reprimand, or admonish" any court member, judge, or counsel. But since the commander retained his power to bring charges, to appoint court members and counsel, and to review court findings, Article 37 was little more than an unenforceable warning. As critics pointed out at the time, the only way really to eliminate command influence was to eliminate the commander's powers.

The UCMJ also created the Court of Military Appeals, consisting of three civilian judges; this was touted as a highly progressive innovation. But while some of COMA's decisions since 1951 have brought court-martial proceedings closer to prevailing civilian standards of justice, its members could hardly be described as judicial activists, and COMA has had much less impact on military law than, say, the Supreme Court of the past twenty years has had on civilian law.

Many old-line officers felt that even the mild reforms contained in the UCMJ would adversely affect discipline within the military; their fears proved groundless. In 1968, confident that America's defenses would not disintegrate, Congress added some revisions to the Code. One change took the power to appoint judges away from the local commander and gave it to the Judge Advocate General in Washington; another permitted defendants to waive trial by jury and choose to be tried by a single judge. (The army supported this latter reform in the hope that it would relieve hard-pressed officers from jury duty in such numerous open-and-shut affairs as AWOL cases; defense lawyers have taken a liking to it because military judges tend to be more sympathetic to legalistic arguments and a bit less Draconian in their sentencing than regular officers.)

The revisions of 1968 were designed—in the words of Senator Sam Ervin of North Carolina, who sponsored most of them—to make "the brand of criminal justice administered by military courts . . . equal to that of federal and state civilian courts in most respects." They have not had that effect, however, and in the years since 1968 the demand for further reform has been widespread, coming not only from low-ranking GI's and those opposed to the Vietnam War, but from high-ranking professionals as well.

Concrete proposals for reform have been plentiful and sometimes sweeping. Charles Morgan Jr., the ACLU attorney who defended Captain Levy, has gone furthest of all by calling for elimination of all military courts. "You can't reform military justice," Morgan says. "The only way to change it is to take every single function away from the military and into the federal courts." The suggestion is not as unrealistic as it might sound; in West Germany, there have been no military courts since the United States "democratized" the German army after World War II.

Other advocates of reform would civilianize only selected aspects of military justice. Some would narrow the jurisdiction of courts-martial to only those offenses directly related to the maintenance of discipline on the battlefield; the Supreme Court, in *O'Callahan* v. *Parker*, has already begun moving in this direction.[4] The Judge Advocate General of the Army, Major General Kenneth J. Hodson, has suggested turning over to federal courts the offenses of prolonged noncombat AWOL and desertion. "If federal courts prosecute civilian draft-dodgers," he contends, "why should they not prosecute 'military' draft-dodgers?" Hodson also has proposed allowing direct appeal in certain cases from COMA to the Supreme Court.

Such sharing of judicial functions with civilian institutions would not be unique to America if adopted; civilian influence is present in the military judicial systems of many foreign countries. It is not uncommon, for example, for soldiers in other nations to be tried in civilian courts for non-military offenses. In addition, Britain, Canada, Australia, and New Zealand have created civilian appeals tribunals that review, overall, a larger percentage of court-martial decisions than does COMA. In Britain, the Judge Advocate General is himself a civilian, and he, rather than the local commander, is empowered to assign defense counsel.

4. An Army court-martial convicted Sergeant James F. O'Callahan of rape and sentenced him to ten years imprisonment. On petition for habeas corpus, O'Callahan contended that he had been off duty, off base, and out of uniform at the time of the offense; therefore, he was guilty, if at all, of a civilian rather than a military crime. The Supreme Court upheld him in 1969, ruling that courts-martial enjoy jurisdiction only over "service-connected" crimes. The military's definition of "service-connected" crimes remains fairly broad, however.

Even if military judicial functions are kept in military hands, there is still enormous room for reform. Edward F. Sherman, a professor of law at Indiana University and a former captain in the Army JAG Corps, would begin by eliminating from the UCMJ such vague and antiquated provisions as Articles 133 and 134. Article 133, prohibiting "conduct unbecoming an officer and a gentleman," is open to so many interpretations that an officer can never know with certainty when his conduct is illegal. Article 134, which outlaws "all disorders and neglects to the prejudice of good order and discipline" and "all conduct of a nature to bring discredit upon the armed forces," is even worse—it is frequently called "the devil's article" because it allows a commander to punish a soldier for almost anything he wishes. The *Manual for Courts-Martial* gives fifty eight examples of the types of offenses punishable under Article 134; they range from wrongfully kicking a public horse in the belly to possessing a marijuana cigarette. But the list is merely illustrative, not exhaustive, and almost any act can fall within the outstretched tentacles of Article 134 if a commander and a court-martial so find. The article was used, for example, to punish Daniel Amick and Kenneth Stolte for distributing an antiwar leaflet, and against William Harvey and George Daniels for "disloyal" words uttered at a bull session.

Other proposed changes would mitigate the double standard of justice that prevails for officers on the one hand and enlisted men on the other. It is easier under the UCMJ to confine enlisted men than to confine officers; enlisted men may be tried by summary courts-martial while officers may not; in special and general courts-martial, officers are tried by their peers while enlisted men are tried by officers; court-martial sentences involving generals or admirals must be approved by the President. In practice, officers are more often allowed to resign than brought before the bar of military justice, and even when they *are* subjected to trial, court-martial juries are apt to be lenient and understanding (except, of course, when the defendant, like Captain Levy, is not a "member of the club").

The double standard often produces bizarre results. In Vietnam, to give just one example, five soldiers were charged with murdering a Vietnamese prisoner of war; three were the low-ranking enlisted men who had been ordered to kill the Viet Cong suspect, and two were the officers who had issued the orders. The three enlisted men were sentenced to from one to ten years in prison by juries composed of officers and senior NCO's; the officers, Captain Paul C. Ogg and Lieutenant John J. Patrick Jr., were acquitted by juries composed solely of fellow officers.

The key to correcting the double standard and many other inequities of the court-martial system lies in changing the make-up of military juries. Many officers recoil at the mere suggestion of such a change, raising the specter of privates sitting in judgment upon generals and contending that the maturity and educational level of military juries would plummet. Such arguments, however, are largely beside the point. Assuming that justice is best assured by guaranteeing to all defendants the right to an impartial jury of their peers, the question is how best to achieve this right without significantly impairing the military's ability to function.

If a private were tried by a court-martial of twelve privates for the offense of slugging a first sergeant, chances are his jury would not be impartial. On the other hand, a jury of nine colonels would hardly be impartial either. The solution lies, as General Ansell suggested half a century ago, in choosing a jury that reconciles the military's interest in discipline with the defendant's interest in justice. Such a jury would consist of neither all privates nor all officers, but rather a mixture that would give the balance of power to jurors of the defendant's rank. Professor Sherman has proposed a system in which half of a court-martial panel would be composed of soldiers of the same rank as the accused, with two-thirds of the members needed to convict. Other formulas are possible. In no case would privates be trying generals; generals would try generals, and privates, in substantial proportion, would try privates.

As important as the make-up of a court-martial is the manner in which its members are chosen. Under the present system, they are hand-picked by the local commander. A much fairer method would be to select them randomly from a roster of all servicemen, much the way jurors are selected for civilian courts. If, say, four privates first class were needed for a particular court-martial, they could be picked out of a roll or wheel containing the names of all privates first class at the given installation.

Proposals have also been made to reform the status of military defense counsel. A true adversary system cannot flourish in military courtrooms if defense attorneys are assigned, rated, promoted, and transferred upon the whim of the Staff Judge Advocate, who is inherently biased in favor of securing convictions. Senators Mark Hatfield of Oregon and Birch Bayh of Indiana have introduced legislation to create an independent corps of military defense counsel. Others have urged that defense counsel be empowered to seek injunctions, writs of habeas corpus, or other forms of relief in federal courts when they deem such action necessary to protect the interests of their clients.

In like manner, greater independence for military judges has been suggested. Since 1968, judges for general courts-martial have belonged to a field judiciary insulated from the control of local commanding officers. This arrangement is admirable as far as it goes, but can still be improved. Judges do not, for example, have tenure; they may be transferred at any time by the Judge Advocate General in Washington. To protect their independence against all sources of outside pressure, tenure could be granted both to trial judges and judges on the courts of military review—not necessarily for life, but at least for the same term, four years, enjoyed by military chiefs of staff.

Many other changes have been proposed: the recommendations of pre-trial investigators should be binding; more peremptory challenges of prospective jurors should be permitted; the commander's power to overrule judges on matters of law ought to be abolished along with his power to review the decisions of courts-martial; the defense should be given the same right to subpoena witnesses as the prosecution; the appeals process should be speeded up and reasonable standards established for releasing defendants not shown to be dangerous, both before trial and pending appeal; jurisdiction should be granted to federal district courts to hear claims of soldiers that their constitutional rights are being violated.

Almost all of these changes have been resisted by the military. Its arguments are similar to those advanced for hundreds of years: the army is different from civilian society; its purpose is to win battles, not to secure justice for its members. In civilian society, the division of governmental powers is important to prevent abuses and to protect the rights of citizens; in the military, concentration of power in the hands of the commander is essential to the preservation of discipline.

Such arguments might be more convincing if they had not also been made against the abolition of flogging, against the introduction of lawyers into military courtrooms, against the hazing of recruits, and against numerous other practices once deemed essential to the maintenance of discipline. They might also be more persuasive if American soldiers were comparable to the Imperials of Gustavus Adolphus or the redcoats of George III. But we no longer live in an age of muskets and horses and ignorant peasants. Weapons have changed, tactics have changed, and soldiers have changed; now they are citizen-soldiers, conscious of their rights under law. Many do not even go into battle; they are uniformed bureaucrats, technicians, and logisticians.

Experience in the United States and other nations has shown that discipline and morale derive from many sources, including a soldier's respect for his army's fairness. The notion that discipline and justice cannot go together is, to say the least, an insult to the American GI. The real question is not whether discipline will survive but whether the American military will adjust to democracy or continue to insist that democracy adjust to it.

EXCESSIVE BAIL SHALL NOT BE REQUIRED
NOR EXCESSIVE FINES IMPOSED, NOR CRUEL
AND UNUSUAL PUNISHMENTS INFLICTED.

—*Eighth Amendment,*
U.S. Constitution

9. THE MILITARY PRISONS

THE MILITARY needs a place to keep its misfits, rule-breakers, and objectors. To this end it has constructed about 130 military prisons, known as stockades in the Army and Air Force and brigs in the Navy and Marine Corps.

Sitting like a lotus leaf in the middle of San Francisco Bay, about halfway between San Francisco and Oakland, is a romantically named piece of landfill called Treasure Island. In earlier days it was the site of an international exposition and a municipal airport. During World War II, it was taken over by the Navy and is now the headquarters for the Twelfth Naval District.

Only minutes from downtown San Francisco via the Bay Bridge, Treasure Island is an extremely attractive base. Many of the Navy's technical schools are here, and some of the barracks have the aura of college dormitories. From the convivial Admiral Chester W. Nimitz Officers Club, or for that matter, from almost anywhere on the island, Navy men are blessed with a breathtaking panorama of the San Francisco skyline, the rolling hills of Marin County, and that other, far more foreboding island in the bay, Alcatraz.

For all its amenities, Treasure Island does, however, have one thing in common with the Alcatraz of the past: a prison with few rivals for inhospitality. For twenty-five years, the two-story, white building surrounded by a barbed-wire fence was officially known as the Treasure Island Brig. In June 1969, a large sign with a new, high-sounding name was posted in front: NAVAL CORRECTIONAL CENTER, it said. Few people were fooled, least of all the prisoners.

In September 1969, thirty-one current and former inmates filed a lawsuit in San Francisco Federal Court demanding an end to guard brutality at the brig. The plaintiffs submitted sworn affidavits concerning their own experiences.

Seaman Harry E. Clark Jr., told of being beaten because he refused to remove his wedding ring while being strip-searched.

Airman Apprentice Murphy L. Musik, sent to the brig after trying to kill himself with an overdose of tranquilizers, stated that he was "forced to run around the confinement area flapping my arms and making noises while they [the Marine guards] stood on each side of me and hit me with their fists, stating that they were trying to 'shoot me out of the sky.' "

Seaman Robert L. Orth became ill one morning while the prisoners were being exercised in the courtyard:

We were to run twenty times around the brig compound. On the eighteenth lap, I became sick and fell to the ground, weak and regurgitating. The PFC on duty yelled at me, "Get up, you phony motherfucker! Get up and run, you son of a bitch!" I got up and ran some more, but I couldn't make it. I was weak and now had the dry heaves. I fell to the ground once again. The guard kicked me and kept kicking me while I was struggling to get up on my feet and carry out his shouted orders of, "Run, you fucking squid [Marine Corps slang for sailor], run!"

Later that day, the same guard took me into an isolation cell and said, "Are you a faggot, squid? Will you suck my dick, squid?" I answered negatively to all questions and he began to beat me with his fists, hitting me hard in the stomach and chest. After about ten blows, he said, "Are you going to puke in my compound again, fucking squid?" While I was answering, he began to pound on my chest again. This went on for several minutes. I began to think he was going to beat me to death and I fell to the floor. I was ordered to get up, but couldn't. He grabbed me and started shouting in my ear, "I'll kill you, you fucking squid. You want to fight me, squid? Anytime, squid." Then he struck me several more times and told me to get back into the compound.

As we passed the guards at Post 1, he was beaming. He said to one of them, "This is the fucker that puked in my compound, but he knows what I'll do if he does it again. Don't you, squid?" Then he pushed me through the door into the compound. He actually seemed rather proud to have beaten me. He walked up to another guard, rubbing his fist, saying something to him. They both laughed.

The Navy was greatly embarrassed by the lawsuit. It didn't like the bad publicity, and it certainly didn't want a federal judge poking around in its brig. So it promptly formed its own informal investigating board headed by Lieutenant Commander Lewis D. Turner. Behind closed doors, Turner's panel interviewed scores of prisoners, guards, and supervisory personnel, amassing a record of sworn testimony that filled seven bulky volumes and painted an even more gruesome picture than did the prisoners' original charges. Had the Navy's hearings been public, the outrage they would have caused would have been considerable.

The caliber of the Marine guards, the investigation revealed, was mixed: most performed their jobs with discipline and restraint, but there were enough bad apples to spoil the barrel. Sergeant Henry J. Holmes was typical of the good guards. "He was always relatively friendly," said Fireman Recruit Michael L. Bartholomew. "He never harassed people. He never got down on anybody. He used to let us smoke up there in orientation once in a while. He'd even bullshit with us for a few minutes."

Corporal Billie Lewis Slick, a curly-haired Southern white youth, was one of the bad apples. Several prisoners testified that they had been beaten by Slick on various occasions. When Slick was interviewed by the board, he claimed to have great difficulty recollecting any of the incidents recounted by prisoners. In the course of his attempt to explain his convenient lapses of memory, the following colloquy took place:

Q. Would you remember every time you might have been struck by a confinee?
A. No, sir.
Q. Does it happen that often?
A. No, sir. It's just that I fight quite a bit on the outside and if it's anything over two weeks, I usually don't remember.
Q. You say you fight quite a lot on the outside. What is your reason for this?
A. I box.
Q. Do you ever fight any place where it is not normally acceptable for you to fight, like in a bar?
A. I have before, yes, sir. . . .
Q. What is your GCT, Slick? [GCT is the military equivalent of IQ.]
A. I don't know.
Q. Did you graduate from high school?
A. No. . . .
Q. Do you like this job?
A. I don't care for no jobs really in the service.
Q. Do you dislike this one more so than other jobs that you have had other than Vietnam?
A. This is the only job I have had since Vietnam. . . .
Q. Why are you supposed to take the GCT again?
A. I don't know. They called me over to the company office and told me.
Q. Did they say why you were taking it over?
A. They just said it needed to be up four points. [Brig guards must have a GCT score of at least 90.]
Q. For what reason?
A. To stay in the brig, they said. That's all they said.

Some of the guards had better powers of recollection than Corporal Slick. One was Sergeant John L. Engram Jr., whose memory was greatly enhanced by the fact that he was getting out of the Marine Corps the following day. Engram was asked if he thought some of the guards were unfit for brig duty:

A. Yes, sir.
Q. How large a percentage do you think that includes?
A. Not a very large percentage, sir. But the persons they do have who aren't qualified, the first place they send them is over to the Annex [where prisoners are first taken in]. And there's nobody over there to watch and see what they do there, and you can't tell what they're going to do.
Q. What makes you say that there are unqualified persons here? Their education or their personalities?
A. Yes, sir, that mostly. They come in here with the attitude that anybody that comes into the brig is no good to begin with. And they more or less treat them any way they want to.
Q. Do you believe, or do you have any reason to believe, Sergeant, that some of the prisoners have been mistreated?
A. Yes, sir, I do. . . .
Q. What leads you to believe that some of the guards are not qualified? You must have observed them doing something you don't believe is right.
A. Well, I think a lot of the guards here are just sadistically inclined. Just because they've got the man here under confinement, and they know that anybody can't do anything back to them, because if they do they are going to get wrote up for it or something, so they feel that they can do just about anything they want to him.

Some of the worst mistreatment, the Turner board found, occurred in the "sally port"—the entrance to the brig—and in the Annex, where the in processing takes place. Prisoners arriving at the sally port would be made to stand at attention for periods ranging up to several hours, the board was told. They would be screamed at and bullied, derided as "dirty hippies" and "fucking dopers." Guards would be unnecessarily rough in conducting the strip search; they would hit and kick and verbally abuse.

Fireman Lawrence A. Simpson had relatively long hair when he was brought to the brig after having been AWOL. Guards called him a "scrounge," a "hippie," and "unfit human being." While he was standing at attention in the check-in office, testimony indicated, a guard whacked him on the head with a mop. Another guard got a broom and hit him four or five times in the testicles with the brush end.

Electronic Technician Recruit Wayne D. Sheets was made to walk around and quack like a duck when he arrived. "Once," Sheets said, "they had them [the new prisoners] stand in a corner and scream out—I think they were Marines, sir—and they were screaming out: 'I'm a green piece of shit, sir.' They were told any time a sentry came in front of them, they were supposed to say this, 'Sound it off, sir.' "

Airman Apprentice Patrick M. Jones, a sailor who had unsuccessfully applied for discharge as a conscientious objector and then gone AWOL, was pushed up against a canvas-covered gate in the sally port and had his legs repeatedly kicked farther and farther apart. Soon Jones fell down and the guard, a sergeant, ordered him up again. Another sergeant came by and repeated the process:

This time I held on to the bars, so when they started kicking me I wouldn't fall down. They got my legs out as far as they'd go, and there was a curb. My left foot was out so far it hit the curb and couldn't go any farther. But he would just stand there and kick it, you know, kick my ankle. Keep on kicking it, just smashing it into the curb. Then he started giving me his fist, slapping and smashing my head against the canvas. Then he yanked the crotch of my pants up, which hurt my genitals quite a bit.

When Jones was taken inside the Annex, "they mixed up a colored girl's picture with the stuff in my wallet, and they started in: 'Is your girl with soul?' 'You a nigger-lover, boy?' 'Is this your chick?' Finally, I think it was a lance corporal, said, 'It's not his picture.' "

Harassment and mistreatment also extend to the permanent prisoner population, occasionally with similar racist overtones. Personnelman Chief Eugene W. Keedy, one of the Navy counselors at the brig, was asked if prisoners were called by names other than their real name or their confinee number.

A. Oh, yes, sir. This is a continual thing.
Q. What types of names are they called?
A. Well, I have heard a few. Of course the racial bit. They were called "niggers."
Q. The guards called them "niggers"?
A. Yes, sir, And then, again, other pet names that they had invented for confinees. Some people are offended more on this than other people. The Indians, for example. There are some tribes of Indians that really resent this type of ethnic joke. . . . The Sioux get quite hot about it.

Guards would do other things to taunt and annoy the prisoners. Sometimes instead of dry blankets they would hand out wet ones that compounded the discomfort of the nighttime cold. Or they would use the PA system after taps to tease the prisoners. One guard, Corporal Jay B. Carlsen, ordered prisoners to do push-ups on their knuckles. Asked his reason, he explained that "These people just coming in, they got a smart-aleck attitude . . . When they come up to me to ask permission to make a head call or anything like that, well, they come 'diddly-bopping' up every time and they think it's funny . . . And I figure, that's the thing we did in boot camp for correction—a little bit of correction. So I put them down there [on their knuckles] for a while."

Another "correctional" technique was to deprive prisoners of their free time to write letters by extending afternoon exercises into the evening. Sometimes smoking privileges would be denied. Or, in the mess hall, prisoners would be made to stand up and sit down in unison until they did it just right.

One Sunday afternoon, the guards' imaginations took a more bizarre turn. "They [the prisoners] had to wear trash cans inverted over their heads and they had to hold up flags with 'T.I. Brig' written on them, for an hour or two, standing at attention," testified Navy Personnelman Chief Keedy. "They had to parade through the outside area, out there, dressed with their pants legs rolled up and pieces of cloth tied around their necks to resemble Batman and Superman capes."

Throughout the investigation, prisoners stated that they hadn't filed complaints because they knew the guards would retaliate. And when any prisoner left the brig, he had to sign a statement affirming that "I have no specific complaint to make concerning treatment while confined."

Turner and the other board members took all this testimony calmly. They recommended that several unqualified guards be reassigned or disciplined, that the staff be brought up to full complement, and that unannounced inspections of the brig be made during nights and weekends.

The brig commander, Navy Lieutenant William T. Lemond, seemed unfazed. An affable, easy-going man, he was looking forward to retirement in 1970. He had long heard stories of brutality in the brig, but you couldn't take that sort of talk seriously, he felt. Once, prior to the Turner investigation, a chaplain had complained to him about abusive treatment of prisoners. "This place is a hotel compared to the Pendleton brig," Lemond replied.

Not all of the military's prisons are quite as bad as the Treasure Island brig. Physically, the prisons vary. Some resemble concentration camps, with primitive barracks surrounded by barbed-wire fences and watchtowers. Others contain more solid structures built of brick or concrete. The Army's major confinement facility for long-term prisoners, the Disciplinary Barracks at Fort Leavenworth, looks like something out of a Grade B movie. The main building, called "the Castle," was constructed by prisoner labor in the 1920's. It is a wheel-like edifice with eight wings protruding from a central rotunda. The cells in each wing are arranged in tiers—two below ground, six above.

Most stockades, including Leavenworth, contain a special section of cells used for isolating troublesome prisoners. These dungeonlike cubicles are usually little more than six feet in width; a man can barely stretch out in them. Frequently, they are windowless, dimly lit and cold. In some stockades there is a hole in the floor into which the prisoner excretes; in others, the inmates are given buckets.

As in civilian jails life in military stockades is a boring, infuriating routine punctuated by occasional outbursts of violence. All activity is completely regimented. Privacy is nonexistent. Harassment is incessant. Always, the atmosphere is tense.

The prisoner's most trying moments occur upon his arrival at the stockade. It is at this point that the guards are most abusive. Like drill instructors during the first days of boot camp, they try to break down the prisoner so that he will be more docile in the months to come.

This initial period of indoctrination, during which the new prisoner is issued his prison uniform and taught the stockade rules, lasts from four days to a week. Then he joins the general stockade population. He is given a number and is thereafter referred to by that number rather than by name. He must wear an armband or badge testifying to his confinement status: sentenced or unsentenced; minimum, medium, or maximum security. Stockade rules prohibit him from possessing even the smallest items of personal pleasure—pictures of his wife or girl friend, a deck of playing cards, chewing gum or candy.

An average day in a stockade begins at the somewhat unnecessarily early hour of 4:30 in the morning. Rather than making their bunks, the awakened prisoners "stockade" them—fold up the sheets and blankets into a common pile. Breakfast is served at 5. Then the inmates return to their cellblocks for clean-up, physical exercise, or just waiting around.

At 7 there is the morning formation. Prisoners may fall out for sick call or be escorted to their assigned details. If a prisoner has behaved well, he may be rewarded with work outside the stockade—picking up papers, washing cars, cutting the general's lawn. Otherwise, he marches, exercises, or performs meaningless chores inside the compound. Marine Corps and Navy brigs—which are run by the Marine Corps—put special emphasis on exercising, marching, and standing at attention; they also tend to be much stricter than Army stockades.

At Leavenworth, the only Army prison with a comprehensive vocational program, there are jobs for prisoners in sheet metal work, silk screen printing, shoe repair, upholstery, leather work, farming, computer programming, radio and TV repair, and mechanical drawing. Also within the prison walls are a clothing factory and an automobile repair shop. In fact, Leavenworth is probably the best place in the Army to learn a trade, though recruiters are unlikely to mention this. Also not bruited about is another benefit of the Leavenworth vocational program: it is a great boon for officers attending the Command and General Staff College at Fort Leavenworth who can get saddles for the hunt club made in the prison leather shop, have their cars repaired at one-third the commercial rate, and send in their furniture to be reupholstered for next to nothing.

After morning activities, the prisoners return to their cellblocks. There is a head count—one of four held during the day. Then lunch, afternoon work, more marching, another head count, supper, a bit of free time (unless the guards are angry), another head count, and lights out at 9:30.

It is not, one may safely say, a very stimulating or beneficial regimen.

When prisoners are put away, they not only lose physical contact with the outside world, they lose human contact as well. "Prisoners should be encouraged to correspond with their families and other persons interested in their welfare," says Army Field Manual 19–60. "This is important to a prisoner's morale." In practice, however, correspondence with the outside world is severely restricted. All incoming mail is inspected for "seditious or subversive matter"—terms which are rather loosely defined. Letters which support a prisoner's resolve to oppose the war, for example, are often returned to their senders. Outgoing mail is also inspected; it may not mention any names of stockade personnel or "any description of events occurring in or about the stockade." The only privileged communications are with the President of the United States, members of Congress, and defense attorneys.

Visiting is usually limited to one or two hours on Sunday and holiday afternoons with a prisoner's immediate family. Mere friends can't get in. A prisoner's physical contact with his wife is restricted to a brief embrace upon greeting and parting. He is searched before and after seeing visitors.

Prisoners have a right to complain about stockade treatment, but they do so at their own risk. In many stockades there are boxes where inmates can drop a note that will go directly to the stockade commander. But guards know when prisoners complain; in some stockades they must ask a guard for the proper complaint form, or for a pencil to fill it out with.

Guards, of course, are not inherently more vicious or mean than other people; it is simply the nature of their job that makes them antagonists of prisoners. Most of the soldiers assigned to stockade duty are Vietnam veterans, and are usually around 20 to 21 years old, about the same age as the bulk of the prisoners. Like the prisoners, also, they are in their positions involuntarily. Their prime concern is to finish their assignments and get out of the army; they want to do nothing that might get them in trouble with their superiors. One thing their superiors are firm about is that fraternization with prisoners is forbidden.

One of the guards' functions is to observe and pass judgment on prisoners' behavior. The length of time a soldier serves in the stockade and the conditions under which he serves it (he can get a good job or a bad job, be placed in minimum security barracks or in "the hole") depend, at least in part, upon his attitude and behavior—or rather, his *observed* attitude and behavior. Army Field Manual 19–60 states:

Each person assigned to the stockade observes prisoners for evidence pertaining to the following factors:
   (1) *Appearance.* Is the prisoner clean, neat and well-dressed?
   (2) *Bearing.* Does the prisoner have a military bearing, or does he slouch or slump?
   (3) *Conduct.* Has the prisoner exhibited insolent or insubordinate conduct?

(4) *Demeanor.* Is the prisoner cocky, sullen, depressed or exhilarated?

(5) *Efficiency.* How well does he accomplish his assigned tasks?

Guards make notes of deficiencies observed in these areas, and the notes are added to prisoners' personnel files. If a guard particularly dislikes a prisoner's behavior, he can have him placed in an isolation cell. There the prisoner must spend his days without a cot, mattress, or blanket, and with one piece of reading matter—the Bible. He is, in addition, put on a special disciplinary diet known as "rabbit chow," consisting of lettuce, bread, potatoes, dried pancakes, and minute portions of vegetables—no meat, condiments, desserts, or anything to drink except water. If the prisoner is considered especially obstreperous, he may be confined in irons, leather straps, or a straitjacket.

Stockade counselors, who are usually specialists or NCO's with some training in psychology, try to fill out the official picture of each prisoner by compiling information on his background and personality. Counselors are directed to establish rapport with prisoners so as to get them to talk freely about their feelings and problems. The Field Manual explains how to do this: "The counselor guides the prisoner by short questions or exclamations, nods, gestures, or expressions of sympathy, as the situation may require." The counselor also points out to the prisoner the rewards for returning to the straight and narrow, for closer adherence to the values of duty, honor, patriotism. This is the army's concept of "rehabilitation."

Prisoners react to the attention of guards and counselors in various ways. Some play along, pretending to adopt the attitudes demanded of them, letting the counselors think they are helping because, as one former prisoner says, "it makes them feel good." Others laugh in the faces of stockade personnel and display their contempt by being intentionally sloppy, lackadaisical, and disrespectful. A few go further, refusing even to march or to cooperate in any way with those in charge.

Some prisoners' reactions are more desperate. They were unable to endure the abuses, deprivations of freedom, and attacks on their personalities that they suffered while on regular duty; they can endure them even less in the stockade. They may seek to smuggle in drugs through the hospital or other channels, as a means of temporary, internal escape. In extreme cases, they may try suicide.

II

TEN MILES from the Treasure Island brig, on a wooded hill overlooking the Golden Gate Bridge, sit two aging white stucco buildings surrounded by a high cyclone fence topped with barbed wire. This is San Francisco's other military prison, the Presidio stockade, perhaps the best-known stockade in the Army. It is little used today, and a commission of penologists has recommended abandoning it altogether, but until 1970 it was jammed with a fluctuating population of prisoners and guards in a nearly constant state of agitation.

As in every military prison, almost all of the Presidio stockade's inmates were AWOL's—men who for a variety of reasons, had been unable to accept or adjust to the Army's demands. Many were emotionally disturbed kids who should never have been in the Army; some were soldiers who had decided that they could not in conscience take part in what America was doing in Indochina. All were thrown together into fifty-year-old cellblocks that had been built to accommodate, at most, two-thirds their number.

The stockade grew particularly tense during the summer of 1968. The Sixth Army, for which the Presidio serves as headquarters, was granting almost no discharges, and so the prison population soared. Building 1213, which contains most of the cellblocks, was stuffed with up to 120 prisoners, when even by the Army's own standards its maximum capacity was eighty-eight. Prisoners could hardly move without constantly dodging or jostling each other.

There were other continual annoyances. The antiquated building had only four latrines; to go to the bathroom or to take a shower, a prisoner frequently had to wait more than two hours. Much of the time the latrines were backed up with excrement. At times the population rose above emergency levels, and food had to be rationed.

Compounding the constant physical discomfort and stress were frequent instances of harassment by some of the guards. Early in the summer, one inmate was dragged down the stairs in such a manner as to have his head hit every step, apparently because he hadn't got out of bed quickly enough. Another time, guards fired water pistols filled with urine at a prisoner. Conversations among black prisoners were broken up with such comments as "What's this, a Black Panther meeting?" In late June, a prisoner running for the gate was shot by a guard with a .45 and seriously wounded, though there were six or seven other guards within the compound at the time and the one who fired was only ten feet away.

Inevitably, there was a high number of suicide attempts— some genuine, others desperate appeals for psychiatric help or discharge from the Army. One prisoner who kept track counted thirty-three suicide attempts by twenty-one men between May and October 1968. Some drank chrome polish, lye, or other poisons; others slashed their wrists or forearms; some tried hanging.

Official stockade policy in dealing with such attempts was to throw the man into "the hole." One prisoner, Private Ricky Lee Dodd of Hayward, California, slit his forearm with a razor; he was bandaged and sent to segregation, where he proceeded to hang himself with his bandages. He was pronounced dead on arrival at Letterman General Hospital, and is alive today only because a disbelieving doctor succeeded in resuscitating him.

Private Patrick Wright, a prisoner at the time, recalls: "It was a crazy house—people cutting on themselves—everybody yelling—being jumped on all the time—guards telling me, 'I'm going to break your arm'—human excrement all over the latrine floor—guards shorting us on food."

Given conditions within the stockade and the nature of the prisoner population, it was not surprising that a combustible situation existed. In July, a prisoner went on an extended hunger strike; he was placed in segregation. Later in the summer, minor disturbances flared. Prisoners burned mattresses, threw garbage, smashed windows. Many inmates tried to escape.

One of the sickest prisoners in the stockade was Private Richard "Rusty" Bunch, a frail, boyish-looking brooder from Dayton, Ohio. "Rusty was a quiet, religious boy with a high IQ," Bunch's mother said later. "When his best friend was drafted, he decided to enlist. At first, he seemed to enjoy military life. But something—I don't know what—happened to him at Fort Lewis."

Bunch went AWOL, wandered through Haight-Ashbury on drugs, then turned up at his mother's home in Dayton. Mrs. Bunch scarcely recognized her own son. He babbled that he had died twice and been reincarnated as a warlock. She tried to have him hospitalized for psychiatric treatment, but no institution would accept an AWOL soldier. In desperation, she called the Army and received a written promise that her son would receive psychiatric care. But instead, he was thrown into prison, first at Fort Meade, Maryland, then at the Presidio.

It didn't take long for his fellow inmates to realize he was mentally disturbed. Bunch would sit on his bunk in a lotus position and mumble about his reincarnations. He would announce that he could walk through walls, and then walk into them. At night the whole stockade would be awakened by his frantic screams.

One day in October 1968, Bunch asked another prisoner to recommend a foolproof method of committing suicide. The latter, half-jokingly, suggested running away from a shotgun work detail. On Friday, October 11, while on such a detail, Bunch asked a guard, "If I run, will you shoot me?" The guard replied, "You'll have to run to find out." Bunch requested the guard to shoot at his head, then skipped away directly in front of him. He had gone barely thirty feet when the guard killed him with a 12-gauge shotgun blast straight at his back.

When word of the shooting reached the stockade, the prisoners could barely contain their fury. Someone walked over to

Bunch's bunk and found a handwritten note that said, "Well if your not going to give me love at least do me the favor of complete elimination . . . Fuck it, it ain't worth living . . . I've got but one click and it's over." Stockade officials quickly declared the shooting a "justifiable homicide."

That evening a minor disturbance occurred. Captain Robert S. Lamont, the stockade's twenty-five-year-old commander, came by and warned the men that if there was any more trouble they'd be tried for mutiny. The prisoners, however, remained agitated. The killing of Bunch was the culmination of a long train of cruelties that was threatening their sanity and now, they thought, their lives. Some talked of killing a guard or burning down the stockade. By Sunday night, passions had cooled enough for the prisoners to agree upon a nonviolent, orderly demonstration the following morning. The idea was to sit down until someone listened to their grievances.

A list was drawn up with seven main demands: elimination of shotgun details, complete psychological evaluations of all prisoners and guards, removal of racist guards, rotation of guards to prevent the build-up of antagonism, better sanitary facilities, decent food in sufficient quantities, and a chance to tell the press the prisoners' version of Bunch's slaying. Surely, they believed, if only those in authority could know what was going on inside the Presidio stockade, help would be quickly forthcoming. Human beings couldn't be treated this way; *Americans* couldn't be treated this way. If only people *knew*.

On Monday morning, October 14, 1968, there took place in the stockade a peaceful sit-down demonstration that has since become known as the "Presidio mutiny." More than the prisoners could have anticipated, it succeeded in focusing attention not only on their stockade, but on the entire military system.

Of the 123 prisoners in the stockade that morning, nearly a quarter—twenty-seven—took part in the "mutiny." Considering the inevitable reprisals, this was an extraordinary turnout. Conspicuous among the absentees were the black prisoners, who feared that punitive reaction would be harshest against them.

The twenty-seven men represented a good cross-section of

the total population, not only of the Presidio stockade, but of all military prisons. All were AWOL's. Their average age was 19. None came from wealthy, well-educated, or established families; a surprising number, in fact, were sons of career military men. All but five had been unable to finish high school. Several, like many other high school dropouts, had joined the Army on the promise of being given useful vocational training. None received the assignments he had expected.

Three of the twenty-seven could be described as Vietnam War objectors. Private Stephen Rowland of St. Louis, the son of an Air Force lieutenant colonel and one of the two demonstrators with a bit of college, had volunteered for the Army because he wanted training in occupational therapy. A few months later, after being trained as a combat medic, he had applied for discharge as a conscientious objector and been turned down. Private Keith Mather of San Bruno, California, another high school graduate, was one of nine antiwar GI's who six months earlier had publicly tried to resign from the Army. Private Richard Gentile of Hampton, Virginia, stepson of a career Air Force NCO, had served twelve months in Vietnam as a machine-gunner; by the time he got back to the States he was sick of killing. Just the previous Saturday, October 12, with only eighty-four days left in his three-year enlistment, he had violated a post-wide restriction to take part in a San Francisco peace march and subsequently been thrown in the stockade for being eight hours AWOL.

Most of the other "mutineers" were military misfits of various sorts. Some were simply cultural aliens. Private Walter Pawlowski of New York City, a straight-A student in high school, had rebelled against what he considered the absurdity of Army discipline. Private Ricky Lee Dodd was a gentle California flower child who kept running away from the Army that was trying to make him into a killer; he became famous in the stockade for his several bizarre attempts at suicide, including the nearly successful effort to hang himself on his bandages. Private Roy Pulley, of Clear Lake Park, California, an "Army brat" by family background, was a hard-drinking, grass-smoking motorcycle enthusiast who had ridden with the

Hell's Angels. After a run-in with police, he enlisted in the Army to learn airplane maintenance; instead, he was trained as a helicopter door-gunner.

Two of the 27—Privates Billy Hayes and Danny Seals— were Project 100,000 men with known mental deficiencies. Seals, from Auburn, California, was mildly retarded from a childhood brain injury. He had wanted to become a medic, but flunked the course at Fort Sam Houston and went AWOL in a fit of despondency. "It was hard to learn in the Army," he said. "I had to take notes and I couldn't spell."

Two others—Privates Michael Murphy and Larry Zaino— were high school dropouts who had gotten in trouble with the law and joined the Army under pressure from their probation officers. Both had gone AWOL four times before landing in the Presidio stockade.

A juvenile delinquent like Murphy and Zaino, Private Larry Reidel had been involved in numerous scrapes with the law: stealing, assaults, truancy. In the stockade he was always getting into fights with other prisoners. An Army psychiatrist had reported that "no therapeutic, punitive or correctional intervention is going to make this person into anything that approximates a good soldier."

Private Alan Rupert, of Pittsburgh, Pennsylvania, had never been quite sure who his father was. His mother worked in bars and had married twelve different men in fifteen years. Rupert ran away from home countless times and ran away from the Army nine times before winding up in the Presidio stockade.

Private Larry Lee Sales, of Modesto, California, had been pulling burglaries since he was a child, and had spent his youth spinning in and out of reformatories and county jails. In 1967 he entered Modesto State Hospital after having suffered a nervous breakdown. A psychiatrist wanted to commit him to the institution indefinitely, but Sales begged to be allowed to join the Army instead. He thought the Army would "straighten him out." After one day of basic training at Fort Lewis, he realized he had made a great mistake. He ran AWOL to his family, tried to commit suicide, and was taken to the Presidio stockade, where he attempted once again to end his life.

The histories of the other demonstrators are studded with chaotic childhoods, broken homes, low IQ's, emotional distress, and plain hard luck. All the frailties and misfortunes, hatreds and fears of this crazy-quilt collection of kids were climactically heightened by the oppressive conditions of the Presidio stockade. Now, on this October morning, they were reacting—in the words of Dr. Price Cobbs, the San Francisco psychiatrist who co-authored *Black Rage*—"like black people. They knew how it felt to be oppressed. Their response was spontaneous. They reacted in a nonviolent fashion, like Martin Luther King."

The demonstration began simply enough. At 7:30 that morning, the formation for assignment to work details and sick call was held, as usual, in front of Building 1212. There were about eighty prisoners lined up. When the first name for sick call was announced by the sergeant in charge, twenty-seven prisoners broke from formation, sat down in a grassy area, and asked to see Captain Lamont. As they waited, they flashed V-signs, chanted "Freedom, freedom, we want freedom," and sang "America the Beautiful," "This Land Is Your Land," and a very faltering version of "We Shall Overcome," which several of the prisoners had picked up from watching civil rights demonstrations on television.

Soon Lamont arrived, accompanied by a fire truck and an Army photographer who circled the demonstrators, taking pictures from all angles. A company of about seventy-five military policemen also showed up, wearing helmets and carrying nightsticks.

Private Walter Pawlowski, one of the three demonstrators who has since escaped to Canada, stood up and informed Captain Lamont that he wanted to read a list of grievances. The prisoners became quiet. Pawlowski began:

"Captain Lamont, we want the elimination of all shotgun-type details here at the stockade. Two, we want a psychological evaluation of all custodial staff, people who work here at the stockade, prior to their being allowed to work here. Three, we want improved sanitation facilities . . ."

Lamont cut Pawlowski off. He was not interested in griev-ances. He had been tipped in advance about the impending demonstration and was interested only in ending it. He de-manded the prisoners' attention and started to read, from the *Manual for Courts-Martial*, UCMJ Article 94, the article con-cerned with the most heinous of military offenses—mutiny. But as he raised his voice to be heard, the demonstrators chanted louder. They demanded to see Colonel John Ford, the Presidio provost marshal; Terence Hallinan, a local attorney; and the press.

Unable to get the group's attention, Lamont walked to a loudspeaker in an MP patrol car parked outside the stockade and ordered the prisoners to return to Building 1213. They kept right on chanting and didn't budge. Lamont turned to the chief of the fire truck—a civilian—and requested him to hose down the demonstrators. He refused. Finally, Lamont ordered the MP's to escort the prisoners back to their cellblocks. Ac-cording to an Army fact sheet, "no force was required other than physically carrying some of the prisoners off."

According to Article 94, "any person . . . who, *with intent to usurp or override lawful military authority*, refuses, in con-cert with any other person, to obey orders or otherwise do his duty or creates any violence or disturbance, is guilty of mu-tiny." (Emphasis added.) The sentence may be death. All twenty-seven men who sat down that morning were subse-quently charged with this offense.

There followed the longest and one of the most controversial series of courts-martial in American history. Military justice being what it is, all but five—three escaped to Canada and two were found guilty of lesser crimes—were convicted of the charge and given sentences ranging from six months to sixteen years. It was not until more than a year later, when the slow process of military appeals had been completed, that the con-victions were overturned and the sentences reduced to a maxi-mum of one year, already served, for willful disobedience of a lawful order. The military appeals judge, Colonel Jacob Hago-pian, used exceptionally strong language in reversing the court-martial verdicts:

Mindful that a concerted intent to override lawful military authority is a requisite element which must be proved, the facts of this record shout its absence. The words and deeds of the [appellants] do not evince, either singularly or collectively, an intention to usurp or override military authority. Rather, the common thread of evidence throughout this entire voluminous record demonstrates an intention to implore and invoke the very military authority which they are charged with seeking to override.

The demonstrators had, in the end, been vindicated—but only at the cost of enormous personal suffering.

III

NESTLED PLACIDLY amidst the rivers and blue stem grass of the gently rolling Kansas prairie is a large and history-laden Army outpost, Fort Riley. It was here that General George Armstrong Custer organized his campaigns against the Indians. It was here, too, that the United States Cavalry made its home when it was riding on horses—not, as it does today, in helicopters.

With its unspoiled natural setting and elegant limestone buildings, Fort Riley has always been one of the Army's showpieces. Recently it has become a showpiece for another reason: to combat the soaring rate of absenteeism that was overloading stockades throughout the country, the Army established at Fort Riley in 1968 an experimental Correctional Training Facility (CTF) that has attracted the scrutiny of scores of visiting generals, colonels, and penologists.

The Army is not shy about CTF. It describes its efforts there as representing "a bold new concept" in military corrections. CTF's mission is "to return to duty former military offenders as competent, well-motivated soldiers." This is presumably the mission of all military stockades, but the Army knows it doesn't work elsewhere and is determined to make it work at CTF. "No longer does corrections merely mean confinement," says the facility's commander, Colonel George F. Proudfoot. "At CTF trainees are exposed to a retraining and remotivational program that will enable them to solve some of the problems which led to their original offense."

There is no question that, as stockades go, CTF is better than anything else the Army has to offer (with the exception of Leavenworth, which is reserved for long-term prisoners). Physically, it is spacious and not overcrowded. Personnel are picked with care and given extensive orientation. Far from being shorthanded, CTF bulges with an abundance of colonels, majors, captains, and veteran NCO's, as well as military lawyers, chaplains, psychiatrists, and counseling specialists.

Each week about two hundred prisoners are brought to CTF by planes and buses from stockades around the country. Almost all are chronic AWOL's, although there is a sprinkling of conscientious objectors and soldiers convicted of such minor infractions as talking back to an officer or refusing to get out of bed when ordered. Two-thirds of the prisoners originally volunteered for the Army. About forty percent come from broken homes, and twenty percent are Project 100,000 men. A roughly equal number are Vietnam veterans.

Right away, the new arrivals get the message that things are going to be different at CTF. Their handcuffs are removed. They are told that they are now "trainees," not prisoners, although CTF is surrounded by watchtowers and a barbed-wire fence. They are informed that the "privilege" of saluting officers—denied in regular stockades—is theirs again to enjoy.

And the atmosphere at CTF is in fact different. Inmates are not hassled about haircuts. They are permitted to keep soap, fingernail clippers, candy bars, photographs, and other personal belongings that are contraband in most stockades. During free time they are allowed to play table tennis, cards, or parlor games. Though visitor and mail regulations are as strict as in other stockades, CTF trainees may, with an officer's approval, make telephone calls to their wives and families.

More importantly, the Army goes out of its way to convince CTF trainees that it *cares*. Officers are friendly; they are willing to sit and talk informally about trainees' problems. Trainees may even yell at officers without getting punished or reprimanded. Lawyers, chaplains, psychiatrists, and counselors interview each prisoner individually and remain continually available for consultation. An Alcoholics Anonymous program is available for prisoners with drinking problems. All-day religious retreats are offered for those who wish to attend. "We were stunned," says a graduate of CTF. "Everyone was absolutely wonderful and nice. They answered all our questions. It was so weird we started wondering, what's going on here?"

What goes on, of course, is an all-out attempt by the Army to motivate its imprisoned misfits to be obedient and honorable soldiers. CTF tries to do this not through harassment and brusque indifference, as at boot camp, or through malevolent neglect, as at other stockades, but through a combination of attention to personal problems, rigorous training, and subtle psychological conditioning.

The key element is psychological conditioning. This takes many forms. At the simplest level, trainees are bombarded from the moment they arrive with the slogan of CTF: "Duty bound." The words are plastered on the outsides of buildings, on the walls inside, even on the backboards of a basketball court.

A bit more sophisticated are the classroom lectures, motivational movies, and discussions. As in basic training, the men are taught about American history and Army traditions. They receive "character guidance" from the chaplain. And repeatedly, from all sides, they are reminded of the benefits accruing from an honorable discharge, as well as the allegedly dire consequences of receiving a less than honorable discharge.

In group discussion sessions, for example, the social worker takes a low-pressure approach. Sure, the Army's messed you over, he concedes, but look at the alternatives: prison, a bad discharge, a lifelong stigma. He encourages trainees to talk about their personal problems. He may grant that the problems are serious ones, but they are never, he insists, justification for going AWOL. However difficult it may be to adjust to the Army, it is always better to stick around.

This theme is driven home again in a series of meetings with civilian ex-convicts who work at Fort Riley under contract with the Army. The ex-cons are extremely effective. They talk

with the soldiers in their own barracks language, and the trainees identify with them, first of all, because they aren't officers,
and secondly because they've been "through it"—they've got
credentials.

The ex-cons explain to the trainees in down-to-earth terms
that there's something wrong with *them*, not with the Army.
The way to succeed in life, they say, is to go along with the
system. Unless you do, you are going to be a failure.

At one session that a reporter sat in on, the trainees were full
of complaints about the Army. "Man, I goofed," said one. "I
signed up when I was 18 years old. I had no idea that I was
going to be fucked so bad. Now I changed my mind."

"You *can't* change your mind," snapped the ex-con.

The conversation drifted to the subject of "doing time." "It
can take five years to do two if you don't do it right," argued
the ex-con. "It just takes a telephone call from here to put you
in Leavenworth."

At another session, the discussion turned to the problem of
finding a wife if you have a "messed-up" discharge. Various
prisoners contended that when a man and a girl are in love, it
doesn't matter what kind of discharge he's got. The ex-con responded bluntly: "When her stomach is hungry and she needs
shoes on her feet, love goes out the window."

The one type of prisoner who might be able to challenge the
CTF line is the articulate political objector. In the objector's
mind, the real problem lies not with the soldier who doesn't
want to fight but with the Army which seeks to make him fight
in an immoral war. Prisoners who hold such views, however,
usually don't get to express them at CTF. Often they are assigned to details that take them away from the group discussions. Or, as Private James Gordon III found out, they are none
too subtly pressured into silence. Gordon had asked an embar-
rassing question in a citizenship class. After the class, the prisoners were denied their customary smoking break, and as they
entered the next class, a captain told Gordon that this deprivation was his fault. To emphasize his dislike for impertinent
comments, the captain made Gordon spend the next period ly-
ing on his back with his arms and legs held straight in the air.

Though most of its motivational efforts are soft-sell, CTF does not let the prisoners forget what can happen if they don't go along. Near the center of the compound is a two-story building surrounded by coiled concertina wire, and known as the "gray palace." This is a kind of mini-stockade within the larger stockade, and prisoners learn that the gray palace contains segregation cells for recalcitrants who don't cooperate. And just to drive the point home, CTF trainees are taken during their final week for a tour of the nearby Fort Leavenworth Disciplinary Barracks. "It really makes an impact," says a high-ranking officer.

After nine weeks of motivational sessions and an intensive training program that is equivalent to basic training, CTF inmates "graduate" in an elaborate ceremony. They are then released from the facility with their sentences remitted and ordered to report to a regular duty station.

Of those who start the program, about fourteen percent fail to complete it. Of those who do complete it, according to a follow-up study in early 1970, approximately seventy percent report to their next duty station as ordered; the other thirty percent go AWOL again straight out of CTF. Of those who report to their duty assignment, a smaller percentage soon go AWOL or are eventually given bad discharges. Adding together those who don't complete the program, those who go AWOL at the end of the program, and those who go AWOL shortly thereafter, one emerges with a final "salvage" rate of approximately fifty-four percent. Most of those who do go AWOL again are returned to other stockades, and some of them wind up, as they were warned, in the bowels of Leavenworth.

One reason why nearly half of those who pass through CTF never make it as soldiers is that they are firmly and unshakably determined not to. "Most of these guys," says a candid CTF sergeant, "are just waiting till they get out of here so they can split again. Man, they don't want to be in the Army."

Another reason is that, though CTF itself may be a newly planted oasis of lovingkindness, the Army is still the Army. One CTF graduate who was motivated to give the Army a second chance soon sent this shakily handwritten letter to Colonel Proudfoot:

I am AWOL at this time. I am very sorry, but I have, I think, a perfect reason for going.

The day I arrived at my new duty station was the start of an ugly experience. I reported to the CQ [Charge-of-Quarters] of E-2-5 and as I was telling him that I was from CTF the First Sergeant walked in, and I quote the First Sergeant in saying, 'Oh hell, another one of them SOBs.' Well right then and there I felt I was in trouble. . . .

After getting settled, I went back to the orderly room to speak with the First Sergeant about getting a pass. I told the First Sergeant that I needed the pass badly, because of being in confinement for almost five months.

The First Sergeant said . . . that there is no way of getting a pass. I asked him if I could see the CO [Commanding Officer] about getting one, but he said the CO was at a meeting and wouldn't be free that night.

I left then and I was depressed. . . . The first thing that ran through my mind was that I would have to take my own pass, and I did. I was gone for three days and then I reported back to the company.

Well, sir, this is where it really starts. I reported to the First Sergeant and sir, as God is my witness, I am going to try to quote what the First Sergeant said to me. He said, 'So, the *scum* is back! You know what I should do to you? I should beat your ass all around this post. You might as well go AWOL again because I'm going to be on your ass from here on in. You are the rottenest thing that ever came in this company. . . .'

The First Sergeant and the CO were talking about AWOLs after that. But during their talk, the First Sergeant stopped to say, 'Sir, for an example, this man here, and I call him a man only because he's wearing that uniform. He has no guts, probably because his parents raised him wrong. If so, his parents are no good, just like himself. . . .'

Sir, I felt like hitting him or even worse. I never felt so low. Especially when the CO said, 'Yes, Sergeant, it's just *bad luck* when we get people like that.'

Well, sir, I decided I just couldn't stay there, because I would

have done something that would send me back behind bars. Sir,
I don't want to see the stockade or any jail again. I wanted to go
back to duty to stay, but not to be treated like a dog! . . .

Sir, I hope and wish you can help me. I need help real bad. . . .

IV

WHEN ANGRY young men are denied their freedom for extended periods of time, rebellion is almost to be expected.
When, in addition, they are crammed together in overcrowded
and psychologically dehumanizing conditions, rebellion is almost inevitable.

Rebellion can take many forms. At the Presidio stockade, it
was peaceful and constructively oriented. It was peaceful, too,
at the Fort Ord stockade, where, in May 1969, some 150 prisoners staged a "mill-in" around the perimeter of the yard. For half
an hour after the morning line-up they chanted, "Amen, amen,"
until they were ordered individually back to their cellblocks.
At lunchtime, nearly four hundred prisoners refused to eat.
They were protesting the refusal of Fort Ord authorities to let
them talk privately with a team of penologists investigating
conditions in the stockade. Wisely, no charges were brought.

Occasionally, rebellions in military prisons become violent.
In the summer of 1968, prisoners in the Marine Corps brig at
Da Nang, South Vietnam, went on a rampage, burning down
several cellblocks. Two weeks later, at the Army's Long Binh
stockade, several hundred prisoners—most of them black—
swarmed out of their tents, wrecked a mess hall, destroyed an
administrative building, and burned the prison records. When
the stockade commander went in to try to quiet the inmates,
he was severely beaten, almost to death. Guards had to form a
wedge to rescue him. Finally a company of flak-jacketed MP's
arrived and subdued the rioters with tear gas and drawn bayonets. Before the fighting ended, fifty-nine prisoners had been
injured and one killed.

In June 1969, some 150 prisoners at the Fort Dix stockade
burned mattresses, threw footlockers down the stairs, wrecked

furniture, and smashed windows. Other stockade riots erupted at Fort Bragg, Fort Riley (the regular post stockade, not CTF), Fort Carson, and Fort Hood.

At the Camp Pendleton brig, where a kind of law of the jungle reigns between prisoners and guards and among prisoners themselves, there have been five major riots and a couple of near-riots since late 1968. The place is, as the Treasure Island brig commander noted, not exactly a hotel.

The brig sprawls across a barren, slightly sloping hill, surrounded by concertina wire and eight spider-legged watchtowers. Most of the inmates are housed in long tin-roofed huts with chicken wire sides. In the evenings, canvas flaps are dropped to keep out some of the cold ocean air. Toilets and showers are outside the huts, and there aren't nearly enough of them.

Though the Marine Corps has recently taken steps to reduce the overcrowding, there were in 1969 as many as 920 persons confined within the brig at a single time, producing a population density of less than 25 square feet per prisoner. In some huts there were barely 30 inches between double bunks. When a reporter for the Oceanside *Blade-Tribune* toured the brig that September, he was furtively handed a note by a prisoner which said, "This place isn't fit for animals, much less humans. . . . I'll probably get thrown into seg for doing this."

Toward the top of the hill is a windowless concrete building, the most solid structure in the compound. This is the "seg" building, or Maximum Security Unit (MSU), where disobedient prisoners are sent. Inside are forty-eight tiny cells with steel doors and chain fence ceilings through which guards can look in at the prisoners and, when the mood strikes, splash them with water. "There's nothing to do inside MSU," says former Private Bernard Jillson, who was a frequent resident of the building, "so you try to scrounge cigarette butts together, roll them in pages from the Bible, and stare at the walls. Every once in a while, some guy gets a match, lights a cigarette, and throws it from one cell to the next through the screen fence roof. People sneak in hypes [hypodermic needles]. They shoot up drugs, cough syrup, Kool Aid, anything they can steal."

Guards at the brig are usually freshly returned from Vietnam; many of them harass prisoners with abusive language and occasional "thumpings." One prisoner refused to shower; guards took a heavily bristled street brush and brushed him with laundry detergent, causing his back to bleed. Another prisoner in segregation who guards thought was yelling too loud was taped across the mouth, eyes, and face, leaving only a small hole at the nose for breathing. A frequent practice is to order inmates into the "prisoner's down" position—stomach flat on the ground, hands behind back, legs spread in a V—and then to kick them or step on them.

Prisoners, in turn, give the guards as hard a time as possible. If guards order them into formation, they often linger in their huts. If ordered to disperse, they often stick together. On occasion, they riot.

On Saturday night, December 7, 1968, brig officials canceled a movie that prisoners had been looking forward to. In response, a sizable group of inmates tore the place apart.

A month later, on January 6, 1969, inmates rioted because they had been denied their weekend recreation period. About a dozen guards and twenty-five prisoners were injured.

On April 19, 1969, there was a near-riot when a guard was spotted literally crucifying a prisoner on one of the chain link fences. The guard had made him stand on a chair, then had handcuffed his spread-eagled arms to the fence and kicked the chair out from under his legs. Angry fellow prisoners saw what was happening and converged on the scene. Had the man not been immediately taken down from the fence, a bloody clash would have quickly ensued.

On June 22, 1969, a violent racial brawl broke out in the brig. During the afternoon, a black prisoner had been hit by a rock believed to have been thrown by a white prisoner. Several dozen blacks got together and decided to retaliate that night. After the evening count, they stormed out of their huts brandishing broomsticks, bedposts, and knives from the mess hall, attacking white prisoners and guards. Yellow-helmeted MP's were called to put down the melee. One guard was badly beaten, and twenty-one prisoners required medical attention.

This incident was a blow to the many black and white prisoners who recognized that their differences were far less important than their shared deprivations. During the summer months that followed, there was constant discussion among prisoners about the racial situation. "We went around to each hut, rapping that we shouldn't get into another race riot, that we should channel our anger against the conditions," recalls Private John Perkins, a militant black Marine who was in the brig at the time. " 'The next time you motherfuckers riot,' I said, 'just tear this place down and let them build it up again.' "

That, in fact, was almost what happened on September 14, 1969. An article had appeared in *The Nation* the previous week, exposing inhumane conditions in the brig, and Major General Donn J. Robertson, commander of Camp Pendleton, had held a press conference to refute the charges. Robertson had then taken reporters on a guided tour of the brig, but denied them permission to speak with inmates. The prisoners, who had seen the reporters walk through, wanted to show that the magazine article was right and could think of no better way of doing so than by—as the expression has it—"going down."

At 7:30 on the evening of September 14, several hours after the reporters had left, about 150 prisoners from Bravo Company surrounded a supply hut occupied by four guards. The guards, frightened, barricaded themselves inside; the prisoners promptly set fire to the hut. Somehow, the guards managed to escape.

The MP riot squad arrived with nightsticks and CS gas. As prisoners pelted them with rocks, the MP's fired their CS canisters and forced the rioters back into their huts. Some members of Bravo Company, however, climbed the fence into Charlie Company's area and succeeded in spreading the word. No sooner had the MP's finished forcing the Bravo Company men back into their huts than Charlie Company "went down," ripping out telephone wires, smashing furniture, throwing buckets, shoes, lockers, bunks, and all other available objects out the windows. The response, again, was tear gas.

For a few moments the brig remained quiet under a billowing gray cloud of smoke. Then Alpha Company got into the act, turning over bunks and throwing furniture out the windows. Fire trucks were called but weren't used. By the end of the evening, the entire brig was a shambles. One guard was hospitalized for injuries caused by a thrown rock; several other guards and inmates suffered bruises or minor fractures, and four or five were overcome by gas.

For several months thereafter, the brig stayed relatively calm. Some new huts were built, easing the overcrowded situation. The old brig commander was removed and a more experienced commander installed. Guards were given a little extra training. But on August 26, 1970, just as Pendleton officials thought they were getting things under control, a four-hour fist-swinging melee broke out. The Marine Corps officially termed it a "race riot."

V

THE COURT SENTENCES AND WE REHABILITATE, proclaims the sign at the entrance to the Fort Bliss stockade, and the Army manual on corrections echoes this credo: "The correctional facility is responsible for furnishing an atmosphere conducive to change. It is paramount that when discharged from the facility a prisoner leave with less hostility than when he arrived." Yet the fact is that, with the possible exception of CTF and Leavenworth, there isn't a single military prison that "rehabilitates" in any sense of the word. And, rather than departing with diminished hostility, prisoners are far more likely to emerge hardened and embittered against the entire military system, and often against even the most legitimate institutions of their country.

There are two basic reasons why military prisons cannot rationally be expected to rehabilitate: first, the stockade population is such that few of its members can be rehabilitated (that is, in the military sense) even under the best of circumstances; and second, the nature of the stockades themselves is such that almost nothing constructive can occur in them.

Who are the people inside of the stockades? In the wake of the furor set off by the Presidio mutiny trials, the Army appointed a six-man committee of prominent civilian penologists to study the Army penal system.[1] The group examined the characteristics of the stockade population and emerged with some interesting findings.

First, the committee found, Army prisoners are almost uniformly young. The average age of stockade prisoners is 19—slightly below the over-all average age of Army enlisted men, which is 20. The one-year difference is not as important as the fact that in any large sampling of men in their late teens and early twenties, there will inevitably be a significant number who are socially immature, emotionally disturbed, or otherwise unable to adjust to Army life.

Second, the committee found that, although a majority of Army enlisted men are draftees, nearly two-thirds of stockade prisoners are volunteers. "Contrary to the general belief that most of the stockade prisoners whose offense was AWOL were draftees who had little enthusiasm for military service or were completely opposed to serving, sixty-four percent of all stockade prisoners came into the Army by enlistment. Not all of them did so willingly, however. Some were jobless and in other ways a burden on their families, who finally forced them into enlisting to get rid of them. Others were in trouble with the law, perhaps as juvenile delinquents, and were warned by judges that they had better enlist or suffer the consequences."

Third, the committee found that many stockade inmates

1. The committee members were: Austin H. MacCormick, director of the Osborne Association, a national nonprofit organization for correctional improvement; James V. Bennett, former director of the Federal Bureau of Prisons; Sanger B. Powers, administrator of the Wisconsin Division of Corrections; Richard A. McGee, former administrator of the California State Youth and Adult Correctional Agency; Lawrence W. Pierce, former deputy commissioner of the New York City police department; and Dr. E. Preston Sharp, general secretary of the American Correctional Association.

were "clearly not fitted for military duty. Many of them were in the stockades' disciplinary segregation cells. They were in trouble because of emotional instability that made it difficult for them to stand the tensions of military life in general, and confinement in particular." These unfit prisoners included draftees as well as volunteers: "The committee is well aware of the fact that some local boards, having trouble filling their quotas, draft youths with physical and mental inadequacies, and sometimes with severe personality and character defects that doom them to almost certain failure in the Army."

Fourth, the committee found that the overwhelming majority of military prisoners—between eighty and ninety percent —are confined for the offense of AWOL. "Only 5.1 percent were charged with or convicted of what could be classified as crimes in civilian practice: murder, rape or attempted rape, robbery, assault, sodomy, burglary, larceny, etc." Most incarcerated AWOL's are "young and often immature" soldiers who want "to go back home some day with an honorable discharge," but go AWOL out of "boredom, fatigue, home-sickness, desire to see a girl friend back home, anxiety over a young wife, worry over ill or destitute parents . . . trouble with paychecks and allotments, debts for purchases [they] could not afford, and the very common inability to handle two problems with which [they] had little experience before coming into the Army—women and liquor."

Fifth, the committee noted the presence in Army stockades of a sizable number of Vietnam veterans. These are soldiers who complete their tour of duty in Vietnam with good if not perfect records, but find it "difficult to adjust to the wholly different military procedures and activities of posts in the United States."

The other type of prisoner found in stockades is the soldier who is strongly opposed to the Vietnam War. "They are frequently seen in disciplinary segregation because they are contemptuous of rules and regulations, and often deliberately commit such offenses as insubordination. They are often seen also in administrative segregation, being under observation for suicidal gestures or hunger strikes [and] as former drug users.

. . . Many of the anti-war, anti-Army prisoners are determined dissidents in their thinking and actions. They are clever at leading less sophisticated prisoners and devising methods of harassing stockade personnel, the post commanders, and personnel as high up in the Army establishment as they can project their nuisance value. Some of the dissidents claim to be conscientious objectors."

Two other significant points about stockade prisoners stand out. First, a very high percentage of inmates are repeaters: young men who have gone AWOL not once or twice, but over and over again. And second, at any given time a strikingly high proportion of stockade prisoners—fifty-eight percent, on the average—have not as yet been legally convicted of any offense, but are being held in pre-trial confinement.

From these observations about the Army's prison population —they hold more or less equally well for the other three services—several conclusions emerge. First, the great preponderance of military prisoners are not hardened criminals who, if let out on the streets, would stir up a wave of muggings, holdups and rapes. Whatever their shortcomings, they are not a threat to the lives or property of the civilian population. Some, to be sure, are adolescents who have shown delinquent tendencies in the past, but most want nothing more than to find jobs, care for their families, and live out their lives as responsible adult citizens.

Second, it is unjust, and of little benefit to either the army or the individual, to hold behind bars young people whose only real crime is an obvious unfitness for the military. The injustice of such confinement is heightened by the fact that millions of young men who have not volunteered and have not been drafted (often because they are unfit) are free of all military obligation. Unfit prisoners should be cleared out of stockades and discharged from the military as soon as they are identified.

Third, it seems obvious that stockade prisoners are, for the most part, inherently unsusceptible to army-style rehabilitation. When a young man runs AWOL time and again in spite of all the known punishments for doing so, it seems fairly evident that there is a basic incompatibility between his value system and the military way of doing things.

Moreover, the Vietnam War objectors—who are political prisoners in the truest sense—will never be won over by incarceration. The desire of many of them to make life as hard as possible for military authorities is quite understandable, considering what military authorities have done to them. If the rules for conscientious objection were more sensible, most of these men, instead of being "nuisances" to the military, might be making some useful contribution to society.

As for those who have already served in Indochina, these are men who have already more than fulfilled any demands their government has a right to make of them. It is difficult to see any value or justification for denying them their freedom.

If the nature of the prisoner population bodes ill for the prospects of rehabilitation, the nature of the stockades themselves makes rehabilitation virtually impossible.

Stockades are, without exception, physically depressing places. They are staffed by young and inexperienced guards, often recently returned from combat in Indochina, where—to use the phrase of Dr. Albert Kastl, a former psychologist with the Army in Vietnam—they have passed through the "killing barrier" and can accept inhuman and violent treatment of people who break rules.

A few stockades do offer some useful educational programs through which a limited number of prisoners are able to study for their high school equivalency certificates. But for the most part, when prisoners aren't mowing lawns, marching, exercising, or rioting, they are usually sitting around trying to figure out how to get away from or get back at their captors. Often, confinement simply leads to more confinement, as bored and angry inmates get into fights or talk back to guards or disobey orders or try to escape, thereby accumulating additional time behind barbed wire.

With their freedom denied and their basic human rights virtually obliterated, it is difficult to see how anything but hostile attitudes can flourish in prisoners' minds. Dr. Karl Menninger's grim assessment of the effects of civilian imprisonment is even more applicable to the military. "I suspect," Menninger wrote in his book *The Crime of Punishment*, "that all the crimes committed by all the jailed criminals do not equal in total social damage that of the crimes committed against them." In the case of prisoners in military stockades, many of the crimes committed against them might well be described as "cruel and unusual punishment."

Compounding the crimes committed against military prisoners is the fact, cited above, that at any given time nearly sixty percent of them have not even been tried. Most of these, in due course, *will* be tried and convicted, given the batting average of military courts; but in the meantime, they are subjected to the same deprivations, the same inhumanities, as convicted prisoners—and it does not count as time served either on their subsequent sentences or toward their total military obligation.

Moreover, it doesn't take much to get a soldier confined. There are no arraignments, no determinations of probable cause, no right to bail. All that is necessary is that a commanding officer suspect a man of guilt and desire to have him locked up. The weeks and months then served by untried prisoners are, in every sense, dead time.

There are two military prisons where treatment is a little better than usual: the Disciplinary Barracks at Fort Leavenworth and the Correctional Training Facility at Fort Riley. As prisons go, Leavenworth is not that bad. It suffers from the customary vices of all custodial institutions, but its work program is the best in the military. For the purposes of confining and perhaps to some extent rehabilitating genuine criminals—murderers, thieves, rapists, and the like—Leavenworth is probably on a par with the better civilian institutions.

CTF is another kettle of fish. It is the Army's answer to the assertion that chronic AWOL's cannot be "salvaged." Through a kind of force-fed repetition of basic training, sugar-coated with personalized attention, CTF is able to persuade about half of its trainees to go back to duty instead of running away again.

CTF undoubtedly represents a significant step forward in Army correction. But it must be recognized that what it does can only in a very restricted sense be called "rehabilitation." The premise of the CTF program is that it is the prisoner who is at fault because he cannot adjust to the Army; the possibility that there might be something wrong with the Army, or that a young man may be justified in seeking to quit a job when it strongly disagrees with him, is not considered.

Despite its oft-repeated claim that it is helping trainees to define their problems and solve them, CTF is in fact primarily concerned with contributing to the Army's manpower pool rather than with aiding the individual. It seeks to "salvage" young men as soldiers, not as husbands, fathers, or skilled workers. There can, of course, be some overlap; and to the extent that continued military service may be beneficial to a "criminal" offender, CTF may be said to perform a legitimate rehabilitative function. But when continued military duty only augments a misfit's anguish and suffering, CTF is not rehabilitative at all. In such cases, forced training is as wrong as simple confinement.

All this said, it is necessary to consider one final question. What if the real purpose of military prisons is not, as the regulations say, rehabilitation? What if their real function is to create terror—to show men what will happen to them if they don't play their roles as pawns? If such is the case, and the evidence indicates that it is, then the problem of stockades must be considered from a different perspective.

If military prisons are basically intended to scare non-prisoners into line, then they must, of necessity, have a bad reputation. To have a bad reputation, they must deserve it. They must be unpleasant, dehumanizing, and more undesirable, when coupled with the dishonor associated with being judged a criminal, than combat in far-off places. The weaker the affirmative sources of troop motivation—patriotism, belief in a cause—the greater the need for a frightful answer to the GI's inner query, "What happens if I don't go along?"

Most people would agree that, distasteful as obedience-through-fear-of-punishment can be, it is on occasion both necessary and legitimate. World War II, for example, was a war which the nation almost universally supported and which, unlike some other wars that America has been involved in, *had* to be won. There were, consequently, defensible reasons for making the threat of punishment for nonperforming soldiers credible. And credible it was. Not only were military prisons primitive and overcrowded, as many of them still are today; sentences were exceedingly severe. The median sentence for wartime AWOL was 3.4 years; for desertion, it was five years (though after the war was over, most prisoners were granted clemency). Forty-nine soldiers were sentenced to death for desertion, and one—Private Eddie Slovik—was actually executed.

There are times, however, when imprisonment as a means of motivating soldiers is not only distasteful, but of questionable legitimacy as well. When there is no attack on the nation or threat of attack, when there is no attack against a close democratic ally, and when there is no declaration of war, how do you justify imprisoning a horde of emotionally confused adolescents for the sake of scaring others into combat? How do you justify incarcerating citizens because of their political or moral beliefs? When the means are inherently repugnant, one must examine the ends. When the end is of dubious legitimacy, it becomes impossible to justify the means.

Granting that the imprisonment of military offenders for the purpose of frightening others into combat is *sometimes* justifiable, the operative question is how to distinguish between right times and wrong. This is not as difficult a problem as it might seem. A standard principle of law is that punishment for a crime must be in proportion to the seriousness of the crime, and that the seriousness of a crime is measured in the context of the time and circumstances in which it occurs. Military law recognizes this principle too. Under the Uniform Code of Military Justice, certain crimes—notably desertion and willful disobedience of a superior commissioned officer—may be punished by death during war, but not during peace. Further, the Code provides that war must have been officially declared by Congress before a death sentence can be imposed.

What is needed in addition to this differentiation in the application of the death penalty is a similar distinction with regard to imprisonment. At a time, as at present, of non-defensive, undeclared war, to flee from military service is not such a serious or socially dangerous crime that the nation's survival requires it to be punished by incarceration. By changing the law to reflect the distinction between declared, defensive war and its absence, the near-insoluble problem of running a humane, rehabilitative military confinement system could be swiftly overcome: almost all of the prisoners, except for the few who were genuine criminals, would be let out.

PART V

THE VETERAN LEGIONS OF ROME WERE AN OVERMATCH
FOR THE UNDISCIPLINED VALOR OF ALL OTHER NATIONS,
AND RENDERED HER MISTRESS OF THE WORLD.
NOT THE LESS TRUE IS IT, THAT THE LIBERTIES OF
ROME PROVED THE FINAL VICTIM TO HER MILITARY TRIUMPHS;
AND THAT THE LIBERTIES OF EUROPE, SO FAR AS THEY HAVE
EVER EXISTED, HAVE, WITH FEW EXCEPTIONS,
BEEN THE PRICE OF HER MILITARY ESTABLISHMENTS.

—James Madison

10. TOWARD A DEMOCRATIC ARMY

AFTER EACH major war that America has fought, the nation has agonized over its military system. Men newly returned to civilian life grumbled about army regimentation, about officer privilege and court-martial injustice. Military leaders, in turn, interpreted each war as a lesson that the nation ought to be better prepared for the next one.

The post-Vietnam agony will, for many reasons, be more intense than those of the past. Popular dissatisfaction with the military after World Wars I and II was mitigated by the general feeling that the wars had been worth fighting and that something had been won; no such consciousness prevails today. The unpleasant memories of earlier returning warriors were salved by showerings of national and international gratitude; the Vietnam veteran returns to his community as quietly as he was spirited away. He is not a hero, just a kid who got caught up in the system. There are no airport welcomes, no parades, not even, as one GI lamented, girls eager to sleep with him. The sense of helplessness, of being "taken" by "them" and made to do unnatural things, as Paul Meadlo's mother remarked, is greater than ever before.

The nature of the debate over America's military system will also be different this time. There will be concern, as in the past, with seeking an accommodation between an autocratic military institution and a democratic society. But there will be an important new element to consider. World Wars I and II were old-fashioned conflicts in the sense that Congress declared them and then created an army to fight them. Korea and Vietnam were different, raising new questions of constitutionality, popular control, and protection of citizens' rights—questions which were not fully pondered after Korea but which have acquired great urgency now.

Americans in the 1970's have become painfully aware, not merely that military service is distasteful, which comes as no surprise, but of how well-founded was the Founding Fathers' admonition that large standing armies are a menace to liberty. For Americans are today confronted with an enormous problem of control—the problem of how to make the military the people's instrument instead of watching helplessly as the military uses people as *its* instruments.

Re-establishing controls and safeguards will not be easy. There will be great resistance to change. It will be repeated *ad nauseam* that civilians are incompetent to advise professional soldiers on how to run an army. The patriotism of those who work for change will be impugned. The Armed Services committees of the House and Senate, so attentive to the care and feeding of generals, will most likely be quite unreceptive to the idea of protecting average citizens. But there should be no question that changes can be made if the nation sets its mind to do so. The Armed Services committees can, if necessary, be by-passed. Floor amendments to military legislation can be the avenue to statutory reform. Many changes can be made by the military itself under pressure from GI's and the public.

There is even some reason for optimism. Not only are attitudes toward the military shifting within America as a result of Vietnam; the international situation itself is in flux, offering an opportunity to re-evaluate America's role in the world and hence the size and shape of its military establishment.

Inspiration can be drawn, moreover, from West Germany, a nation which not only sits at the very edge of the Soviet empire but which is heir to a far more militaristic tradition than is America. At America's urging, West Germany began rearming in 1955; but the United States and Bonn's new leaders agreed that the Bundeswehr would be a democratic army, designed in such a way that it could not get out of control, that soldiers' rights would be protected, and that there would be no resurgence of militarism to bring Germany and the world to ruin once again.

To protect the civil liberties of soldiers and to assist in maintaining parliamentary control of the military, a special office was created, that of Military Commissioner of the Bundestag, similar to the Swedish military ombudsman. The Military Commissioner is elected by the legislature, and functions independently of the defense ministry and of the military itself. German law provides him with far-reaching authority. He may respond directly to complaints of soldiers or intervene on his own initiative when information reaches him that soldiers' rights have been violated. He may inspect military installations without warning, examine official documents, and request that reports be made to him. His powers are well-respected within the Bundeswehr. "Once," recalls a German private quoted in *Newsweek*, "we found the noncoms had scattered our gear all over the barracks to teach us not to be sloppy. When we threatened to take it to the commissioner, half the officers in the camp came to convince us that it wouldn't happen again."

The rights of German soldiers were spelled out in the Soldier's Law of 1956, a law grounded on the principle that soldiers are not a special caste but rather civilians in uniform, possessing almost all the rights of non-uniformed citizens, including the right to run for elective office and to join a soldiers' labor union. "There is no longer any difference between 'soldier' and 'citizen,' " declares the Soldier's Law. "Both stand side by side as 'fellow citizens.' The soldier enjoys the rights of man that the Basic Law [Bonn's constitution] declares unchangeable." Perhaps most significantly, the basic law guarantees the right to conscientious objection on nonreligious grounds.

During training, the new German army places heavy emphasis on *innere Führing*—"inner guidance." Recruits are informed that blind obedience is not a sacred virtue; they are reminded of the Nuremberg principle that individual soldiers are ultimately responsible for their acts; they are taught that the German officers who plotted to assassinate Hitler were the true military heroes of World War II, and that the role of the military in contemporary Germany is purely a defensive one.

The architects of the Bundeswehr also eliminated peacetime courts-martial, created a civilian chaplains' service, abolished the goose step, and revived an institution dating from the Weimar Republic, the so-called *Vertrauensmann*, or soldiers' representative, an enlisted man elected by the members of each company to act as spokesman before the company commander. Under the Soldier's Law, a unit commander must consult the *Vertrauensmann* in all matters pertaining to discipline and complaints; he may also use the representative to obtain a sense of the enlisted men's feelings and to inform them of such things as schedules and missions. The *Vertrauensmann* serves a one-year term and cannot be removed from his position or punished by the commander.

Germany's military reforms were, to be sure, the result of a devastating defeat—something the United States has fortunately not yet suffered. But if the nation of Frederick the Great and Clausewitz could deliberately create an army respectful of soldiers' rights and internally rigged against militarism, it seems logical to assume that the nation of Madison and Jefferson can do the same.

Where to begin? A growing number of legislators believe that an important first step would be to restore Congress's now largely forfeited powers in the war-making sphere. But more, obviously, needs to be done.

Somewhat surprisingly, however, there has been a noticeable

dearth of ideas about what further steps can be taken. John Kenneth Galbraith, in a breezy booklet entitled *How to Control the Military*, recommends little more than the election of liberal-minded Congressmen and Presidents; apparently he sees the problem as soluble merely through a change in personalities rather than through institutional reform. Merlo J. Pusey, in a thoughtful work entitled *The Way We Go to War*, urges enactment of a War Powers Act reaffirming the exclusive right of Congress to send troops into combat. Colonel James A. Donovan—co-author with General David M. Shoup of the 1969 *Atlantic* article "The New American Militarism," and author of a subsequent book, *Militarism, U.S.A.*—advocates cutting military manpower levels, reducing defense appropriations, and pursuing a less aggressive American foreign policy.

All these measures are unquestionably necessary; none of them, however, deals directly with the problem of protecting citizens against the illegitimate exercise of military power. Nor do they, individually or collectively, guarantee that the military will be an instrument of legitimate national defense and not of the ambitious foreign-policy aims of the President. The only true protection, as Madison recognized nearly two centuries ago, must lie in an effective system of counterbalanced powers, and ultimately in the people themselves. If the old institutional roadblocks to illegitimate military power have crumbled, new ones must be built. And if Madison's vision of an armed citizenry rising en masse against a standing federal army is no longer practicable, then the citizenry must be enabled to protect itself with legal rights instead of guns.

There has been one very prominent proposal put forward that would go far toward protecting citizens against the military—the idea of an all-volunteer army. Support for the proposal comes from many quarters. Liberals such as Professor Galbraith and Senators McGovern and Hatfield endorse it; so do conservatives like William F. Buckley Jr. and Senator Barry Goldwater. So, too, in principle, does Richard M. Nixon, a right-of-center pragmatist, and so, unanimously, did a middle-of-the-road presidential commission headed by former Defense Secretary Thomas S. Gates, Jr.

Each faction has different reasons for supporting an end to the draft. The conservatives quite persuasively argue that conscription is a gross infringement upon individual liberty. The liberals, tormented by Vietnam, maintain with equal persuasiveness that no one should be compelled to fight in a war that is immoral, undeclared, and non-defensive. They also see an end to peacetime conscription as a way to limit the military's size, and thus its power. The pragmatists put forward a number of largely technocratic arguments for an all-volunteer army. Their underlying objective is not to control the military but to appease the restlessness of students.

One can hardly disagree with most of these goals. Questions arise, however, about whether an all-volunteer army would really limit the President's power to engage in wars such as Vietnam, whether it would really protect all citizens against military infringement of their rights, and whether it would be socially just and democratically sound.

It is argued, accurately, by many liberal advocates of an all-volunteer army that conscription in its present form gives the President a blank check on the nation's manpower, allowing him to commit American troops without regard to public or congressional support for his policies. With an all-volunteer army, they continue, the President could not embark upon a large-scale military adventure without in due course coming to Congress and requesting a draft. This would give Congress a chance to say no; it would, in effect, force the President to obtain a congressional declaration of war. This was the arrangement, it is said, that prevailed before World War II and there is no reason why we shouldn't go back to it.

These arguments carry considerable weight. Their strength is premised, however, on the assumption that an all-volunteer army would necessarily be a small one. Such an assumption is questionable. There is hardly a Congressman or military leader today who foresees under any circumstances an army of less than two million men; most talk in terms of a two-to-three million man force—one quite ample for embarking upon Vietnam-type interventions.

Moreover, most plans for an all-volunteer army envision the

retention of a stand-by draft; male citizens would still be registered and classified by local draft boards, and in times of need they could be called. Presumably, congressional authorization would be required before the President could dip into the draft pool, but even so, such an arrangement would hardly be the same as that which prevailed before World War II. By retaining the stand-by draft, Congress would implicitly have told the President, "We are ready to come to your aid when needed."

A very small all-volunteer force without a stand-by draft— in other words, a genuine return to the pre-World War II system—would be much more preferable, but given the improbability of such a solution, it is important that the public not be beguiled by similar-sounding substitutes. An all-volunteer army that is both large and readily expandable might well make it *easier* for a President to commit American troops to non-defensive combat. Such an army would be composed of soldiers who saw themselves, and were seen by others, as professionals. An essential characteristic of the professional soldier is that he does not care where or whom he fights; his concern is only with technique, with victory, and with money. And how many civilians would care, and how deeply, about Vietnam-type wars if their sons and brothers were not being conscripted to fight them?

It is also doubtful that a large, expandable all-volunteer army would protect all citizens against the injustices associated with military service. In times of peace, it is true, such a system would eliminate the ugly mechanism of coercion. But without a provision for conscientious objection to non-defensive and undeclared wars, it would not protect innocent volunteers from being used in combat situations which they found morally repugnant, nor would it protect draftees against a similar fate if the stand-by draft were suddenly activated.

Moreover, without peacetime conscription, the military would have to procure its manpower entirely through recruitment. If unemployment is high and military manpower needs are small, recruiting is a simple and relatively honest task; in the 1930's, for example, the army was literally turning people away, and there were few recruiting abuses. Under present and foreseeable conditions, however, recruitment is likely to be as unfair a procurement process as is conscription. Military advertising based on phony motivational appeals would inundate the airwaves. Without the threat of induction to spur enlistments, hard-pressed recruiters would make promises of all sorts to entice volunteers, and many young men would be accepted into the service who never should be.

There are still other reasons for questioning the desirability of an all-volunteer army—whether large or small, whether backed by a stand-by draft or not. Its advocates seem to be under the mistaken impression that because no one would be forced to enlist in the military, the rights of all citizens would thereby be protected. A more accurate analysis would indicate that it is only the rights of those young people endowed with sufficient cultural, economic, emotional, and educational advantages to resist the appeals of military recruiters that would be protected.

The magic word "all-volunteer" is often used to conjure up visions of a highly motivated force of regulars, well paid, well adjusted, and unplagued by malcontents. In the lengthy report of the Gates commission, for example, there can be found several statements such as the following: "A force made up of men freely choosing to serve should enhance the dignity and prestige of the military. Every man in uniform will be serving as a matter of choice rather than coercion." Apparently, the Gates commission did not take a very close look at the army today. If it had, it would have found thousands of volunteers as eager to "unvolunteer" as any unwilling draftee. It would have found young soldiers who had naïvely signed up, or thought they had signed up, for airplane mechanics training and then found themselves in the infantry; others who joined because a judge offered them a choice between the army and the county jail; still others who were runaways, or kids from broken homes. It would have come across Project 100,000 men with fifth-grade reading abilities who had fallen humiliatingly behind their buddies in training. It would have discovered that sixty-four percent of the AWOL's now imprisoned in military stockades are volunteers, as are about the same percentage of deserters known to be in Canada and Sweden. It would have found, in short, that the majority of Regular Army enlisted men impatiently count their days till separation and resent their loss of liberty as much as the majority of men who have been drafted—indeed, that many volunteers are more embittered than draftees because they were led to expect something other than they got.

An all-volunteer army would do nothing to protect these citizens' rights or ensure their well-being. It would not eliminate the injustices of military service so much as it would remove those injustices from the sight of those who prefer not to see and experience them—primarily the sons of the educated white middle class.

It is argued, in a somewhat elitist tone, that those young people most susceptible to being induced to join the army would have the most to gain from military service, or at least have less to lose. This is undoubtedly true; and the fact that it is true is in itself a sad commentary on American society. But is it proper that the nation should be defended by those who have been favored by it the least? Is not the burden of common defense something that all segments of society should share equally, or at least run an equal risk of sharing? How well is justice served by ending conscription but replacing it with a recruiting system that feeds on the poverty, ignorance, and gullibility of disadvantaged youngsters?

Proponents of an all volunteer army hold out the hope of creating a painless military; they ask Americans to believe that, simply by paying the price, the distastefulness of military service can be made to vanish. The Gates commission, for example, talks of upgrading financial compensation and other conditions of service so that participation in the military becomes "a rewarding opportunity, not . . . a burden." If military service could really be made a rewarding opportunity, there would be little reason to do away with the draft. And if the draft *is* suspended, more volunteers than at present will be obliged to go into combat, thus making military service even less of "a rewarding opportunity" for those who volunteer than it is now.

There is, in short, no such thing as a large painless military. The more socially just course lies not in trying to hide the pain, or transfer it, but in sharing the pain and seeking, through reform of the army, to reduce it. The surest way *not* to reform the army is to move at once to an all-volunteer force. Change within the military can come only from outside pressures and internal fermentation. Both these stimuli would dry up if the draft were eliminated.

II

WHAT, THEN, can be done?

Political wisdom and simple humanity require that America construct a competent, defense-oriented army that causes minimum damage to liberty and to individual personality. Such an army can be built if several basic principles are accepted:

1. The purpose of maintaining a military establishment is not to project the United States into the arena of world politics but to defend the freedom and security of the American people. To the extent that all citizens have an obligation to serve as soldiers, it is a defensive obligation only—not an obligation to serve as world policemen.

2. For the purpose of limiting the claims that the military can rightfully make upon citizens, a distinction must be made between defensive and non-defensive wars. To make this distinction workable, it should be established by statute that all wars are non-defensive until Congress determines otherwise. In making such a determination, Congress would also have to take significant steps to mobilize the nation; in other words, a finding of defensive war could not be merely a semantic exercise.

3. The concept of the citizen-soldier must be revived and strengthened. In the early days of the republic, the citizen-

soldier was a part-time militiaman who defended his community and fought for liberty but did not venture forth on far-flung military expeditions. The role of the modern citizen-soldier should be analogous: to fight not for money or glory but when and only when the nation's defense demands it. The great crime of the American military as presently constituted is that it justifies its authority over citizens in terms of citizen-soldier obligations, but treats and uses its soldiers as professionals.

4. The purpose of conscription is not to surrender to the President unchecked power to send American soldiers anywhere he chooses. It is to assure that the burden of filling the ranks is shared equitably by all segments of the population, to inject into the military as much civilian influence as possible, and to build an army of citizen-soldiers, not of professionals.

5. Large standing armies, whether drafted or all volunteer, are inherently aggressive; small standing armies are inherently defensive. The size of America's standing army should be determined with this in mind. It should also be recognized that the real strength of America—missiles and air power aside—lies in its geographical isolation, its control of the surrounding oceans, and its ability to mobilize its manpower and economy.

6. It is not the purpose of the army to strengthen the moral fiber of youth or rescue citizens from the unemployment rolls. These tasks are the proper concern of such civilian institutions as the family and government agencies like the Job Corps.

7. The two things that most degrade the enlisted man are his total lack of power over his own life and the constant attack by the army on his personality. The former is to some degree inevitable; the latter is not. All efforts should be made to minimize both.

8. The army has a right to expose its soldiers, in a mild way, to political and sociological ideas that may motivate them to be better fighters. However, these ideas must have a democratic bent. They should encompass the notion that obedience to authority is not a sign of manhood or lasting civic virtue, but merely a temporary military expedient. And they should include a careful explanation that, even in the military, the

duty to obey is not absolute; it is tempered by the soldier's right not to participate in non-defensive, undeclared wars, and by the Nuremberg principle that when, as at Mylai, soldiers are ordered to commit war crimes, it is their duty not to obey.

9. Along with the army's right to educate, the soldier's right to receive and freely discuss ideas other than those officially propagated must be preserved.

With these principles as guidelines, it is possible to set forth some recommendations for reform. The following proposals are not offered as flawless solutions, but in the hope that they will stimulate discussion and action.

THE DRAFT. Historically, almost every nation that has adopted permanent conscription has marched down the road toward militarism. Prussia came first; America and the Soviet Union are recent examples. In most cases—countries like Sweden and Switzerland are the exceptions—conscription served not to civilianize the military but to militarize the civilian population. It is time this process was reversed.

Where conscription has paved the way to powerful armies uncontrollable by the people, the basic reason has been the use of draftees as professionals, rather than as defensive citizen-soldiers. This anomaly can be corrected through two important reforms: the establishment of conscientious objection to non-defensive, undeclared wars as a basic political right, and the imposition of strict limits upon the power of the President to conscript.

— A fixed ceiling should be placed on the number of men that can be drafted each month, and the induction of additional men permitted only with specific congressional approval. Thus, Congress might authorize the President to draft up to ten thousand men per month. If at any time the President wanted more than this number, he would have to come to Congress, stating the reasons for his request. He might be required to do this monthly, or perhaps only quarterly. In either case, Congress would retain the power to review periodically the President's use of the draft. It would be able to say "stop" *before* the President completed a massive build-up overseas, instead of finding itself confronted with *faits accomplis*. And it would be able to express and act on popular concern about the use of American soldiers, not once every four years when the draft law was up for renewal, but every month or every three months, while it was still possible to *do* something.

— Operation of the draft should be as equitable as possible. Generally speaking, the present lottery system is adequate from the standpoint of equity, although certain occupational deferments could be eliminated and hardship deferments could be liberalized. As for college deferments, they are in a sense inequitable, but as long as college students are subject to the lottery upon graduation or departure from school, there is something to be said for infusing the army with older, better-educated soldiers.

CONSCIENTIOUS OBJECTION. Crucial to establishing effective control of the military and protection of the individual is a revised definition of conscientious objection. The right to refuse participation in non-defensive, undeclared wars should be a political right having nothing to do with a man's conception of God. It should be a right founded first of all upon the principle that when there is no compelling need for the state to impose upon a citizen's conscience, the state should not do so, and secondly upon the principle that citizens in a democracy must have at least one effective safeguard against illegitimate military power.

Obviously, such a political right would be broader in its application than the existing right of religious objectors to be excluded from combat, but it would not go nearly as far in excusing citizens from military service as would an all-volunteer army. It would apply only to those who objected to a particular war for *reasons of conscience*—not to soldiers or civilians who simply don't like the army. It would not apply in peacetime, except to absolute pacifists; it would not apply to wars in which the nation was under attack (although even during such wars, Congress might find it wise, as Britain did during World War II, to assign sincere objectors to noncombatant jobs). It would allow the army to obtain and to train soldiers for use in defense of the nation while protecting the citizen-soldier's right not to be used against his will for non-defensive purposes.

To implement the right to conscientious objection, a system of independent civilian councils should be created, similar to the British tribunals. The sole function of these councils would be to pass on the sincerity of soldiers and draft-age civilians seeking conscientious objector status. The councils would not judge the content of the applicant's ideas, but simply whether their opposition to military service or to a particular non-defensive war was deeply held. Those men found to be con-scientious objectors would be assigned to alternate forms of service deemed of value to society. This could include noncom-batant military service (though not necessarily in the medical corps) for those not objecting to it.

A slightly different proposal, suggested by Representative Jonathan Bingham of New York, is also worth considering. Bingham has introduced legislation that would grant to young male citizens three options: enlist in the military, volunteer for an equivalent form of national service, or take a chance on the draft lottery. Bingham's plan has the advantage of relieving the government of the task of judging the sincerity of young men's beliefs; the conscientious objector would demonstrate his sin-cerity by choosing civilian service, usually for a longer period than military service. The plan, however, has one important disadvantage that it shares with the all-volunteer army: it would effectively remove from the army many of those reluctant citizen-soldiers whose presence is needed to promote change and preserve civilian influence.

NATIONAL GUARD. The role of the National Guard as a strictly defensive force should be restored. In recent years, federalized

National Guard units have been sent to Korea and Southeast Asia to fight in non-defensive wars, thus violating the spirit and possibly even the letter of the Constitution. New legislation should specifically prohibit the President from sending Guard units outside the United States unless there has been a congressional declaration of defensive war.

RECRUITING. Recruiting should continue along with conscription as a source of military manpower. However, citizens should be protected against deception and fraud. Potential enlistees very often have an implicit trust in their government and in persons who wear the uniform of their government. That trust should not be abused.

— There is probably no way to prevent the armed services from using Madison Avenue advertising techniques that appeal to such deep-rooted desires as the urge to "become a man" and to get away from home. Radio and television stations which broadcast recruiting commercials, however, should be required to present a reasonable number of announcements sponsored by citizens' groups advocating alternatives to military service. Several lawsuits are currently under way to obtain the right to reply to military commercials; the lawsuits are based on the "fairness doctrine" of the Federal Communications Commission, under which, for example, broadcasters were required to present anti-smoking announcements in response to cigarette commercials.

— The monthly quota system which places so much pressure on recruiters should be abolished; it should be just as important for recruiters to find *qualified* volunteers as to obtain an arbitrary number of bodies. If voluntary enlistments are insufficient, additional qualified men can be drafted.

— In judging whether potential volunteers are qualified, recruiters should examine not only aptitude test scores but other factors such as emotional stability and family problems. If there is a good chance the prospective enlistee will

not adjust to military life, the recruiter should be expected to warn him of the dangers. Military service is not a great boon for everyone; recruiters should not pretend that it is.
— Recruiters should explain the true probabilities of receiving specific assignments, and should be required to put all promises in writing. The government ought to publish monthly a statistical analysis of the number of volunteers assigned to different military occupational specialties, and these figures should be shown to each prospective volunteer.
— The only truly effective way to insure against deceptive recruiting practices is to provide an escape hatch for deceived volunteers. Thus, an enlistee should be given the right to change his mind—perhaps up until the second week of basic training. If he discovers that the army is not what he has been led to believe it was, he can opt out before too much money has been invested in his training. If he decides to stay, he will do so in the knowledge that the responsibility for this decision is fully his. Those who opt out would remain liable to the draft. (Britain has a comparable scheme under which a young man may try out the army for up to four days before making a definite commitment to stay on.)
— The law prohibiting fraudulent enlistment, which now applies only to enlistees, should be extended to cover recruiters as well. Recruiters found to have made false or misleading promises should be demoted, fined, or otherwise punished by the army. In addition, they should be made liable to damage suits in civilian courts by defrauded volunteers.
— The above policy changes ought to be established by Congress through a new "truth-in-recruiting" law.

TRAINING. It is the function of military training to develop the physical and technical capabilities required for the job of soldiering; it is not its function to restructure a young man's personality or turn him into a robot.

— The identification of manliness with obedience, and with the willingness to kill, should cease.

— Trainees should be taught the Nuremberg principle—that
it is the soldier's responsibility and duty to disobey illegal
orders, such as orders to kill defenseless civilians or prisoners.

— Physical brutality, hazing, and other forms of abuse should
be eliminated from Marine Corps boot camp and wherever
they appear in the other services. Existing rules against
abuse of recruits should be enforced; drill instructors who
violate these rules should be severely punished. Since courts-
martial are inherently partial to drill instructors and tend to
give light sentences when they convict at all, recruits should
be enabled to bring suit for damages in civilian courts.

WORKING CONDITIONS. One of the great problems of large standing armies is that there is not much for soldiers to do while
they sit around waiting for war—just a lot of tedious chores,
inspections, and what is generally referred to as "Mickey
Mouse." It is not unnatural for boredom and frustration to set
in. On top of the lack of meaningful work is a constant stream
of petty harassments and invasions of privacy. By the end of a
noncombat day in the army, an enlisted man does not have
much sense of dignity left.

— In noncombat and nonalert situations, soldiers should be
given a five-day, forty-hour work week.

— There is no reason why ninety percent of the duty assignments in the United States cannot be in the geographical
area of a soldier's choice. The army should use computers
or other management tools to assure that as many soldiers
as possible are stationed near home, if that is what they
desire. Such a policy would, among other things, significantly reduce the number of AWOL's.

— After a certain period of time in the service—say, one year
—a soldier ought to be granted a number of days of "free
leave." These would be days when he would not require
official permission to be absent; he could, in effect, call in
sick. Thus, if a soldier, like a postal employee, wanted to

visit his home and did not have an approved reason, he could do so anyway for a short period of time. This, too, would cut down on AWOL's.

— Unmarried soldiers with routine jobs should be permitted to live off-base.

COUNTERVAILING POWER. Much of the unrest within the army stems from soldiers' lack of any say regarding their living and working conditions. A military force must of necessity be autocratic on the battlefield, but it does not follow that commanders should possess total power over soldiers' lives at all times. Enlisted men need some means both of expressing their grievances and of remedying the abuses that inevitably accompany unchecked power.

— A civilian ombudsman should be stationed on every major base. Unlike the Inspector General, he would not be a member of the commanding general's staff, but would be responsible instead to a chief ombudsman chosen by Congress. He would have the power to investigate specific complaints and to issue cease-and-desist orders. He would also serve as the eyes and ears of Congress on the base and make periodic reports—which would be available to the public—on the responsiveness of commanding officers to soldiers' needs and rights.

A plan similar to the above has been proposed by Representative Mario Biaggi of New York. He has introduced, along with several other Congressmen, legislation to create an eleven-member Military Justice Commission that would hear grievances, investigate charges of brutality, and protect the constitutional rights of servicemen. Commission members would be appointed by the President; five would be military officers, five others civilian jurists, and the eleventh would be recommended by the first ten. The Commission could issue cease-and-desist orders and would possess other punitive powers.

— Several groups within the GI movement have proposed that enlisted men elect their own officers, as was the custom in many early American militias. Such a reform is neither necessary nor desirable; it is more important to have professionally competent officers than popular ones. However, the members of each company could and should elect an enlisted leader who would have powers and responsibilities similar to those of the West German *Vertrauensmann*. He would have tenure of office and immunity from punishment; he would represent the enlisted men's interests before company commanders and would have access to the commanding general and the civilian ombudsman.

— To deal with the interests of enlisted men on a post-wide basis, elected councils of enlisted men should be authorized. These councils would advise the commanding general on broad matters of personnel policy and post regulations. Such councils have already been established at two installations—Fort Carson and Sandia Base, New Mexico—with favorable results.

— Enlisted men should be allowed to join unions. Soldiers in Sweden, Austria, and West Germany have this right; policemen and firemen in the United States have it, as do other federal employees.

Enlisted men's unions—they would in fact be more like employee associations than true trade unions—would be barred from collective bargaining; strikes, too, would be illegal, since they would be tantamount to mutiny and could be punished as such. But unions could serve as channels for resolving grievances, expressing soldiers' views, and lobbying Congress for GI rights.

CHAPLAINS. The Constitution forbids the enactment of any law "respecting an establishment of religion" and asserts that "no religious test shall ever be required as a qualification to any office or public trust under the United States." Yet chaplains in the army hold military rank, perform military duties, and are paid with taxpayers' money. The presence of chaplains in the armed forces—in spite of the clear language of the Constitution—is justified on the grounds that, since the government takes soldiers away from their habitual places of worship, it incurs an obligation to provide them continued access to spiritual guidance. This reasoning is valid so far as it goes; but it does not follow that the present system is the best way to meet that obligation.

— The military chaplains corps is unconstitutional and should be abolished.

— Clergymen of all faiths should be made available to servicemen at home and on the front lines. These clergymen should be civilians; if necessary, they could undergo a certain amount of military training before visiting a combat zone. Their sole function should be to provide spiritual succor to the troops; they should not teach "character guidance," give religious sanction to policies of the state, or advise the commander on conscientious objection or other matters. Their salaries and expenses should be defrayed through free-will offerings of GI's, donations by the various religious denominations, and perhaps, like the USO, through United Fund contributions.

DISCHARGES. Prevailing military policy is that once a man has been sworn into the army, he is to be held onto at all costs. The military is thus the only employer in America that does not fire misfits and does not allow disgruntled employees to quit. This policy is based on the belief that discipline will suffer if men are released from duty before the normal end of their enlistments; the sufferings of the individual are not considered. In fact, however, discipline is not greatly aided by the retention of misfit soldiers, especially when retention means imprisonment; and the misfit himself is hardly aided at all.

— Except in times of declared war, all soldiers who are clearly unsuitable for military service—either as determined by psychiatrists or made evident by repeated bad behavior, absenteeism, or suicidal tendencies—should be discharged at once. This includes prisoners in stockades.

— When less than honorable discharges are given, they should "expire" after a period of five years and honorable discharges should then be issued. No citizen, in other words, should be hindered in earning a livelihood for more than half a decade, simply because he cannot adjust to the demands of the military.

— It should be possible for enlisted men to resign from the army after a certain period of time—perhaps two years into a three-year enlistment, three years into a longer enlistment, or after combat duty is completed—just as officers, who are presumably more valuable, are presently allowed to resign. Besides introducing an element of voluntarism into extended military service, it would have the effect of keeping the army on its toes: nothing could stimulate better treatment of enlisted men more than the fear of losing them.

AWOL's. Absenteeism is the great military "crime"; it is what fills stockades past the bursting point.

— Many AWOL offenses could be averted, as indicated above, by more enlightened leave policies and by stationing more soldiers close to home. Others could be prevented by more attentive treatment of young recruits.

— Illegal absences motivated by objection to non-defensive, undeclared wars will disappear when a fair policy regarding conscientious objection is adopted.

— There will still be soldiers who run away out of sheer dislike for military service. Some of these, if they have not gone through basic training and do not appear to be in too much agony, might be sent to centers like the Correctional Training Facility at Fort Riley. Those who are clearly unsuitable and in distress should be discharged.

STOCKADES. Military prisons rehabilitate almost no one. They do, to some extent, serve to deter GI's from straying too far out of line; but this is a repugnant way to motivate soldiers and is intolerable in a democracy, short of all-out war.

— The Disciplinary Barracks at Fort Leavenworth and the Naval Correctional Institution at Portsmouth, New Hampshire, should be retained for genuine criminals with long-term sentences.

— Punishment other than imprisonment should be allotted to soldiers whose offenses consist essentially of incompatibility with the military. Where appropriate, they should be fined, demoted, discharged, and/or assigned to civilian work of value to the community—a kind of punitive parole. This would effectively empty most stockades except in time of declared war.

— A small number of criminal prisoners with short-term sentences for such offenses as assault or petty theft would continue to be kept in some stockades. In the operation of these post confinement facilities, every effort should be made to eliminate brutality. Guards should be carefully trained and given short working hours. They should wear name tags so that prisoners can identify those who mistreat them. Guards who abuse prisoners should be harshly punished by the army and made liable to damage suits in civilian courts.

— The "diminished rations" diet should be abolished. Shotgun details outside stockade walls should be eliminated; the chances that someone will be needlessly hurt are too great.

— Incoming mail should be inspected for dangerous objects, but neither incoming nor outgoing letters should be read; that includes letters of complaint sent to higher officers, ombudsmen, or Congressmen. Visitors other than relatives should be permitted.

— Frequent unannounced inspections should be conducted by commissioned officers and civilian ombudsmen.

Rights. In a somewhat backhanded way, Congress recognized the second-class status of soldiers by passing after World War II what was glowingly referred to as the GI Bill of Rights. This was a measure providing educational, medical, and financial benefits, not to soldiers but to veterans. The bill was based on the unusual notion that benefits are equivalent to rights, and even more ironically, that citizens can't enjoy rights *while* they are soldiers—they must wait until afterwards.

— Congress should append to the Uniform Code of Military Justice a new GI Bill of Rights dealing, not with veterans' benefits, but with the actual rights of soldiers. Such legislation, like the Soldier's Law in West Germany, should spell out the conditions under which certain rights could be curtailed; but it should make clear that off-duty soldiers, stationed in the United States in times of peace or undeclared war, are entitled to the full complement of rights guaranteed by the Constitution. Federal courts should be authorized by statute to protect the constitutional rights of soldiers, and punishment should be authorized for military officers who interfere with the exercise of guaranteed rights.

— In the prosecution of soldiers accused of wrongly exercising First Amendment rights, the burden should be placed on the military to prove that a palpable danger to national security is created by the defendants' spoken or printed words. When the nation is not engaged in a declared, defensive war, only illegal acts or words that directly incite illegal acts should be punishable.

— Those antiquated and overly vague articles of the UCMJ which have been used to abridge soldiers' rights should be repealed—namely, Article 88 (prohibiting "contemptuous words" by commissioned officers against government officials), Article 133 (prohibiting "conduct unbecoming an officer and a gentleman"), and Article 134 (prohibiting "all disorders and neglects to the prejudice of good order and discipline").

— Since the military has far more power to keep watch over

its members' movements than does civilian society, it should establish a system for granting reasonable pre-trial bail and release from prison pending appeal.

COURTS-MARTIAL. Military justice must be brought into line with the constitutional requirement that "in *all* criminal prosecutions, the accused shall enjoy the right to a speedy and public trial, by an *impartial* jury. . . ." (Emphasis added.)

— Court-martial juries should be selected randomly by an independent judicial administrator, not hand-picked by the commander who convenes the trial. At least half of a jury's members should be men of the same rank as the accused. A three-fourths majority should be required to convict, and unanimity should be required to impose sentences of imprisonment for more than six months.
— An independent corps of military defense counsel should be created, separate from local Staff Judge Advocates. The personnel of this corps should be rated on the quality of their legal work, not on how well their zeal or arguments are appreciated by commanding officers.
— All counsel should wear civilian clothes at courts-martial in order to eliminate the influence of rank in dealings with the judge and jury.
— Military defense lawyers should be authorized to seek relief in federal courts if it is in the interest of their clients to do so.
— Military judges, including appeals judges, should be granted tenure. The power of commanders to overrule judges on matters of law should be abolished.
— The commander's power to review verdicts and sentences should be transferred to an independent judicial officer or panel.
— The recommendations of Article 32 investigators—the military equivalent of grand juries—should be binding.
— The appeals process should be greatly speeded. In cases

where infringements of constitutional rights are involved, direct appeals to the federal courts should be authorized.

CIVILIAN ACTIVITY. As important as any institutional reform is continued civilian concern about citizen-soldiers.

— Army bases tend to be in isolated locations, far from the press and public view. Civilians and newsmen should visit military bases frequently; they should attend courts-martial, talk with GI's, and just look around. Military regulations and practices restricting peaceful access by civilians to bases should be eliminated. (At some bases, for example, civilians with long hair or peace decals on their cars are generally denied entrance.)
— Civilians should also keep an eye on recruiting stations. Counseling services should be established for potential volunteers as well as draftees; young men thinking of enlisting should be helped to know what they are getting into and warned about deceptive recruiting practices.
— Law schools should offer courses in military law, and legal aid programs should be established for GI's, similar to the programs in poverty areas.

III

A FINAL word should be said about a broader question—namely, what kind of nation does America wish to be? The nature of its military system, the conduct of its foreign policy, the priorities it places on social needs—all are related to this deeper problem. Does America wish to rise to world dominance as did, each in its time, Rome and Spain and England? Or does it wish to be a land of farmers, workers, artists, and teachers, living in harmony with one another and at peace with the world? Is its prime concern to be the power struggle among states or the relationship between citizens and the state?

In the republic's youth, there was no doubt about the course that America would take. Blessed with a bounteous land, unencumbered by the chains of feudalism, separated by two oceans from the petty ambitions of kings and emperors, America felt it would be different from all civilizations before it. It would be a land of promise and openness where people would come and work and enjoy in freedom the fruits of their labor, a land where life, liberty, and the pursuit of happiness would truly be the birthright of every citizen.

That, at least, was the dream, and for a while it seemed almost too easy to attain. But soon many Americans began thinking in grander terms, of a "higher" or "manifest" destiny as measured from a global perspective. At first, there appeared to be no contradiction between internal democracy and external power; it seemed possible for America, rich as it was, to be two nations at once, the nation of Thomas Jefferson and the nation of Theodore Roosevelt, the home of the Statue of Liberty and the practitioner of gunboat diplomacy, a beacon of hope for oppressed Europeans and the suppressor of Philippine independence.

Through a generation of world wars this two-nation vision persisted; Presidents in the 1960's spoke of guns and butter, of wars against Communism and wars against poverty. Yet reality pressed in on this vision. There were riots in the cities, erosions of the democratic process, growing power of the military in many phases of American life. It became clear that America could not be all things to all men; not the new Rome and the last great hope for mankind. It would have to make a choice.

And so the debate has raged, not always in clear-cut terms, but essentially between those who, like Richard Nixon, see America as a magnificent war-diplomacy machine, the ultimate embodiment of Clausewitz's teaching, "pacifying" the world with its arsenal of might; and those who hark back to an earlier vision, who say "Let us keep our house in order and be, not the most feared people in the world, but the most admired."

The debate is not, as is often claimed, between isolationists and internationalists, but between two different traditions of internationalism, one which might be traced to James K. Polk and Theodore Roosevelt, and another which draws inspiration from Thomas Jefferson, Woodrow Wilson's Fourteen Points, and, more recently, J. William Fulbright. One tradition views America's role in the world in terms of power, the other in terms of ideals. One speaks of carrying a big stick, the other of "decent respect for the opinions of mankind." One places primacy on solitary grandeur, the other on collective endeavor. One sees foreign policy as almost an end in itself; the other views foreign policy as merely a means to an end, the end being the preservation of democratic values and processes within America.

The choice, in my mind, is not difficult to make. A democracy can fight and win wars, as America has proved, but it cannot be a nation chronically at war. America can flex its muscles, it can flaunt its virility, it has the capability of being the biggest and toughest player at the Old World game of *Realpolitik;* but if it continues on this path, it will not remain democratic for long, and in the end it will lose the game anyway, as all previous competitors have.

A pessimist might reasonably argue that man is by nature a combative animal, that there is no escaping the Darwinian struggle among nations, that the fittest must prevail until someone fitter comes along. He may be right. But should we not cling to the hope that America can be different; that because of its unique endowments and geography, its history need not be a rerun of past rises and falls?

This is what the Founders envisioned—a growing, prospering, steady-state democracy, changing, yes, but essentially ahistorical, transcending and standing free of the conflicts that so largely characterize human history. Their vision now has nearly been spoiled; their great experiment has nearly failed. Nearly, but not yet.

BIBLIOGRAPHY

BOOKS

Cornell, Julien D.: *The Conscientious Objector and the Law*. New York. John Day; 1943.

Cunliffe, Marcus: *Soldiers and Civilians: The Martial Spirit in America, 1775–1865*. New York: Little, Brown; 1968.

Donovan, James A.: *Militarism, U.S.A.* New York: Scribner's; 1970.

———: *The United States Marine Corps*. New York: Praeger; 1967.

Duncan, Donald: *The New Legions*. New York: Random House; 1967.

Galbraith, John Kenneth: *How to Control the Military*. New York: Signet; 1969.

Ganoe, William A.: *History of the United States Army*. New York: Appleton-Century; 1936.

Gardner, Fred: *The Unlawful Concert. An Account of the Presidio Mutiny Case*. New York: The Viking Press; 1970.

Goffman, Erving: *Asylums*. Garden City: Doubleday; 1961.

Hammer, Richard: *One Morning in the War*. New York: Coward, McCann and Geoghegan; 1970.

Hayes, Denis: *Challenge of Conscience: The Story of the Conscientious Objectors of 1939–1949*. London: Allen and Unwin; 1949.

Heller, Joseph: *Catch-22*. New York: Simon and Schuster; 1961.

Hersh, Seymour M.. *My Lai 4*. New York: Random House; 1970.

Huie, William Bradford: *The Execution of Private Slovik*. New York: Signet; 1954.

Huntington, Samuel P.: *The Soldier and the State*. Cambridge: Harvard University Press; 1964.

Kaufman, William W.: *The McNamara Strategy*. New York: Harper and Row; 1964.

Kreidberg, Marvin A., and Merton G. Henry: *History of Military Mobilization in the United States Army, 1775–1945*. Washington: Department of the Army; 1955.

Langley, Harold D.: *Social Reform in the United States Navy, 1798–1862*. Urbana: University of Illinois Press; 1967.

Madison, James: *Notes on Debates in the Federal Convention of 1787*. Athens, Ohio: Ohio University Press; 1966.

———, Alexander Hamilton, and John Jay: *The Federalist Papers*. New York: Mentor; 1961.

Marshall, S. L. A.: *Men Against Fire*. New York: William Morrow and Co.; 1947.

Millis, Walter: *Arms and Men: A Study in American Military History*. New York: Putnam; 1956.

———, ed.: *American Military Thought*. Indianapolis: Bobbs-Merrill; 1966.

Pusey, Merlo J.: *The Way We Go to War*. Boston: Houghton-Mifflin; 1969.

Rivkin, Robert S.: *GI Rights and Army Justice*. New York: Grove Press; 1970.

Schissel, Lillian, ed.: *Conscience in America: A Documentary History of Conscientious Objection in America, 1775–1957*. New York: Dutton; 1968.

Sherrill, Robert, *Military Justice Is to Justice as Military Music Is to Music*. New York: Harper and Row; 1970.

Stafford, Robert T., Frank J. Horton, Richard S. Schweiker, Garner E. Shriver, and Charles W. Whalen Jr.: *How to End the Draft*. Washington: The National Press; 1967.

Taylor, Telford: *Nuremberg and Vietnam: An American Tragedy*. Chicago: Quadrangle Books; 1970.

Waldman, Eric: *The Goose Step Is Verboten: The German Army Today*. New York: The Free Press; 1964.

Weigley, Russell F.: *History of the United States Army*. New York: Macmillan; 1967.

———: *Towards an American Army: Military Thought from Washington to Marshall*. New York: Columbia University Press; 1962.

Williams, T. Harry: *Americans at War: The Development of the American Military System*. Baton Rouge: Louisiana State University Press; 1960.

Wittels, Mike: *Advice for Conscientious Objectors in the Armed Forces*. Philadelphia: Central Committee for Conscientious Objection; 1970.

ARTICLES

Alger, John: "The Objective Was a Volunteer Army." *Institute of U.S. Naval Proceedings*, February 1970.

Alsop, Stewart: "The Dreadful System." *Newsweek,* August 31, 1970.

Barnes, Peter: "The Army and the First Amendment." *The New Republic,* May 24, 1969.

———: "The Presidio 'Mutiny.' " *The New Republic,* July 5, 1969.

———: "All-Volunteer Army?" *The New Republic,* May 9, 1970.

Bishop, Joseph W., Jr.: "The Quality of Military Justice." *New York Times Magazine,* February 22, 1970.

Bourne, Peter B.: *Psychosocial Phenomena Observed in Basic Training With Implications for Later Personality Effect.* Paper delivered at American Orthopsychiatric Association convention, New York, April 2, 1969.

Bresler, Robert J.: "The War-Making Machinery." *The Nation,* August 17, 1970.

Clark, Blair: "The Question Is, What Kind of Army?" *Harper's,* September 1969.

Clausen, Roy E., Jr., and Arlene K. Daniels: "Role Conflicts and Their Ideological Resolution in Military Psychiatric Practice." *American Journal of Psychiatry,* September 1966.

Datel, William E., and Stephen T. Lifrak: "Expectations, Affect Change, and Military Performance in the Army Recruit." *Psychological Reports,* June 1969.

Ervin, Sam, Jr.: "The Military Justice Act of 1968." *Wake Forest Intramural Law Review,* May 1969.

Fincher, Jack: "The Hog-Tied Brig Rats of Camp Pendleton." *Life,* October 10, 1969.

Glasser, Ira: "Justice and Captain Levy." *Columbia Forum,* Spring 1969.

Greenberg, I. M.: "Project 100,000: The Training of Former Rejectees." *Phi Delta Kappan,* June 1969.

Henry, James D.: "The Men of 'B' Company." *Scanlan's,* February 1970.

Kester, John G.: "Soldiers Who Insult the President: An Uneasy Look at Article 88 of the Uniform Code of Military Justice." *Harvard Law Review,* June 1968.

Lifton, Robert Jay: "Vietnam: Betrayal and Self-Betrayal." *Trans-Action,* October 1969.

Lyon, Waldo B.: *Military Service and American Youth: Some Reflections After Seven Years of Psychological Evaluation of Marine Corps Recruits.* Paper delivered at American Orthopsychiatric Association convention, New York, April 2, 1969.

Moyer, Homer E., Jr.: "Procedural Rights of the Military Accused: Advantages over a Civilian Defendant." *Maine Law Review,* Vol. 22, No. 1, 1970.

Polner, Murray: "18-Minute Verdict: Military Justice and Constitutional Rights." *Commonweal*, March 28, 1969.
Rechy, John: "GIs for Peace: The Army Fights an Idea." *The Nation*, January 12, 1970.
Rigg, Robert B.: "The Permissive Army." *Army*, January 1970.
Rosenberger, John W.: "How the Soldiers View Vietnam." *The Progressive*, March 1968.
Scott, Jim: "GI Guinea Pigs Risk Death." *Army Times Family Magazine*, April 1, 1970.
Sherman, Edward F.: "The Civilianization of Military Law." *Maine Law Review*, Vol. 22, No. 1, 1970.
——: "Dissenters and Deserters." *The New Republic*, January 6, 1968.
——: "Buttons, Bumper Stickers and the Soldier." *The New Republic*, August 17, 1968.
Sherrill, Robert: "Must the Citizen Give Up His Civil Liberties When He Joins the Army?" *New York Times Magazine*, May 18, 1969.
Shoup, David M., and James A. Donovan: "Our New American Militarism." *The Atlantic*, April 1969.
Sullivan, Daniel P.: "Soldiers in Unions—Protected First Amendment Right?" *Labor Law Journal*, September 1969.
Warren, Earl: "The Bill of Rights and the Military." *New York University Law Review*, April 1962.

GOVERNMENT DOCUMENTS

Department of the Army: *Doolittle Board Report*, Senate Doc. No. 196, 79th Cong., 2nd Session. Washington: U.S. Government Printing Office, 1946.
Department of the Army, Office of the Adjutant General: "Guidance on Dissent," memorandum to commanders, May 28, 1969.
Department of the Army, Office of the Deputy Chief of Staff for Personnel: *Project Volunteer in Defense of the Nation*, unclassified executive summary of Department of the Army analysis of all-volunteer army. Washington; 1970.
Department of the Army, Special Civilian Committee for the Study of the United States Army Confinement System: *Report*. Washington: 1970.
Department of the Army, U.S. Army Correctional Training Facility: *Military Offenders Sent to the U.S. Army Correctional Training Facility—A Follow-Up Study*. Fort Riley, Kansas: 1970.

Department of Defense: *Manual for Courts-Martial,* 1969 ed. Washington: 1969.

Department of Defense: DoD Directive 1300.6, "Conscientious Objectors." Washington: May 10, 1968.

Department of Defense: DoD Directive 1325.6, "Guidelines for Handling Dissent and Protest Activities Among Members of the Armed Forces." Washington: September 12, 1969.

Department of Defense: DoD Directive 1344.10, "Political Activities by Members of the Armed Forces." Washington: September 23, 1969.

Department of Defense, President's Commission on an All-Volunteer Armed Force (Gates commission): *Report.* Washington: U.S. Government Printing Office, 1970.

Department of Defense, Office of the Assistant Secretary for Manpower and Reserve Affairs: *Project 100,000: Characteristics and Performance of "New Standards" Men.* Washington: 1969.

Department of the Navy, Treasure Island Naval Station: *Report of informal Board of Investigation inquiring into alleged maltreatment of confinees in the Naval Correctional Center.* San Francisco: 1969.

Department of the Navy, U.S. Marine Corps Recruit Depot: San Diego, *Standing Operating Procedure for Recruit Training.* San Diego: 1968.

Library of Congress, Legislative Reference Service: *Military Justice: A Summary of Its Legislative and Judicial Development.* Washington: 1969.

U.S. Court of Military Appeals and the Judge Advocates General of the Armed Forces: *Annual Report, 1969.* Washington: 1970.

U.S. House of Representatives, Armed Services Committee, 91st Congress, 2nd Session: *Inquiry into the Reported Conditions in the Brig, Marine Corps Base, Camp Pendleton, California.* Washington: U.S. Government Printing Office, 1970.

U.S. House of Representatives, Armed Services Committee, 91st Congress, 2nd Session: *Report of the Armed Services Investigating Committee of the Investigation of the My Lai Incident.* Washington: U.S. Government Printing Office, 1970.

U.S. Senate, Armed Services Committee, 90th Congress, 2nd Session: *Hearings on Military Deserters.* Washington: U.S. Government Printing Office, 1968.

U.S. Senate, Subcommittee on Constitutional Rights, 88th Congress, 1st Session: *Report on Constitutional Rights of Military Personnel.* Washington: U.S. Government Printing Office, 1963.

U.S. Senate, Subcommittee on Constitutional Rights, 89th Congress, 2nd Session: *Hearings on Military Justice*. Washington: U.S. Government Printing Office, 1966.

U.S. Senate, Committee on Foreign Relations, 91st Congress, 1st Session: *Report on National Commitments*. Washington: U.S. Government Printing Office, 1969.

INDEX

A

A NOTE ABOUT THE AUTHOR

Peter Barnes, the West Coast Editor of *The New Republic*, is 29. He holds a B.A. degree from Harvard College and an M.A. from Georgetown University. Before joining *The New Republic*, he was a staff correspondent of *Newsweek*, a writer for Eugene McCarthy during the 1968 presidential campaign, a reporter for the Lowell (Massachusetts) *Sun*, and an Associate Nieman Fellow. He currently lives in San Francisco.

A NOTE ON THE TYPE

This book was set on the Linotype in Janson, a recutting made direct from type cast from matrices long thought to have been made by the Dutchman Anton Janson, who was a practicing type founder in Leipzig during the years 1668–87. However, it has been conclusively demonstrated that these types are actually the work of Nicholas Kis (1650–1702), a Hungarian, who most probably learned his trade from the master Dutch type founder Dirk Voskens. The type is an excellent example of the influential and sturdy Dutch types that prevailed in England up to the time William Caslon developed his own incomparable designs from them.

The book was composed, printed, and bound by The Haddon Craftsmen, Inc., Scranton, Pennsylvania. Typography and binding design by CLINT ANGLIN.